Emil Otto, Rodes Massie, Edward Southey Joynes

**Exercises for Translating English Into German**

Emil Otto, Rodes Massie, Edward Southey Joynes

**Exercises for Translating English Into German**

ISBN/EAN: 9783337735197

Printed in Europe, USA, Canada, Australia, Japan

Cover: Foto ©Paul-Georg Meister /pixelio.de

More available books at **www.hansebooks.com**

*THE JOYNES-OTTO GERMAN COURSE.*

# EXERCISES FOR TRANSLATING

# ENGLISH INTO GERMAN

BY

DR. EMIL OTTO

*WITH NOTES AND VOCABULARY*

BY RODES MASSIE
*Professor of Modern Languages, Richmond College*

EDITED BY

EDWARD S. JOYNES
*Professor of Modern Languages, Vanderbilt University*

NEW YORK
HENRY HOLT AND COMPANY
F. W. CHRISTERN
BOSTON : SCHŒNHOF & MŒLLER

COPYRIGHT
BY HENRY HOLT
1878

# NOTE.

This book is based on Dr. Otto's "MATERIALS FOR TRANSLATING ENGLISH INTO GERMAN."

The helps for the learner vary considerably from those in the original, in consequence of their being made more in conformity with American requirements. The references to OTTO's GERMAN GRAMMAR are much fuller, and the field of the book's usefulness is further enlarged by numerous references to WHITNEY'S GERMAN GRAMMAR.

For the occasional translations of difficult words, in the original work, a full vocabulary has been substituted in this one.

As the original German of a few of the selections in the "MATERIALS" had already found its way into EVANS' OTTO'S GERMAN READER, other selections have been substituted for them in this volume.

# CONTENTS.

### ANECDOTES, STORIES, ETC.

|  |  | PAGE |
|---|---|---|
| 1. | The Sensible Child. | 1 |
| 2. | True Politeness. | 1 |
| 3. | Ariosto. | 1 |
| 4. | Young Napoleon. | 2 |
| 5. | The Good Excuse. | 2 |
| 6. | The Traveler and the Boatman. | 2 |
| 7. | The Scholar Outdone. | 3 |
| 8. | Simplicity. | 3 |
| 9. | Excessive Politeness. | 3 |
| 10. | Troy. | 3 |
| 11. | The Dangerous Wound. | 4 |
| 12. | The Romans. | 4 |
| 13. | The Ass and the Wolf. | 4 |
| 14. | Stentor. | 5 |
| 15. | The Fearful Menace. | 5 |
| 16. | Dr. Franklin. | 5 |
| 17. | Dean Swift and his Servant. | 6 |
| 18. | Honesty. | 7 |
| 19. | Ignorance. | 7 |
| 20. | The Place by the Fire. | 8 |
| 21. | Arrogance Punished. | 8 |
| 22. | The Treasure-Diggers. | 9 |
| 23. | The Emperor as Attorney. | 9 |
| 24. | Cross Questions. | 10 |
| 25. | Female Heroism. | 11 |
| 26. | The Two Merchants. | 12 |

|     |                                           | PAGE |
|-----|-------------------------------------------|------|
| 27. | Peter the Hermit                          | 13   |
| 28. | Filial Affection of a Page                | 14   |
| 29. | Delicacy of King Alphonso                 | 14   |
| 30. | Walter Scott at School                    | 15   |
| 31. | Diamond cut Diamond                       | 16   |
| 32. | Humanity of Louis XIV                     | 17   |
| 33. | The Cunning Cutler                        | 18   |
| 34. | Abstraction, or Absence of Mind           | 18   |
| 35. | The Value of Time                         | 19   |
| 36. | The Bagpiper Revived                      | 20   |
| 37. | Mercury and the Woodman                   | 21   |
| 38. | The Dog and the Eels                      | 22   |
| 39. | The Dervise and the Atheist               | 22   |
| 40. | The Queen of Spain has no Legs            | 23   |
| 41. | The Wolf and the Lamb                     | 24   |
| 42. | Honorable Conduct of King John of France  | 25   |
| 43. | A Dog's Will                              | 26   |
| 44. | Ventriloquy                               | 27   |
| 45. | The Page and the Cherries                 | 28   |
| 46. | The Lounger                               | 29   |
| 47. | Cruelty of King John                      | 30   |
| 48. | Real or Intrinsic Value                   | 31   |
| 49. | A Very Singular Excuse                    | 32   |
| 50. | How to Catch a Pickpocket                 | 32   |
| 51. | A Singular Precaution                     | 33   |
| 52. | Gratitude                                 | 34   |
| 53. | The Same Subject Continued                | 35   |
| 54. | Noble Blood. A Lesson for Pride           | 36   |
| 55. | The Same Subject Continued                | 37   |
| 56. | The Mysterious Englishmen                 | 38   |
| 57. | The Same Subject Continued                | 39   |
| 58. | The Same Subject Continued                | 40   |
| 59. | The Lost Camel                            | 41   |
| 60. | The Whistle (by Franklin)                 | 42   |

|     |                                              | PAGE |
| --- | -------------------------------------------- | ---- |
| 61. | The Same Subject Continued.................. | 43   |
| 62. | Benevolence.................................. | 44   |
| 63. | The Same Subject Continued.................. | 44   |
| 64. | Respect for the Bible....................... | 45   |
| 65. | The Same Subject Continued.................. | 46   |
| 66. | The British Empire.......................... | 47   |
| 67. | The Youthful Martyr......................... | 48   |
| 68. | A Lesson.................................... | 48   |
| 69. | Rabelais, a Traitor......................... | 49   |
| 70. | Misery of Inactivity........................ | 50   |
| 71. | Hazael, King of Syria....................... | 50   |
| 72. | Desperate Patriotism........................ | 51   |
| 73. | Curious Expedient........................... | 52   |
| 74. | The Storks.................................. | 53   |
| 75. | The Giant and the Dwarf..................... | 54   |
| 76. | Rotterdam in Winter......................... | 55   |
| 77. | A West Indian Slave......................... | 57   |
| 78. | The Bishop and his Birds.................... | 58   |
| 79. | The Same Subject Continued.................. | 59   |
| 80. | A Mystery Cleared Up........................ | 60   |
| 81. | Dionysius the Tyrant........................ | 61   |
| 82. | Napoleon and the British Sailor............. | 62   |
| 83. | Avarice Punished............................ | 63   |
| 84. | Pœtus and Arria............................. | 64   |
| 85. | The Same Subject Continued.................. | 65   |
| 86. | Origin of the Chimney-Sweepers' Holiday..... | 66   |
| 87. | The Same Subject Continued.................. | 67   |
| 88. | Memory...................................... | 68   |
| 89. | Accident at Prince Schwartzenberg's Hotel... | 69   |
| 90. | Ingratitude and Avarice Punished............ | 70   |

## Letters.

|     |                                              |    |
| --- | -------------------------------------------- | -- |
| 91. | Returning some Books........................ | 72 |
| 92. | From an Uncle to his Nephew................. | 72 |

| | | PAGE |
|---|---|---|
| 93. | Answer..................................... | 73 |
| 94—96. | Letters on Several Subjects................ | 73 |
| 97. | Information on Going to London............. | 76 |
| 98. | Answer..................................... | 76 |
| 99. | Informing a Mother of her Son's Illness....... | 77 |
| 100. | On a Journey to Marseilles................... | 78 |
| 101. | From Lord Byron to his Mother.............. | 79 |
| 102. | Mr. Sterne to Mr. Panchard................. | 80 |
| 103. | Another Letter.............................. | 80 |
| 104. | Mary Stuart to Queen Elizabeth.............. | 81 |
| 105—106. | Two Other Letters....................... | 82 |
| 107. | Dr. Johnson to Mr. Elphinstone............. | 84 |
| 108—109. | Two Other Letters....................... | 85 |
| 110. | Lord Chesterfield to his Son................. | 86 |

### HISTORICAL EXTRACTS.

| | | |
|---|---|---|
| 111. | Franklin.................................... | 88 |
| 112. | Patriotism of Regulus....................... | 89 |
| 113. | The Same Subject Continued................ | 90 |
| 114. | Copernicus.................................. | 91 |
| 115—117. | History of Catharine, First Empress of Russia................................... | 93 |
| 118—120. | Combat between the Horatii and Curiatii. | 97 |
| 121—124. | Captain Cook........................... | 100 |
| 125—130. | Discovery of America.................... | 105 |
| 131. | Columbus' First Return to Europe............ | 112 |
| 132—138. | Life and Writings of Oliver Goldsmith... | 114 |
| Notes...................................................... | | 123 |
| VOCABULARY................................................ | | 131 |

# EXERCISES FOR TRANSLATING
# ENGLISH INTO GERMAN.

### 1.
### The Sensible Child.

A bishop once[1] said to a very sensible child, "My child, I will[2] give you[3] an apple if[4] you tell me where[5] God is." The child answered: "And I will give you[3] two if you tell me where[5] he is not."

### 2.
### True Politeness.

When[1] President Jefferson was once[2] walking[3] on the street, he[4] returned with the expression of civility the salutation of a negro who[5] was passing[3] by. "How!" said a merchant who accompanied him, "Your Excellency condescends to[6] salute a slave?" "I should be really sorry," answered the President, "to[6] allow myself to[6] be surpassed in politeness by a slave."

### 3.
### Ariosto.

Ariosto built a small house for himself.[1] Being[2] asked

by[3] his friend how[4] he, who[4] described fine palaces in his "Orlando," could[5] content himself with so small an[6] edifice? "Words are cheaper than stones," replied the philosophic bard.

## 4.
## Young[1] Napoleon.

Napoleon already in his youth often[2] gave very striking answers. When[3] he went for the first time to the Lord's Supper, the archbishop[4] scrupled to administer it[5] to him, because[3] his Christian name, Napoleon, was[6] not in the calendar. "What!" cried Bonaparte, promptly, "there is[7] a very great multitude of[8] Saints, and the year has only three hundred and sixty-five days!" The archbishop, astonished at[9] this exclamation, administered the communion to him.

## 5.
## The Good Excuse.

Sheridan being[1] once[2] on[3] a visit at[4] a friend's in[5] the country, an old maid had[6] taken[7] it into her[8] head to[9] accompany him on a walk. First[10] he pleaded the bad weather. But soon afterwards[10] the lady caught[11] him in[12] the attempt to[13] steal[14] away without her. "Aha!" said she, "I see verily[15] it has cleared up." "Yes, indeed,"[16] rejoined he, "it has cleared up enough for one, but not enough for two."

## 6.
## The Traveler and the Boatman.

A traveler came to[1] a ferry, and hired a boat to take[2] him across. The water being[3] rather more agitated than was agreeable to him, he asked the boatman if any person was[4] [ever] lost in[5] the passage. "Never," replied the boatman, "never. My brother was drowned here last week,[6] but we found him again the[7] next day."

## 7.
### The Scholar₂ Outdone.₁

A little girl came to¹ a scholar who² was quite busy in his study, to ask³ him for⁴ some⁵ fire. "But you⁶ have nothing," said the doctor, "to⁷ take it in;"⁸ and while he was gone⁹ away to⁷ look for something for¹⁰ this purpose, the little girl stooped¹¹ down at the fire-place, and, taking some¹² cold ashes in one hand, laid the glowing coals on them¹³ with the other. The doctor seeing¹⁴ this, threw down his books in¹⁵ astonishment, and exclaimed: "With¹⁶ all¹⁷ my learning, I should not have found out this experiment."

## 8.
### Simplicity.

"Patrick, you fool," cried a man to his neighbor, "what makes¹ you steal after that rabbit, when² your gun has no lock [on]?" "Hush! hush! my dear, the rabbit does not know that."

## 9.
### Excessive Politeness.

Queen Elizabeth was¹ once making a journey in England: and on² her approaching³ the city of⁴ Coventry, the mayor, with a numerous cavalcade, went out to meet⁵ her. On⁶ their return they had to pass over a wide brook, and the mayor's horse, being⁷ thirsty, attempted several times to drink, but his cavalier prevented him.⁸ The queen observing⁹ it, said to him: "Pray, Mr. Mayor, permit³ your horse to drink." The mayor, bowing⁹ very humbly, replied, "Madam, it would be the highest presumption for my unworthy horse to drink before your Majesty's royal steed has satisfied his thirst."

## 10.
### Troy.

Troy was a famous city. When¹ Priam was king, the

Greeks came to the city. They besieged it ten years without success. They could not take it by force,² because³ its walls were high and broad : but at last it was taken by the stratagem of a wooden horse. This horse being⁴ filled with armed men, was admitted into the city as a gift to⁵ Minerva. In the middle of the night, when all were asleep,⁶ the armed men came out of the belly of the horse and burned the city.

## 11.
### The Dangerous Wound.

A surgeon was brought to a gentleman who¹ had received a slight wound in a duel. He ordered² his servant to go home³ with⁴ all conceivable haste to⁵ fetch a certain plaster. The patient turned somewhat pale, and said : "I hope there⁶ is really no danger." "Yes, indeed, to be sure there is really some⁷," said the surgeon, "for if the boy does not make haste, the wound will⁸ be healed before he gets⁹ here again."

## 12.
### The Romans.

Romulus built the city of¹ Rome. The inhabitants were called Romans, and were accounted² very brave men. They loved their country, and fought to defend it. They chose³ rather to die than lose their liberty. It⁴ was dearer to them than life⁵. They carried on many wars with the Carthaginians, with various success. At last⁶ the Carthaginians were conquered, and the city of Carthage was destroyed.

## 13.
### The Ass and the Wolf.

An ass had the misfortune to meet¹ a hungry wolf. "Have mercy on² me," said the trembling animal; "I am a poor sick beast: look what a great thorn I have run³ into my⁴ foot !"

"Really, you quite grieve me," replied the wolf. "Conscientiously speaking,⁵ I feel myself compelled to put you out of your misery."

He had scarcely spoken, when⁶ he tore the supplicating donkey to pieces.

## 14.
### Stentor.

In the Grecian army it¹ was usual to have three men in each battalion to² communicate the commands of the officers to the men. Of these, one³ carried a standard, and another a trumpet. But in the confusion and din of battle, neither⁴ a signal could be seen, nor a trumpet heard. The third man (who⁵ for this purpose was the strongest in the army) communicated then the commands by word⁶ of mouth. Homer relates of⁷ one of these men, Stentor by⁸ name, that he shouted as⁹ loud as fifty other men. Hence a man with a powerful voice is said¹⁰ to possess the voice of Stentor, or a Stentorian voice.

## 15.
### The Fearful Menace.

A student of¹ medicine, having² lost an important lawsuit, broke out into the most violent language against his judges, and said³ it might⁴ really yet cost more⁵ than a thousand men their lives. He was immediately apprehended on account of this fearful menace, and was asked for⁶ an explanation. "Nothing is clearer,"⁷ said he; "having⁸ been⁹ deprived¹⁰ of all my property, I have no other resource left¹¹ me but¹² to become a physician."

## 16.
### Dr. Franklin.

Dr. Franklin, in the early¹ part of his life, when he was a² printer, had occasion to³ travel from⁴ Philadelphia to⁴

Boston. On his journey, he stopped at one of the inns, the landlord of which[5] possessed all[6] the inquisitive curiosity of his countrymen. Franklin had scarcely sat down to supper, when[7] his landlord began to torment him with questions. He, well knowing[8] the disposition of these people, and aware[9] that answering[10] one question would only pave the way for twenty more,[11] determined to stop[12] the landlord at once, by[13] requesting to see his wife, children and servants. When they were summoned, Franklin solemnly said : "My good friends, I sent[14] for you here to give you an account of myself : my name is Benjamin Franklin ; I am a printer, nineteen years of age ; reside at[15] Philadelphia, and am now going to Boston. I sent for you all, that[16] if you wished for any further particulars, you might ask, and I inform you: which done,[17] I hope that you will permit[18] me to eat my supper in[19] peace."

## 17.
### Dean Swift and his Servant.

As the late Dean Swift, attended[1] by a servant, was once on a journey, they put up at an inn where[2] they lodged all night;[3] in the morning[3] the dean[4] called for[5] his boots; the servant immediately took[6] them to him uncleaned. When the dean saw them, he said: "How is this, Tom ?" "As you are going to ride, I thought they would soon be dirty again." "Very well," said the dean, "go and get[7] the horses ready."

In the mean time, the dean ordered the landlord to let his man have no breakfast. When the servant returned, he asked if[8] the horses were ready. "Yes sir," answered the servant. "Go, bring them out[9] then," said the dean. "I have not had my breakfast yet, sir," replied Tom. "Oh no matter for that,"[10] said the dean, "if you had, you would soon be hungry again." They mounted and rode off. As they rode, the dean pulled a book out of his pocket, and began to read.

A gentleman met them,[11] and seeing[12] the Doctor reading,[13] was not willing to disturb him, but passed by, till he met the servant. "Who is that gentleman?" said he to the man. "My master." "I know that, you blockhead," said the gentleman; "but where are you going?" "We are going to heaven, sir," replied Tom. "How do you know that?" asked the gentleman. "Because I am[14] fasting, and my master is praying."

## 18.
### Honesty.

As[1] Marshal Turenne was going along on the ramparts one night,[2] he was assailed by a gang of robbers, who took everything from him except[3] a valuable diamond, which they left him on his promise to give them the next day[4] a hundred louis d'or. In the course of the day one[5] of the robbers[6] had the audacity to come to[7] him in his residence, and, in the midst of a large company, to demand[8] of him the fulfillment of his promise. Turenne had[9] the money paid out to him, and gave him time to get[10] off, before he related the adventure. Everybody seemed surprised at[11] such procedure. "An honest man," said he, "should never forfeit his word, when he has given it even to scoundrels."

## 19.
### Ignorance.

Korsakof, a favorite of the Empress Catherine, had a handsome face and an extremely elegant[1] figure, but as[2] for the rest[2] was entirely without knowledge. As soon as he was called to[3] the court, he conceived that a man like[4] him must[5] of course have also a library. Accordingly[6] he sent without delay to the most celebrated book-seller in St. Petersburg, and notified him that[7] he wanted[8] some books for his house, of which the empress had just made him a present. The book-seller asked him what sort[9] of books he would[10] have. "That you understand better than I," he answered, "that is indeed your business; but there[11] must be large books below and small ones[12] above, as they are at[13] the empress's."

## 20.
### The Place by[1] the Fire.

A traveler[2] arrived a very cold evening[3] at[4] an inn. All[5] the places around the fire were occupied, and no one of the guests showed as if he would[6] resign his place to him. The traveler therefore called the hostler, and ordered him[7] to give his horse six dozen[8] oysters. "Oysters!" said the hostler, "but surely[9] a horse does not eat oysters." "Do what I tell you," replied the traveler; "you[10] will no doubt see." The hostler went to the stable to[11] give the horse the oysters, and all the guests now left their places to[11] see the horse eat[12] oysters. Meanwhile the traveler took possession of the best place by the fire. Presently the hostler came in again, and said the horse would[6] not eat any oysters. "That's true,[13] no doubt,"[13] said the traveler; "then[14] bring me the oysters, and give the horse a peck[8] of oats."

## 21.
### Arrogance Punished.

Immanuel Kant, the celebrated Königsberg[1] philosopher, was[2] eating one day[3] at the public table in an inn; a young nobleman of[4] the neighborhood, who was-in-the-habit of making-his-appearance everywhere with[5] great pretension,[5] was[2] sitting opposite him. The dishes[6] were served, among them, too, one which especially enticed the appetite of the guests. The young nobleman seemed to think that upon such[7] a delicacy only *his* palate had a claim; for[8] he seized without[9] more ado[9] a pepper-box and shook[10] it over the dish, adding[11] dryly: "I like[12] this dish with pepper." All the rest[13] of the guests were as[14] much amazed as[14] shocked at[15] this presumption; but Kant, with the most perfect calmness, seized his snuff-box, shook it also over the dish, and said quite[16] as dryly: "And I like it with snuff."

## 22.
### The Treasure-Diggers.

"Hear,[1] children!" said a sick man, who gained much by the cultivation of the vine; "in our vineyard lies a treasure; only dig for[2] it." "In[3] what spot?" thus all asked; "tell the place." "Dig, dig!" He died at[4] this word.

Hardly was the old man carried to the tomb, when[5] there[6] was digging[6] day and night; with mattock, hoe and spade, the vineyard was scratched around[7] and about.[7] Not[8] a clod was left undisturbed;[8] the earth was[9] even thrown through the sieve; rakes were[9] dragged this[10] way and that[10] after every pebble. But no treasure[11] was discovered, and every one considered himself deceived.

Yet scarcely did the next year appear, when[5] it was perceived with surprise that every vine bore threefold. Not[12] till then[12] did the sons learn wisdom; and now, year in, year out, they dug out more[13] and more[13] treasure.[14]

## 23.
### The Emperor as[1] Attorney.

An old soldier, who had long served under the Emperor Augustus, and especially had fought for him in the decisive battle of[2] Actium, was involved in a lawsuit[3] that threatened[4] to be interminable.[4] When he was[5] to appear before the court-of-justice, he applied on the public street to the emperor, and begged him for[6] assistance. Augustus called one[7] of his retinue,[7] and transferred to him the cause of the defendant. But the old soldier was not content with[8] this,

1*

and cried with a loud voice: "O emperor, when thou in the battle of Actium wast[9] in danger, I sought out no substitute, but fought for thee in my own person." At the same time he bared his scarred breast to point to the wounds he had received for the emperor. The latter was touched at[8] this. Not to appear ungrateful, he went with the defendant before the tribunal, defended him with warmth and zeal, and thereby helped him to his rights.[10]

## 24.
### Cross Questions.

Frederick the Great paid so much[1] attention to[2] his regiments of guards, that he knew personally every one of the soldiers. Whenever he saw a fresh one,[3] he used to put the three following questions to[4] him: "1st,[5] How old are you? 2d, How long have you been[6] in my service? 3d, Are you satisfied with your pay and treatment?" It happened that a young Frenchman, who did not understand three words of German, enlisted[7] into the Prussian service, and Frederick, on[8] seeing him, put the usual questions. The soldier had learned the answers, but in the same order as the king generally interrogated.

Unfortunately,[9] on[10] this occasion Frederick began with the second question: "How long have you been in my service?" "Twenty-one years," replied the Frenchman. "What!" said the king, "how old are you then?" "One year," was the reply. "Upon my word," said Frederick, "you or I must be mad." "Both," replied the soldier, according to[11] what he had been taught. "Well," said the astonished monarch, "this is the first time that I was ever called a madman by one of my guards: what do you mean by[12] it, sir?" The poor fellow, seeing the king enraged, told him, in[13] French, that he did not understand a word of German. "Oh! is it so?" said Frederick; "well, learn it as soon as possible, and I have no doubt that you will make[14] a very good soldier."

## 25.
### Female Heroism.

Robert, a gamekeeper, residing[1] in a solitary house near Weilheim, had one day[2] gone to[3] church with[3] his family, leaving[4] at[5] home a daughter aged sixteen. They had not been long gone, when there appeared at the door an old man, apparently half dead with[6] cold. Feeling[7] for his situation, she let him in and went into the kitchen to prepare him some soup. Through a window, which communicated[8] with the room in which she had left him, she perceived that he had dropped[9] the beard he wore, when he entered, and that he now appeared as a robust man, and was pacing[10] the chamber with a poniard in his[11] hand.

Finding[12] no mode of escape,[13] she armed herself with a chopper in one hand, and the boiling soup in the other; and entering[14] the room where he was, first threw the soup in his[15] face, and then struck[16] him a blow on his neck with the chopper, which brought[17] him insensible to the ground.

At[18] this moment another knock at the door occasioned her to look out of an upper window, when she saw a strange hunter who demanded admittance, and on her refusal threatened to break open the door. She immediately took her father's gun, and as[19] he was proceeding to put his threats into execution, she shot him through the right shoulder, on which[20] he made[21] his way back into the forest. Half an hour afterwards a third person came and asked after an old man who must[22] have passed that way. She said she knew nothing of him; and as he was proceeding to break open the door, having[12] by useless threats endeavored to prevail upon her to open it, she shot him dead on the spot.

The incitements to her courage being now at[5] an end, her spirits began to sink, and she fired and screamed from the windows, until some persons were attracted to the house; but nothing could induce her to open the door until the return[23] of the family from church.

## 26.
### The Two Merchants.

A Persian merchant, having[1] occasion to travel on business,[2] deposited a hundred-weight of[3] silver with[4] a neighbor. On[4] his return he asked[5] to have[6] it restored to him. "Your silver!" said the other, "alas! I have it no longer: I regret to say that a rat has devoured the whole; I was very angry with my servants, but what could I do? Every one is liable to accidents."

The merchant was astonished at this prodigy; but, nevertheless, pretended[7] to believe it. Some days after, meeting the child of his perfidious neighbor, he carried him to his house, concealed him, and invited the father to dinner. The latter excused himself, and bursting into tears, said: "I beg of you to allow me to decline. Never again shall I know happiness. I had an only son, whom I loved better than my life; alas! how shall I speak it? I have him no longer. He has been stolen from me: have pity on[8] my misfortune."

The merchant replied: "Yesterday evening about[9] dusk, a screech-owl pounced upon your son, and carried him off to[10] some ruin." "How can I credit," said the father, "that an owl could ever carry off so large a[11] booty? If necessary, my son could have caught the bird." "I can't pretend[12] to tell you how," replied the other, "excepting that I saw it with my own eyes, and I must observe that I cannot perceive[13] what[14] right you have to doubt it when I say so (*es*). What can there be remarkable in a screech-owl's carrying off[15] a child weighing but fifty pounds, when a rat will devour silver, and a whole hundred-weight too?"

The other, comprehending what he meant, gave the merchant his silver, who returned him his hopeful son.

A similar discussion happened[16] between two travelers. One of them was of the class which sees nothing but through a magnifying-glass, and finds everything gigantic.

I have seen," he says, "a cabbage larger than a house." "And I," says the other, "a saucepan as large as a church." The first laughs at him; the other replies: "Softly, friend, softly, the saucepan was made on purpose to boil your cabbage."

## 27.
## Peter the Hermit.

Peter the Hermit, a native of Amiens, in Picardy, was a man of[1] great zeal, courage, and piety. He had made a pilgrimage to[2] the holy sepulchre at Jerusalem, and beheld with indignation the cruel manner in[3] which the Christians were treated by the Infidels, who were in the possession of the place. Unable to repress his resentment, he entertained,[4] upon his return, the bold design of freeing[5] the whole country from the Mahometan yoke, and of restoring to the Christians the land where their religion was first propagated. He first proposed his views to Martin II, at that time[6] pope, who assisted this bold enthusiast in his aims.

Peter, warmed with a zeal that knew no bounds, began to preach the Crusade, and to excite the princes of Christendom to the recovery of the Holy Land. Bare-headed, and bare-footed, he traveled from court to court, preaching as[7] he went, and inflaming the zeal of every rank of people. The fame of his design being thus diffused, prelates, nobles, and princes, concurred in[5] seconding it; and, at (in) a council held at Clermont, where the pope himself exhorted to the undertaking, the whole assembly cried out with one voice, as if[8] by inspiration: *It is the will of God. It is the will of God.* From that time, nothing was seen[9] but[10] a universal migration of the western nations into the east: men of all ranks flew to arms with the utmost alacrity, and bore the sign of the cross upon their right shoulder, as a mark of their devotion to[11] the cause. GOLDSMITH.

## 28.
### Filial Affection of a Page.

The emperor Charles V. had a page named Athanasius d'Ayala, whose[1] father had had the imprudence to engage[2] in a conspiracy against his monarch; he was proscribed, his property confiscated, and he himself was obliged to flee. Athanasius was yet very young, not being[3] more than fourteen, and consequently did not[5] receive any[5] salary at court; his tender heart was deeply afflicted at the situation of his father, who was reduced to poverty, and he had no means of[6] sending him assistance. At length, unable to support the idea of[7] the sufferings of his parent, the young Athanasius sold the horse that was allowed him for his exercises[8], and sent the money to his father.

The horse was soon missed and the page interrogated; but he obstinately refused to give any account of him.[9] The emperor, being informed[10] of the circumstance, ordered[11] Athanasius to be brought[11] before him, and insisted[12] on knowing what he had done with the horse. The youth immediately fell on his knees, and bursting into tears confessed the whole, saying, "I hope that your majesty will pardon me, for, if my father has forgotten his duty to his king, he is nevertheless my father, and nothing could excuse me if I were[13] to forget my duty towards him."

## 29.
### Delicacy of Alphonso, King of Aragon.

Alphonso, king of Aragon, went one day to[1] a jeweler's to purchase some diamonds for (αἰδ) presents to[2] a foreign prince. He was accompanied by several courtiers, and the jeweler spread his finest diamonds and other precious stones before them without hesitation. The prince, after making his purchases, retired; but he had scarcely left the house when[3] the jeweler came[4] after him, and requested he would do him the honor to return for a moment, as he had something important to say to him. The prince and his courtiers re-entered, and the jeweler then said that a diamond of great value had been taken by [some] one of his attendants.

Alphonso looked sternly at those who accompanied him, saying, "Whichsoever[5] of you has stolen the diamond, he deserves the most severe punishment; but the publication of his name might[6] perhaps tarnish the reputation of an honorable family; I will spare them that disgrace." He then desired the jeweler to bring a large pot full[7] of bran. When it was brought, he ordered every one of the attendants to plunge his right hand closed into the pot, and to draw it out quite open. It was done; and, the bran being sifted, the diamond was found. The prince then addressed them, saying: "Gentlemen, I will not suspect any one among you; I will forget the affair: the culpable[8] person cannot escape the torment of his guilty conscience."

### 30.
### Walter Scott at School.[1]

When this celebrated author was at school,[1] he was very laborious; yet it appears that his intellect was not brilliant, and that his great success in after-life[2] was owing to[3] his indefatigable perseverance.

The following anecdote is[4] found in his autobiography lately published.

"There was," says Walter Scott, "a boy in my class who stood always at the top, and I could not, with all my efforts, supplant him. Day came after day, and still he kept his place: at length I observed that, when a question[5] was asked him, he always fumbled with his fingers at[6] a particular button on the lower part of his waistcoat while[7] seeking an answer. I thought therefore if[8] I could remove the button slyly, the surprise at[9] not finding[9] it might derange his ideas at the next interrogation of the class, and give me a chance of taking him down. The button was therefore removed without his perceiving[10] it. Great was my anxiety to[9] know the success of my measure, and it succceeded but[11] too well.

"The hour of interrogation arrived, and the boy was questioned: he sought, as usual, with his fingers, the friendly button, but he could not find it. Disconcerted he looked down, the talisman was gone, his ideas became confused, he could not reply. I seized the opportunity, answered the question, and took his place, which he never recovered, nor[12] do I believe he ever suspected the author of the trick.

"I have often met with him since we entered the world, and never without[13] feeling my conscience[14] reproach me. Frequently have I resolved to make him some amends by rendering[15] him a service; but an opportunity did not present itself, and I fear I did not seek one with as much ardor as I sought to supplant him at school."

## 31.
### Diamond cut Diamond.[1]

A gentleman of Oliver Cromwell's domestic-establishment had conceived a great affection for the Protector's youngest daughter; the young lady did not discourage him, and at length he proposed a secret marriage, as there was no hope of obtaining her father's consent. A person[2] having[3] discovered the secret, communicated it to Cromwell, who gave him orders to watch, and to let him know the next time[4] the gentleman and his daughter should[5] be together. This happened on[6] the following day, and Cromwell, being informed of it, entered suddenly his daughter's room, where he found the gentleman on his[7] knees before her.

The Protector in a fury demanded an explanation of his conduct, and the other, with great presence of mind, replied: "May[8] it please your highness, I have a great affection for your daughter's chamber-maid; but she refuses to give me her hand; so, thinking this young lady had great influence over her, I was soliciting that she would[9] intercede for me."

"Oh!" replied Oliver, "if that's the case, I will see what I can do for you." And calling the young woman, he said to her: "Why do you refuse the honor of marrying Mr. White? he is my friend, and I insist[10] that you give your consent." The young woman, who had no[11] objection, blushed deeply and Cromwell said: "Ah! I see how it is, a little coquetry; go call me the chaplain." The chaplain came, and Oliver ordered him immediately to marry[12] Mr. White and the chamber-maid. Mr. W. was obliged to submit or to expose himself to the vengeance of Cromwell, who, however, to render the bride more attractive, gave her a portion of five hundred pounds.

### 32.
### Humanity of Louis XIV.

During the reign of Louis the Fourteenth, an Italian chemist named[1] Poli came to Paris, and having obtained an audience of[2] the king, informed him that he had discovered a composition ten times more destructive than gunpowder. Louis was fond of[3] chemistry, and ordered the Italian to prepare the composition, and to make the necessary experiments on[4] a certain day in his presence.

It was done, and everything succeeded according to the wishes of Poli, who then observed to the king that it would give him a great superiority over his enemies. "It is true," said Louis, "and your invention is very ingenious; but mankind already possess sufficient means of destroying[5] each other; you shall be handsomely rewarded for your trouble and ingenuity, but I charge you, for the (zur) honor of human nature, never to divulge your secret."

## 33.
### The Cunning Cutler.

There is[1] at London, in a place called Charing-cross, a very fine statue in[2] bronze of Charles the First on[3] horseback. After the revolution and the decapitation of that monarch, the statue was taken down and sold to a cutler, who undertook to demolish it. He immediately manufactured a great number of knives and forks with bronze handles, and exposed them in his shop as the produce of the statue which was supposed[4] to have been melted. They were so rapidly bought, both[5] by the friends and[5] the enemies of the late monarch, that the cutler soon made[6] a fortune, and retired[6] from business.[7]

Soon after the restoration it was[8] proposed to erect a new statue to the memory of[9] the unfortunate king. The cutler, hearing of this, informed the government that he could spare them the trouble and expense[10] of casting a statue, as the old one was yet in his possession, and that he would sell it to them at a moderate price. The bargain was concluded; and the statue, which he had secretly preserved, was re-elevated on the pedestal at (in) Charing-cross, where it now stands.

## 34.
### Abstraction, or Absence of Mind.

Among the many curious examples of abstraction-of-mind, we have the following laughable one[1] of the celebrated English philosopher, Newton.

Being one morning deeply engaged in the study of some difficult problem, he would not leave it to[2] go and breakfast with the family. His housekeeper, however, fearing that long fasting might make him ill, sent one of the servants into his room, with an egg and a saucepan of water. The servant was told[3] to boil the egg, and stay while her master ate it; but Newton, wishing to be alone, sent her away, saying⁴ he would cook it himself. The servant, after placing it by-the-side-of his watch on the table, and telling him to let it boil three minutes, went out; but fearing he might forget,⁵ she returned soon after, and found him standing by the fire-side, with the egg in his hand, his watch boiling⁶ in the saucepan, and he quite unconscious⁷ of the mistake he had committed.

## 35.
## The Value of Time.

King Alfred, who ascended the throne of England in¹ 871, and who, like² Charlemagne, by his magnanimity and wise government, acquired the title of the Great,³ was a prudent economizer of time, well knowing⁴ that a moment lost can never be recovered. Alfred wished to divide the day into equal portions, in order to appropriate a certain space-of-time to the accomplishment of the different objects he had in view.

This was not an easy matter,⁵ as clocks were at that time nearly unknown in Europe, and quite unknown in England. It is true that in⁶ fine weather the flight of time could be marked, in some⁷ degree, by the course of the sun; but in the night, and when the sun was hidden by clouds, there were no means of judging.

The king, after much reflection and many experiments, ordered⁸ a certain quantity of wax to be⁸ made into six candles of equal length and thickness, which, being⁹ lighted one after the other (as he had found by experience), would¹⁰ last from midday to midday. On each of these candles he marked twelve divisions or inches, so that he knew nearly how the day was going, as the consumption of each candle marked the expiration of a sixth part, or about four hours, and each division or inch denoted the lapse of twenty minutes.

By these means Alfred obtained what he desired, an

exact admeasurement of time; and the improvements which took place during his reign, show that both the king and his people had learned[11] to appreciate its value.

## 36.
## The Bagpiper Revived.

The following event happened in London during the great plague, which in 1665 carried off nearly 100,000 of the inhabitants.

A Scotch bagpiper used to get his living by[1] sitting and playing his bagpipes every day on the steps of St. Andrew's church[2] in Holborn. In order to escape the contagion, he drank a great deal of gin; and, one day, having taken more than usual, he became so drunk that he fell fast asleep on the steps. It was the custom, during the prevalence of that terrible disease, to send carts about every night to collect the dead, and carry them to a common grave or deep pit, of which several had been made in the environs of London.

The men passing[3] with the cart up[3] Holborn-hill, and seeing the piper extended on the steps, naturally thought it was a dead body, and tossed him into the cart among the others, without observing[4] that he had his bagpipe under his arm, and without paying any attention to[5] his dog, which followed the cart, barking and howling most[6] piteously.

The rumbling of the cart over the stones and the cries of the poor dog soon awoke the piper from his drunken lethargy, and not being able to discover where he was, he began squeezing[7] his bagpipe and playing[7] a Scotch air, to the great astonishment and terror of the carters, who immediately fetched lights, and found the Scot sitting erect amid the dead bodies, playing his pipes. He was soon released and restored to his faithful dog. The piper became, from[8] this event, so celebrated, that one of the first sculptors of that epoch made a statue of him and his dog, which is still to be seen[9] in London.

## 37.
## Mercury and the Woodman.

A man was felling a tree on the bank of a river, and by chance let his hatchet slip out of his hand, which dropped nto the water and immediately sank to[1] the bottom. Be-.ng, therefore, in great distress for[2] the loss of his tool, he sat down and bemoaned himself most lamentably.

Upon this, Mercury appeared to him, and, being informed of the cause of his complaint, dived to the bottom of the river, and, coming up again, showed the man a golden hatchet, demanding if that were his. He denied[3] that it was. Upon which Mercury dived a second time, and brought up a silver one.[4] The man refused it, alleging, likewise, that this was not his. He dived a third time, and fetched up the hatchet the man had lost; upon[5] sight of which[6] the poor man was overjoyed, and took it with all humility and thankfulness.

Mercury was so pleased with the fellow's honesty, that he gave him the other two into the bargain[7] as a reward for his just dealing. The man goes to his companions, and, giving them an account of what[8] happened, one of them went presently to the river and let his hatchet fall designedly into the stream; then, sitting down upon the bank, he commenced weeping and lamenting, as if he had been really and sorely afflicted.

Mercury appeared as before, and, diving, brought him up a golden hatchet, asking if that were the hatchet he had lost. Transported at[9] the sight of the precious metal, he answered yes, and went to snatch it greedily. But the god, detesting his abominable impudence, not[10] only refused to give him that, but[10] would not[11] even let[12] him have[12] his own hatchet again.[12]

## 38.
### The Dog and the Eels.

A person[1] had a poodle-dog so intelligent that he was frequently sent on errands; they[2] used to write on a piece of paper what was wanted, and giving him a basket in his mouth, he would[3] go[3] and punctually execute[3] his commission. One day the servants wished to have some sport with him, and writing an order for three pounds of live eels, sent poor[4] Fidèle to fetch them, one[5] of the servants following at some[6] distance. The eels were put into the basket, and the poor dog trotted off with them; but he had not gone far, when he saw some[6] of them slipping over the edge; he set the basket down and tapping them with his paw, made them go in:[7] he then took up his load and set off[5] towards home.[8] In a few moments several of the eels were on the pavement, and poor Fidèle, beginning to be enraged, took them up in his mouth, shook them well, and put them again into the basket; which was scarcely done, when others had crawled out. At length, quite out of patience, he put down the basket, and taking the eels one by[9] one between his teeth, bit them till they were incapable of crawling out; after this he took them home, but from that day would never more go to market.

## 39.
### The Dervise and the Atheist.

Atheists are those ridiculous and impious persons[1] who, contrary to the evidence of their senses, pretend not to believe in[2] the existence of God.

One of them was disputing with a dervise, and said to him: "You tell me that God is omnipresent, yet I cannot[3] see him anywhere;[3] show him to me, and I will believe it. Again I say that a man ought not to be punished for[4] his crimes by your laws, since you say that everything is done by the will of God. You say also that Satan is punished by being condemned to hell-fire; now, as he is said[5] to be[6] of that element, what injury can fire do to itself?"

The dervise, after a moment's reflection, took up a large lump of earth, struck the atheist a violent blow with it, and then left him. The latter went directly to the cady, complained of the injury, and demanded justice. The dervise was summoned to answer,[7] why, instead of replying to the man, he had struck him "What I did," replied the dervise, "was in[8] answer to his ridiculous questions. Of what does he complain? He says he has a pain; let[9] him show it, if he wishes us to believe him: he accuses me of a crime, yet he said that a man ought not to be punished by our laws, since everything, according to our doctrine, was under the direction of God: he complains that I have injured him by striking him with a piece of earth; and he maintains that an element can do no harm to itself: of what then does he complain?" The atheist was confounded, and retired amidst the railleries of the auditors.

To be convinced of the hypocrisy of those infidels, we should see one of them on a bed-of-death; it would be a lesson for the others.

### 40.
### The Queen of Spain has no Legs.

When the German princess Marie of Neuburg, who became wife of Philip IV. of Spain, was on her way to Madrid, she passed through a little town, in Spain, famous for[1] its manufactory of gloves and stockings. The citizens and magistrates thought they could not better express their joy for the reception of their new queen, than by presenting her a sample of those commodities for which their town was remarkable. The major-domo, who conducted the princess, received the gloves very graciously; but when the stockings were presented, he flung them away with indignation, and severely reprimanded the magistrates of the deputation for[2] their indecency.

"Know," said he, "that a queen of Spain has no legs."

The young queen, unacquainted with the etiquette, customs and prejudices of the Spanish court, imagined that they³ were⁴ really going⁴ to cut off her legs. She burst into tears, begging they would conduct her back into Germany, for she could never endure such an operation, and it was with great difficulty that they appeased her. The king, it is said,⁵ never laughed more heartily than at⁶ the recital of this adventure.  HUME'S ESSAYS.

## 41.
## The Wolf and the Lamb.

One¹ hot, sultry day, a wolf and a lamb happened² to come, just at the same time, to a clear brook to quench their thirst. The wolf stood upon the higher ground³ and the lamb at some distance from him down the current.⁴ However,⁵ the wolf, having a mind⁶ to pick⁶* a quarrel with him, asked him why he⁷ troubled the water, and made it so muddy that he could not drink; and at the same time demanded satisfaction.

The lamb, frightened at⁸ this threatening charge, told him, in a tone as mild as possible, that he could not conceive how that could be; since the water which he drank, ran down from the wolf to him, and therefore it could not be disturbed so far up the stream.

"Be that as it may,"⁹ replied the wolf, "you are a rascal, and I have been told¹⁰ that you treated¹¹ me with¹¹ ill language¹¹ behind my back about half a year ago." "Upon my word," says the lamb, "the time you mention was before I was born." "That may¹² be," replied the wolf; "but it was no later than yesterday that I saw your father encouraging the hounds that were pursuing me." "Pardon me!" answered the lamb, "my poor father fell a victim to the butcher's knife upwards of a month since."¹³ "It was your mother, then,"¹⁴ replied the savage beast. "My mother," said the innocent lamb, "died on the day¹ I was born." "Dead or not," vociferated the wolf, as¹⁵ he gnashed his teeth in¹⁵* rage, "I know very well that all the breed¹⁶ of you hate me, and therefore I am determined to have¹⁷ my revenge." So saying, he sprang upon the poor innocent, defenseless thing, tore it to pieces and devoured it.

### 42.
### Honorable Conduct of King John of France.

The name of¹ John does not appear to have been in favor, either² in the royal families of England or² of France, as we find but³ one monarch of that name in each of those countries, unless we reckon the John who reigned but³ four days in France, from⁴ the 15th to⁴ the 19th of November, 1316.

The characters⁵ of the other two Johns were very opposite to each other. John of England was cruel, vindictive, rapacious, and cowardly; and, during a reign of nearly seventeen years, was perpetually at⁶ war with his subjects. John of France, on the contrary, whose reign was nearly as long (from 1350 to 1364), occupied himself so much about⁷ the welfare of his people, that he acquired the surname of¹ the Good.

John, after fighting heroically at the battle of Poictiers, had the misfortune to be made prisoner by the English. He was taken to London, where he remained until a treaty was signed, by which he agreed to pay three millions of gold crowns for⁸ the ransom of himself and the other prisoners, and to leave Gascony, Calais, Guines, and several other places in possession of the English.

The king was then set at liberty, and returned to France, leaving⁹ the dukes of Anjou and Berry, his sons, the duke of Orleans, his brother, and the duke of Bourbon, his cousin, as hostages for the payment of the ransom. Some difficulties having arisen as¹² to the execution of the treaty, the princes obtained permission to go over to Calais on parole, saying they should be better able to explain and terminate the differences there than in England. The duke of Anjou, however, violated his parole, and fled to Paris.

John, highly[13] displeased at[14] such want-of-faith, immediately returned to London, and delivered himself prisoner to ₂Edward ₁king of England, saying: "*If honor is banished from every other place, it ought to remain sacred in the breast of kings.*"

Edward assigned the palace[15] of the Savoy[15] to the king for his residence; but he was soon after attacked by an illness which in a few weeks terminated his existence. His body was sent to France with a splendid retinue, and buried at the Abbey of St. Denis, which is the general burial-place of the French monarchs, as Westminster Abbey and Windsor Castle are[16] for the sovereigns of England.

## 43.
## A Dog's Will.

A gentleman in the country possessed a valuable dog, which had twice saved him from drowning, and several times protected him against thieves; he was consequently much attached to[1] him. At length the poor animal became old and died, and the master, in memory of his fidelity, buried him at the end of his garden, which was near the church-yard; he also had[2] a monument placed[2] over him, with an epitaph in the following words: "Here lies one whose virtues rendered him more worthy of[3] consecrated ground than many who are there interred."

Some busy persons immediately informed the magistrate, denouncing the gentleman as an atheist. The magistrate sent[4] for him, reproached him with[5] his impiety, and threatened to accuse him before the ecclesiastical court. The gentleman began to be alarmed, but recollecting himself,[6] he said to the magistrate: "Sir, your observations are very just, and if my dog had not possessed almost human intelligence, I should merit the punishment with which you threaten me. It would be tiresome to relate to you the history of the faithful creature, but the last act of his life will convince you of his extraordinary intelligence: would you believe it, sir, that he made a will, and among other things, has left you a hundred pounds, which I now bring you!" "Indeed!" replied the magistrate, "he was a most astonishing dog, and you have done [extremely] well in[7] paying[8] honor to his remains; it would be well if everybody had lived so as[9] to merit the inscription that is[10] seen on his tomb."

## 44.
## Ventriloquy.

Ventriloquy is the art of speaking inwardly without any[1] apparent motion of the lips or other organs of speech, and of disguising the voice so as[2] to make[3] it appear that[4] of another person, as if[5] it came from another place.

Some years ago there was in England a man named Hoskins who possessed this art in a very eminent degree, and by the aid of it frequently amused himself at the expense of others. He was once traveling on foot in the country, and overtook on the road a carter driving a cart with a load of hay. After walking some time and conversing with the countryman, Hoskins imitated the crying of a child. As there was not any child to be seen,[6] the carter appeared surprised, and asked Hoskins if he had not heard it; he replied yes, and almost at the same instant the cry was repeated. It appeared this time to come from[7] among[7] the hay in the cart, and the ventriloquist insisted that the carter had concealed a child there.

The poor fellow, astonished and alarmed, stopped his horses and unloaded the cart truss by[8] truss; no child, however, was found, and he reloaded it; which he had scarcely done when[9] the cry was again distinctly heard.

The countryman, frightened[10] out of his wits,[10] immediately took[11] to his heels,[11] and running to the nearest village, told the villagers that he had met the devil on the road, and begged them to go and assist him to recover his cart and horses which he had left in his clutches. The peasants immediately set off armed with pitch-forks and flails, and soon arrived in sight of the supposed devil, who having a wooden leg could not run away. After some difficulty, he persuaded them to let him approach and convince them that he was really a human being.

They were for a long time incredulous, and the experiments he made of his art, increased their belief of[12] his diabolic knowledge. At length, fortunately for Hoskins, the village curate arrived, and explained the matter to the satisfaction of the peasants, who then agreed to accompany the ventriloquist to the next public house, where he treated them with beer and a lunch. Soon after this, Hoskins was engaged[13] at several of the London theatres, where he exhibited his art to the astonishment of the multitude, as ventriloquy was at that time almost unknown, particularly in the provinces.

## 45.
### The Page and the Cherries.

A basket[1] of fine cherries having been sent to Frederick, king of Prussia, at a time when[2] that fruit was extremely carce, he sent them, by one of his pages, to the queen. The page, tempted by the beauty of the cherries, could not resist tasting,[3] and finding them delicious, devoured the whole, without reflecting on (über) the consequences.

A few days afterwards, Frederick asked the queen how she had liked[4] the cherries. "Cherries?" said her majesty, "what[5] cherries?" "Why,[6] did not Clist, the page, bring you a basket the other day?" "No," replied the queen; "I have not seen any." "Oh! oh!" said his majesty, "I will give the lickerish rogue something more savory;" he then went to[7] his room, and wrote the following note to[8] the officer of the royal guard: "*Give the bearer[9] twenty-five lashes, and take[10] his receipt for them.*"[11] He then called Olist, and told him to[12] take the note to the guard-house and wait for an answer.

The page, however, fearing that all was not right (a guilty conscience needs no accuser), determined to send the note by another hand, and just as he was going out, at the palace door, he met a Jew[13] banker who was well known at court, and asked him to carry the note. The Jew, glad of an opportunity of obliging[14] any one at the palace, immediately set off. On his arrival at the guard-house, the officer read the note, told the messenger to wait, and called out the guard. The Jew, thinking it[15] was to do honor to him, as a messenger from court, begged the officer not to give himself any unnecessary trouble. "I do not," replied he; "those ceremonies are quite necessary, as you will find." He then ordered the guard to seize the Jew, and give him twenty-five lashes, which was immediately done. The Jew, with his honor[16] and his back severely wounded, was going[17] away; but the officer told him he could not let him depart till he had given a written acknowledgment for what he had received. The Jew was obliged to comply, for fear of having another account to settle. The affair soon reached the ears of the king, who, though he could not help laughing heartily at the adventure, was obliged to confer some favors on the hero of it, as the Jews frequently advanced him considerable sums of money, in cases of necessity.

## 46.
### The Lounger.

The following story, told of Franklin's mode of treating "loungers" is worth[1] putting[1] into practice occasionally, even in this age and generation. One morning, while

Franklin was preparing his newspaper for[2] the press, a lounger stepped into the store, and spent[3] an hour or more in[4] looking over the books, etc., and finally, taking one into his hand, asked the shop-boy the[5] price. "One dollar," was the answer. "One dollar!" said the lounger, "can't you take less than that?" "No, indeed; one dollar is the price." Another hour had nearly passed, when the lounger asked: "Is Mr. Franklin at home?" "Yes; he is in the printing-office." "I want to see him," said the lounger. The shop-boy immediately informed Mr. Franklin that a gentleman was in the store waiting to see him.

Franklin was soon behind the counter, when the lounger, book[6] in hand, addressed him thus: "Mr. Franklin, what is the lowest you can take for this book?" "One dollar and a quarter," was the ready answer. "One dollar and a quarter! Why, your young man only asked a dollar." "True," said Franklin, "and I could have[7] better afforded to take a dollar then, than to be taken out of the office." The lounger looked surprised, and wishing to end a parley[8] of his own making,[8] said: "Come,[9] Mr. Franklin, tell me what is the lowest you can take for it?" "A dollar and a half," was the reply. "A dollar and a half! Why, you offered it yourself for a dollar and a quarter." "Yes," said Franklin, "and I had better[10] have taken that price then, than a dollar and a half now." The lounger paid the price, and went about[11] his business, in case he had any, and Franklin returned into the printing-office.

## 47.
### Cruelty of King John.

The Jews, since their dispersion, have been frequently treated with cruelty by Christian kings. John of England being much in want of money, and knowing that many of the Jews in his kingdom were very rich, taxed them very heavily, and threw[1] them into prison, to remain[2] there till they would pay. Several of them gave all[3] they possessed: but the king was not satisfied, believing they had yet money concealed: he therefore ordered them to be[4] tortured, until they would acknowledge it.

Some were deprived of an eye, and one in particular, from whom a sum of ten thousand marks was demanded, was treated with yet greater cruelty. The king ordered that one of his[5] teeth should be pulled out every day, till he paid the money. The Jew, not being disposed to reduce himself to poverty, resisted during a whole week, and thus lost seven of his teeth; but unable to bear the pain any longer, he consented on the eighth day, and thus preserved[6] the rest of his teeth at the expense of his fortune: otherwise he would have soon lost all his teeth. Happily[7] for that people they live now in a less barbarous age. No one need fear punishment unless he deserve it.

### 48.
### Real or Intrinsic Value.

A lady who had more money than good sense, was very fond, when she was in the country, of showing[1] her jewels and other finery, in order to astonish the peasants, and give them an idea of her riches and superiority. One day a miller, who brought flour to the house, expressed his admiration of[2] an elegant watch that she wore, and this flattered[3] her pride so much that she showed him a superb diamond-necklace and bracelets.

The miller, after looking at them for some time with admiration, said: "They are very beautiful, and, I dare say,[4] very dear." "Indeed, they are very dear; how much do you suppose they cost?" "Upon my word, I cannot guess," replied he. "Why, they cost more than 20,000 francs." "And what is the use of these stones, madam?" "Oh, they are only[5] to wear."[5] "And do they not bring[6] you anything, madam?" "Oh, no." "Then," replied the miller, "I prefer the two great stones of my mill; they cost me a thousand francs, and they bring me four hundred francs a year, and, besides that, I am not afraid that anybody will steal them." The lady was shocked at² the vulgarity of his ideas, and the miller was astonished that any one could let⁷ so much money remain⁷ idle in such useless baubles.⁸

## 49.
### A Very Singular Excuse.

An Irishman, accused of having stolen a gun, was taken, and brought¹ to justice.¹ On the day of trial he was reflecting on² what² defense he should make before the judges, when he saw a fellow-prisoner return from the court, having been tried³ for³ stealing a goose. "Well," said the Irishman, "how have you come off?"⁴ "Oh!" replied the other, "I am acquitted." "What defense did you make?" "Why, I told the judge that I had brought up the goose from the time it⁵ was a gosling, and that I had witnesses to prove it." "Very good, indeed," said Paddy, who was at that moment called into court⁶ to take his trial;⁷ "wait a short time for me, I shall soon be acquitted."

He was then conducted to the bar, the accusation was read, and the judge asked him what he had to say in his defense. "My lord," replied the Hibernian, "I have brought up that gun ever since it was a pistol, and I can bring witnesses to prove it." The judge, however, and the jury were not sufficiently credulous, and poor Paddy was condemned to be transported.

## 50.
### How to Catch a Pickpocket.¹

A merchant in London, who used to walk very much in the city, the streets of which are always crowded and infested by pickpockets, was continually losing either his pocket-book, his snuff-box, or his purse, without ever being² able to discover the thief. At last he thought of a very ingenious method which promised success. He went to a fishing-tackle shop and bought some strong fish-hooks, which he had³ sewed fast in his pocket with⁴ the points turned downwards, so that anybody might put his hand into the pocket, but could not draw it out without being caught.

Thus prepared he went out as usual to go on 'change,⁵ desiring one of his clerks to follow him at a short distance, to be ready in case he should catch a fish. On⁶ passing up Lombard-street, he felt a slight tug at his coat, and immediately set off⁷ to run, but was prevented by something holding⁸ him back. He turned and saw the pickpocket, and said: "Why do you hold my coat, sir? let me go, I am in a great hurry." At the same time he attempted to snatch the flap from him, which drove the fish-hooks further into his hand, and he cried out: "Oh! oh! sir, I cannot, you are tearing my hand to pieces; pray let me go." "Ah! ah!" said the merchant, "I have then caught the fish that has so frequently bitten; you are the pike, or rather the shark."

By⁹ this time the clerk had come up, and a crowd being assembled around them, had a hearty laugh at the fisherman and fish, whose fin was so firmly hooked that he was obliged to go with the merchant to a surgeon and have³ the flesh cut to disengage the hooks. The gentleman was satisfied with the trick, and did not send the pickpocket to¹⁰ prison; but ever after that¹¹ he could walk safely through the city, with his pocket-book, purse, or snuff-box.

### 51.
### A Singular Precaution.

Two young men¹ set out together on a long journey; one of them was a great spendthrift, but the other being very economical, it was agreed, for their mutual benefit, that the latter should have charge of the purse. The spendthrift soon found himself embarrassed, wishing to buy all the curiosities he saw, and not having money to do it. They slept both in the same room; and one night, after they had been some time in bed, the prodigal called to his friend, saying: "William, William!" but William did not answer, till he heard him call very loud, and fearing he might disturb the people of the house, he said "Well, what do you want?" "Are you asleep?" said the other. "Why?" said William. "Because, if you do not sleep, I want to borrow a pound[2] of you." "Oh, I am fast[3] asleep," he replied, "and have been for some time."

Finding William inexorable, the other frequently got[4] out of bed[4] in the night, and looked about[5] the room for his purse, but could never find it. At last they arrived at the end of their journey, which, by the economy of William, had cost but very little: his companion was much pleased, since he knew that if he had kept the purse, it would have been much more expensive. He then said to William: "Tell me, now that there is[6] no more danger, where you hid the money every night, for I frankly confess that I have often endeavored to find it." "I expected that," said William, "and therefore I always waited till you were in bed; and, after putting[7] out the light, I hid the purse in your own pocket, knowing that you would not seek it there, and took care to rise in the morning before you were up."[8]

The young man acknowledged that he was pleased with the trick his companion had played him;[9] but told him it would, in future, be necessary to find another hiding-place.

## 52.
### Gratitude.

The lieutenant of the police of the caliph Manoun related to one of his friends the following story of an event which had happened to himself.

' I was one evening," said he, "with¹ the caliph when a note was brought which seemed to irritate him very much. After reading it he said to me: 'Go into the next room; you will find a prisoner; keep him in safe custody to-night, interrogate him, and bring him before me to-morrow morning, or answer it² with your head.' I took the man to my own apartment and asked him his country.³ 'I am,' replied he, 'of Damascus.' 'Indeed,' said I, 'that town is dear to me, for I owe my life to one of its inhabitants.' 'Your story,' replied he, 'must be interesting, will you tell it me?' 'I will,' said I; 'it is as follows:'

"'Being once at Damascus, I had the misfortune to displease the caliph, and was pursued by the officers of justice. I escaped out⁴ of⁴ a back window, and sought refuge in another part of the town, where a citizen received me with kindness, and at⁵ the risk⁵ of his life, concealed me in his house till the pursuit was over; then he furnished me with money and a horse, to enable me to join⁶ a caravan that was going to Bagdad, my native city. I shall never forget his kindness, and I hope before my death to find an opportunity of proving my gratitude.'

"'That opportunity is at this moment offered to you,' said my prisoner. 'I am the person who had the pleasure of rendering you that service.' He then related to me some circumstances that convinced me he had been my protector. I asked him by what calamity he had excited the caliph's displeasure. 'I have had,' replied he, 'the misfortune to offend an officer who has great influence at court, and he, to revenge himself, has charged⁷ me with an intention⁸ against⁸ the life of the caliph,⁸ for which, though innocent, I shall no doubt pay with my head.'

## 53.
### The Same Subject Continued.

"'No, generous friend,' said I, 'you shall not be sacrificed; you are at liberty; take this purse, return to your family, and I will answer to the caliph.' 'Do you then,' said he, 'think[1] me capable of sacrificing your life that I have once preserved? No, the only favor that I will accept is that you will endeavor to convince the caliph of my innocence: if you fail,[2] I will go and offer him my head, for I will not escape and leave you in danger.'

"I went directly to the caliph, who, as soon as he saw me, demanded my prisoner and sent for the executioner. 'My lord,' said I, 'an extraordinary circumstance has happened concerning him.' 'I swear,' cried he, 'if you have[3] let him escape, your head shall pay for it.' With great difficulty I persuaded him to listen to me, and I then related how my prisoner had saved my life at Damascus; that I had offered him his liberty as a proof of my gratitude, and that he would not accept it for fear of exposing me to his (the caliph's) displeasure. 'My lord,'[4] added I, 'it is improbable that a man of such generous sentiments should be capable of the crime imputed to him; deign[5] then[6] to demand the proofs of it before you condemn him.'

"The caliph expressed his admiration of the conduct of my friend; a strict inquiry was made, and he was found innocent; the accuser was beheaded, and my friend appointed to his place; which he filled[7] with honor till the day of his death."

## 54.
## Noble Blood: A Lesson for Pride.

A very good king, who loved his subjects, and whose constant care was to make them happy, and to show that he considered them as his family, had a son whose disposition was so contrary to that of his father that he despised all those who were beneath him, considering[1] himself a superior creature, and[2] that those whom fortune had placed under him were unworthy of his notice, or fit only to be the slaves of his will. Unfortunately his education had been confided to men who had not had sufficient courage to correct his impetuous and haughty temper, and the good king, his father, saw him arrive at the age of manhood, possessing[3] a character and opinions which, if ever he came to reign,[4] would change his faithful subjects to enemies, and make his throne a seat of thorns instead of roses.

At length the prince married a foreign princess and became a father; and the king, by[5] the advice of one of his faithful courtiers, thought this a favorable opportunity to give him a lesson on[6] the nobility of birth. For this purpose, on the morning after his child was born, another infant of the same age, dressed exactly in the same manner, was placed in the cradle by the side of it.[7]

The prince, on rising, went to see his little son, but what[8] was his surprise on[9] finding two children resembling each other so much that he could not distinguish his own! He called the servants, and finding them equally embarrassed, he gave way to his rage,[10] swearing that they should be all discharged, and severely punished.

## 55.
### The Same Subject Continued.

The king, his father, arrived at the same instant, and hearing the complaints of the prince, he said smilingly to him: "How is it possible you should mistake and not recognize your own child? is there any other of such noble blood? can any other child resemble him so as[1] to deceive you? where then is your natural superiority?"

Then taking the infant prince in his arms, he said: 'This, my son, is your child, but I should not have been able to distinguish him from the other little innocent if precautions had not been taken [2] by tying a ribbon round his leg: in what then, I ask you again, consists our superiority? It arises[3] only from good conduct and good fortune."

The prince blushed, owned he was wrong, and promised

to entertain more philanthropic sentiments; but the king fearing he might relapse, took[4] an opportunity of giving him another[5] lesson. A short time after, the prince being indisposed, the doctor advised him to[6] be bled,[6] and having to bleed one of the pages on the same day, the king ordered the blood to be preserved in separate bowls. A few hours after, when his son was with him, the king sent for the doctor, and having ordered the two bowls to be brought, desired him to examine the blood, and tell him which was the purest. The doctor, pointing at one of the bowls, said: "That is far more pure than the other." "That blood," said the king to his son, " was taken from the veins of your page, and is, it[7] appears, more pure than yours, because, no[8] doubt, he lives more simply and more conformably[9] to the laws of nature:[9] you see then that by[10] birth all men are equal; they acquire superiority in[11] proportion[11] as they cultivate their minds and render themselves useful to mankind."

## 56.
### The Mysterious Englishmen.

In the year 1767 two Englishmen landed at Calais; they did not go to Dessin's hotel, which was at that time much frequented by their countrymen, but took up their lodging at an obscure inn kept by a man named Dulong. The landlord expected every day that they would set off for Paris; but they made no preparations for[1] departure, and did not even inquire what was worth seeing at Calais. The only amusement they took was to go out sometimes a shooting.

The landlord began after a few weeks to wonder at[2] their stay, and used to gossip of an evening with his neighbor, the grocer, upon the subject. Sometimes they decided that they were spies, at other times they[3] were suspected to be[3] run-aways. However they lived well, and paid so liberally, that it[4] was at last concluded they were fools.

This was confirmed in the opinion of Mr. Dulong, by a proposition which they soon after made to him.

They called him into their room and said: "Landlord, we are very well satisfied with your table and your wine, and, if the lodging suited us, we should probably remain with[5] you some time longer; but unfortunately all your rooms look into the street, and the smacking of postilions' whips and the noise of the carriages disturb us very much."

## 57.
### The Same Subject Continued.

Monsieur Dulong began to feel alarmed and said if[1] it were possible to make any arrangements to render them more comfortable, he would gladly do it. "Well then," said one[2] of them, "we have a proposal to make which will be advantageous to you; it will cost some money, it is true, but we will pay half[3] the expense, and our stay will give you an opportunity of[4] re-imbursing yourself." "Well," said the landlord, "what is it?" "Why," said the Englishmen, "your garden is very quiet, and if you will run up a wall in the corner, you can easily make us two rooms, which is all we shall want; the expense will not be great, as the old wall that is there will form two of the sides, and your house will be worth so much the more."

Dulong was glad to find so easy a method of[4] preserving uch profitable guests: the rooms were constructed, the Englishmen took possession, and appeared very comfortable; living[5] in their usual manner to the great satisfaction and profit of the landlord; though[6] he was at a loss to imagine why they should shut themselves up in such an obscure corner. Thus[7] passed about two months, when one day they told him that they were going on a shooting excursion, and that, as they should be absent perhaps three days, they would take abundance of ammunition. The next morning they set off with their guns on their shoulders, and their shot-bags heavily loaded; the landlord wishing them (a) good sport. They told him that they had left some papers in the apartment, and therefore they took the key with them.

The three days passed, and so[8] did[8] the fourth, fifth, sixth, and seventh, without the return of the strangers. M. Dulong became at first uneasy, then suspicious, and, at last, on the eighth day, he sent for the police officers, and the door was broken open in presence of the necessary witnesses. On the table was found the following note:

## 58.
## The Same Subject Continued.

"Dear Landlord: You know, without doubt, that your town of Calais was in the possession of the English during two hundred years; that it was at length retaken by the Duke of Guise, who treated the English inhabitants as our Edward the Third had treated the French; that is, he seized their goods[1] and drove them out. A short time ago[2] we discovered among some old family-papers some documents of one of our ancestors, who possessed a house at Calais where yours now stands. From these documents we learned that, on[3] the retaking of Calais, he was obliged to flee; but in hopes of[4] being able to return, he buried a very considerable sum of money close to a wall in his garden: the paper contained also such an accurate description of the spot that we doubted not of[4] being able to discover it. We immediately came to Calais, and finding your house on the spot indicated, we took lodgings in it.

"We were soon convinced that the treasure was buried in the corner of your garden; but how[5] dig for[6] it without[7] being[7] seen? We found a method; it was the construction of the apartment. As soon as it was completed, we dug up the earth and found our object in the chest which we have left you. We wish you success in your house, but advise you to give better wine, and to be more reasonable in your prices."

Poor Dulong was dumb with[8] astonishment; he looked at his neighbor the grocer, and then at the empty chest; they both shrugged up their shoulders, and acknowledged that the Englishmen were not quite such fools as they had taken[9] them[9] for.

Judge[10] not the actions of any one without knowing the motives.

### 59.
### The Lost Camel.

A dervise was journeying alone in the desert, when two merchants suddenly met him. "You have lost a camel," said he to the merchants. "Indeed we have," they replied. "Was he not blind in[1] his right eye, and lame in[1] his left leg?" asked the dervise. "He was," replied the merchants. "Had he lost a front tooth?" said the dervise. "He had," rejoined the merchants. "And was he not loaded with honey on one side, and wheat on the other?" "Most certainly he was," they replied; "and as you have seen him so lately, and marked him so particularly, you can, in all probability, conduct us to him." "My friends," said the dervise, "I have never seen your camel, nor ever heard of him but from yourselves." "A pretty story, truly!" said the merchants; "but where are the jewels which formed part[2] of his cargo?" "I have neither seen your camel nor your jewels," repeated the dervise. On[3] this, they seized him and forthwith[4] hurried[4] him before the cadi, where, on the strictest search, nothing could be found upon him, nor could any[5] evidence whatever[5] be adduced to convict[6] him, either of falsehood or of theft.

They were then about[7] to proceed against him as a sorcerer, when the dervise with great calmness thus addressed the court: "I have been much amused with your surprise, and own that there has been some ground for your suspicions; but I have lived long, and alone; and I can find ample scope for observation, even in a desert. I knew that I had crossed the track of a camel that had strayed from its owner, because I saw no mark of human footsteps on the same route; I knew that the animal was blind of one eye, because it had cropped the herbage only on one side of the path, and I perceived that it was lame of one leg, from the faint impression [8]that particular foot had produced upon the sand; I concluded that the animal had lost a tooth, because wherever it had grazed, a small tuft of herbage was left[9] uninjured, in the centre of his bite. As to[10] that which formed the burden[10] of the beast, the busy ants informed me that it was corn on the one side, and the clustering flies, that it was honey on the other."

GOLDSMITH.

## 60.
## The Whistle.
A TRUE STORY WRITTEN FOR HIS NEPHEW BY DR. FRANKLIN.

When I was a child seven years old, my friends on a holiday filled my pockets with coppers. I went directly to[1] a shop where they[2] sold toys for children; and being charmed with[3] the sound of a whistle that I saw by[4] the way[4] in the hands of another boy, I voluntarily offered him all[5] my money for one. I then came home, and went whistling all[6] over[7] the house, much pleased with my whistle, but disturbing the whole family. My brothers, and sisters, and cousins, understanding the bargain I had made, told me that I had given four times as much for it as it was worth. This put[8] me in mind[8] what good things I might[9] have[10] bought[10] with the rest of the money; and they laughed at me so much for my folly, that I cried with[11] vexation, and the reflection gave me more chagrin than the whistle gave me pleasure.

This, however, was afterwards of[12] use to me, as the impression continued (blieb) on my mind; so that often when I was tempted to buy some[13] unnecessary thing,[13] I said to myself, *Don't give too much for the whistle;* and so I saved my money.

As I grew up, came into the world, and observed the actions of men, I met with[14] many, very many, who *gave too much for the whistle.*

When I saw any one fond[15] of popularity, constantly employing himself in political bustles, neglecting his own affairs, and ruining them by that neglect; *He pays, indeed,* say I, *too much for his whistle.*

## 61.
### The Same Subject Continued.

If I knew a miser, who gave up every kind[1] of comfortable living,[1] all the pleasures of doing[2] good to others, all the esteem of his fellow-citizens, and the joys of benevolent friendship, for[3] the sake[3] of accumulating wealth; *Poor man,* say I, *you do indeed pay too much for your whistle.*

When I meet a man-of-pleasure, sacrificing[4] every laudable improvement of the mind, or of his fortune, to mere corporeal[5] sensations,[5] *Mistaken man,* say I, *you are providing[6] pain for[6] yourself instead of pleasure: you give too much for your whistle.*

If I see one fond of fine clothes, fine furniture, fine equipages, all above his fortune, for which he contracts debts, and ends his career in prison; *Alas,* say I, *he has paid dear, very dear, for his whistle.*

When I see a beautiful, sweet-tempered girl, married to[7] an ill-natured brute[8] of a husband:[8] *What a pity it is,* say I, *that she has paid so much for a whistle!*

In short, I conceived that a great part of the miseries of mankind were brought upon them by the false estimates they had made of the value of things, and by their giving[9] too much for their *whistles.*

## 62.
## Benevolence.

The following anecdote of the Duke of Montagu is very remarkable and laudable. During a walk in Saint-James's Park, the duke observed a middle-aged man continually walking to and fro or sitting in a melancholy attitude on one of the benches. Wishing to know something more of him, the duke approached him several times, and endeavored to draw him into conversation,[1] but without success; his only answers were: "Yes, sir; No, sir; I don't know; I believe so," etc.

Determined to obtain some information concerning him, the duke ordered one of his servants to follow him home, and to make all the inquiries[2] he could.[3] The servant, on his return, informed his master that he had learned that the gentleman was a [military] officer with a numerous family; and having nothing but half-pay to support them, he had sent them to a distant part of England, where they could live more cheaply than in London; that he transmitted them the greater part of his pay, and lived as he could himself at London, in order to be near the war-office, where he was soliciting promotion.

The duke, after having obtained further information concerning the residence of the family, determined to do something for the officer, and to procure him an agreeable surprise.

## 63.
## The Same Subject Continued.

In a few days, the preparations being complete, he sent one of his servants into the park to tell him that his master had something of importance to communicate, and requested[1] that he would[1] call on him. The astonished officer followed the servant, and was introduced to the duke, who then told him that a lady of his acquaintance, and who knew his circumstances and was greatly interested² in his welfare, wished very much to see him; that the lady was³ to dine that day at⁴ his house,⁴ and that he would introduce him to her. The officer had scarcely recovered from his surprise when⁵ dinner was announced; the duke conducted him to the dining-room, where, to his great astonishment, he found his wife and family, who were equally amazed and delighted at⁶ meeting him so unexpectedly.

It appears that the duke had sent a messenger to bring the family to London, without permitting any communication with the husband; and that they had but⁷ just⁷ arrived. After the mutual embraces and felicitations, the duke interrupted them, and presenting a paper to the officer, said to him: "Sir, I have discovered that you are a worthy man, and that your present means are not sufficient to support your amiable family; promotion in the army is slow in time of peace; I have a snug little country-house and farm at your service; accept it, go and take possession, and may you live happily." At the same time he presented him a paper in which he acknowledged that he gave the house and grounds to Mr. —— and his heirs forever.

## 64.
### Respect for the Bible.

A little boy, a Sunday scholar, was one day sent by his mother to¹ a shop for² some soap. The shop-woman, having weighed it, took a leaf from the Bible that was ³placed on the counter for⁴ waste paper; at which⁵ the boy was greatly astonished, and vehemently exclaimed: "Why, mistress, that is the Bible!" "Well, what if it be?"⁶ replied the woman. "It is the Bible," repeated the boy, "and what are you going to do with it?" "To wrap up the soap." "But mistress, you should not tear⁷ up⁷ that book, for it is the Bible!" cried the boy with peculiar emphasis. "What does that signify? I bought it for waste paper, to use⁸ in the shop."

The little boy with still[9] increasing[9] energy exclaimed "What, the Bible! I wish it were mine! I would not tear it up like[10] that."[10] "Well," said the woman, "if you will pay me what I gave for it, you shall have it." "Thank you," replied the boy, "I will go home and ask my mother for some money."

Away he went and said: "Mother, mother, please[11] give me some money!" "What for?" said his mother. "To buy a Bible," he replied, "for the woman at the shop was tearing up the Bible, and I told her she should not do it; then she said she would sell it to me. O mother, do[12] give me some money to buy it, that it may not be torn up!"

## 65.
### The Same Subject Continued.

His mother said: "I am very sorry, I cannot, my dear boy, I have none." The child cried, still[1] begged for[2] some money, but in vain. Then, sobbing, he went back to the shop and said: "My mother is poor, and cannot[3] give me any[3] money; but, O mistress, don't tear up the Bible, for my teachers have told me that it is the Word of God!" The woman, perceiving the boy to be[4] greatly concerned, said: "Well, don't cry, for you shall have the Bible, if you will go and get its weight in waste paper." At[5] this unexpected, but joyful proposal, the boy dried up his tears, saying: "That I will, mistress, and thank you too."

Away he ran to his mother and asked her for[2] some paper: she gave him all she had; and then he went to all his neighbors' houses and begged more: and having, as he hoped, collected enough, he hastened with the bundle under his arm to the shop, and on[6] entering exclaimed: "Now, mistress, I have got[7] the paper." "Very well," said the woman, "let me weigh it." The paper was put into one scale, and the Bible into the other. The scale turned[8] in the boy's favor,[8] and he cried out, with tears of joy in his eyes: "The Bible is mine!" and seizing it, he exclaimed: "I have got it! I have got it!" and away he ran home to his mother, crying as he went: "I have got the Bible! I have got the Bible!"

## 66.
### The British Empire.

The British Empire, exclusive[1] of its foreign dependencies, consists of the islands of[2] Great Britain and Ireland, and of the smaller islands contiguous[3] and subordinate to them. Great Britain, the largest and by far the most important of the British Islands, is divided into the kingdoms of[2] England and Scotland. The former occupies[4] its southern, most fruitful and extensive, and the latter its northern, more barren and smaller, portion. After the withdrawal of the Romans from Great Britain, these two divisions became separate and independent states, between which the most violent animosities frequently subsisted.

In consequence of the marriage of Margaret, daughter of Henry VII. of England, to[5] James IV. king of Scotland in 1502, James VI., king of Scotland, ascended the English throne upon[6] the demise of queen Elizabeth in 1604. But notwithstanding this union of the crowns, the two kingdoms had distinct and independent legislatures till 1706, when, under the auspices[7] of queen Anne, a legislative union of England and Scotland was completed. In many respects, however, the institutions of the two countries still continue[8] peculiar. The common-law[9] and the judicial establishments of England differ much from those of Scotland; the prevailing religion and the church-establishment of the former are also materially different from those of the latter; and the manners and customs of the two countries, though gradually[10] assimilating,[11] still preserve many distinguishing features.

## 67.
### The Youthful Martyr.

In the third century, a child named Cyril, of Caesarea, showed uncommon fortitude. He called on the name of Jesus Christ continually, and neither threats nor blows could restrain him. Many children of his own age persecuted him; and his own father drove[1] him out of his house, with the applause of many for his zeal in[2] support[2] of paganism. He was at length summoned to appear before the judge, who thus addressed him: "My child, I will pardon your faults; your father shall receive you again; it is[3] in your power to enjoy your father's estate, provided you are wise and regard your own interest."

"I rejoice to bear[4] reproaches," replied Cyril, "God will receive me—I am glad that I am expelled out of our house—I shall have a better mansion—I fear not death, because it will introduce me to a better life."

Divine grace enabled him to witness this good confession. He was ordered[5] to be bound[6] and led, as it were,[7] to execution. The judge, hoping that the sight of the fire would overcome his resolution, had given secret orders to bring him back again. Cyril remained inflexible. The humanity of the judge induced him still to continue his remonstrances.

"Your fire and your sword," said the young martyr, "are insignificant—I go to a better house and more excellent riches—dispatch[8] me presently, that I may enjoy them." The spectators wept. "You should rather rejoice," continued he, "in conducting[9] me to my punishment; you know not what a city I am going[10] to inhabit, nor what is my hope."

He went to his death amidst the admiration of the whole city.

## 68.
### A Lesson.

A friend of Dean Swift one day sent him a turbot, as a present, by a servant who had frequently been on similar errands, but who had never received the most trifling mark of the Dean's generosity. Having gained¹ admission,¹ he opened the door of the study, abruptly put down the fish, and cried very rudely: "Master has sent you a turbot.' "Young man," said the Dean, rising from his easy-chair, "is that the way you deliver your message? Let me teach you better manners: sit down in my chair, we will change situations, and I will show you how to behave² in future."

The boy sat down, and the Dean, going to the door, came up to the table with a respectful pace, and, making a low bow, said: "Sir, my master presents his kind compliments, hopes you are well, and requests³ your acceptance³ of a small present." "Does he?"⁴ replied the boy; "return⁵ him my best thanks,⁶ and there's half-a-crown for yourself."

The Dean, thus drawn⁷ into an act of generosity, laughed heartily, and gave the boy a crown for his wit.

## 69.
### Rabelais, a Traitor.

This celebrated wit was once at a great distance from Paris, and without money to bear his expenses thither.¹ The ingenious author being thus sharp-set,² got together a convenient quantity of brickdust, and having disposed³ of it into several papers, wrote upon one: Poison for Monsieur;⁴ upon a second: Poison for the Dauphin; and on a third: Poison for the King. Having made this provision⁵ for the royal family of France, he laid his papers so that his landlord, who was an inquisitive man and a good subject, might get⁶ a sight⁶ of them.

The plot succeeded as he desired; the host immediately gave intelligence to the secretary of state. The secretary presently sent down a special messenger, who brought up the traitor to court, and provided him, at the king's expense, with proper accommodations⁷ on the road. As soon as he appeared, he was known⁸ to be the celebrated Rabelais, and his powder, upon examination, being found very innocent, the jest was⁹ only laughed at; for which a less eminent droll would have been sent to the galleys.

SPECTATOR.

## 70.
## Misery of Inactivity.

The happiness to be derived[1] from[2] retirement from[3] the bustle of the city to the peaceful scenes of the country,[4] is[5] more in idea than it often proves [to be] in reality. A tradesman in London, who had risen[6] to wealth from the humble rank of life, resolved to retire to the country to enjoy, undisturbed, the rest of his life. For[7] this purpose, he purchased an estate and mansion in a sequestered corner in the country, and took possession of it.

While the alterations and improvements which he directed[8] to be made [8] were going on, the noise of hammers, saws, chisels, etc., around him, kept him in good spirits. But when his improvements were finished, and his workmen discharged, the stillness everywhere disconcerted him, and he felt quite miserable. He was obliged to have recourse to a smith upon his estate for relief to his mind, and he actually engaged to blow⁹ the bellows for a certain number of hours in the day. In a short time this ceased to afford the relief he desired; he returned to London, and acted[10] as a gratuitous assistant to[11] his own clerk, to whom he had given up business.

## 71.
## Hazael, King of Syria.

In the days of Joram, king[1] of Israel, flourished the prophet Elisha. His character was so eminent, and his fame so widely spread, that Benhadad, the King of Syria, though[2] an idolater, sent to consult him concerning the issue of a distemper which threatened his life. The messenger employed on[3] this occasion, was Hazael, who appears to have been one of the princes, or chief[4] men of the Syrian court.

Charged with rich gifts from the king, he presents himself before the prophet, and accosts him in terms of the highest respect. During the conference which they held together, Elisha fixed his eyes steadfastly on the countenance of Hazael, and discerning, by a prophetic spirit, its future tyranny and cruelty, he could not contain[5] himself from bursting into a flood of tears.

When Hazael, in surprise, inquired into[6] the cause of this sudden emotion, the prophet plainly informed him of the crimes and barbarities which he foresaw[7] that he would afterwards commit. The soul of Hazael abhorred, at this time, the thoughts of cruelty. Uncorrupted, as yet, by ambition or greatness, his indignation rose at[8] being[8] thought[9] capable of the savage actions which the prophet had mentioned; and, with much warmth, he replies: "But[10] what ![10] is thy servant a dog, that he should do this[11] great thing ?"[11]

Elisha makes no[12] return, but[12] to point out[13] a remarkable change which was to take place in his condition: "The Lord hath shown me that thou shalt be king of Syria." In the course of time, all that[14] had been predicted came[15] to pass.[15] Hazael ascended the throne, and ambition took possession of his heart. "He smote the children of Israel in all their coasts. He oppressed them during all the days of king Jehoahaz;" and, from what[16] is left[17] on record[17] of his actions, he plainly appears to have proved[18] what[19] the prophet foresaw[20] him to be,[21] namely, a man of violence, cruelty, and blood.   BLAIR.

## 72.
### Desperate Patriotism.

During the wars of Napoleon in Spain, a regiment of the guard of Jerome, ex[1]-king of Westphalia, arrived under the walls of Figueiras.

The general sent a message to the prior to ask[2] if[3] he would prepare refreshments for his officers and men.[4] The prior replied that the men[4] would[5] find good quarters in the town, but that he and his monks would entertain the general and his staff.

About an hour afterwards a plentiful dinner was served,[6] but the general, knowing[7] by[8] experience how necessary it was for the French to be[9] on their guard[9] when eating[10] and drinking with[11] Spaniards, lest they be deceived, invited the prior and two monks to dine with him.

The invitation was accepted in[12] such a manner[12] as[13] to lull every suspicion. The monks sat[14] down to[15] table and ate and drank plentifully with their guests, who after the repast thanked them heartily for their hospitality; upon[16] which[16] the prior rose and said: "Gentlemen, if you have any[17] worldly affairs to settle,[18] there is no time to be[19] lost; this is the last meal you and I shall take on earth; in an hour we shall know the secrets of the world to come."[20]

The prior and his two monks had put[21] a deadly poison into the wine, in which they had pledged[22] the French officers, and notwithstanding the antidotes immediately given by the doctors, in less than an hour every man, hosts and guests, had ceased to live.

## 73.
### Curious Expedient.

Two Irishmen, blacksmiths by trade,[1] went to Jamaica. Finding soon after their arrival that they could do nothing without a little[2] money to begin with, but that with sixty or seventy pounds and industry they might be able to do[3] some business, they hit[4] upon[4] the following ingenious expedient:

One of them made the other black from head to foot. This[5] being done,[5] he took[6] him to one of the negro-dealers, who, after viewing and approving his stout, athletic appearance, made a bargain to pay eighty pounds for him and prided[7] himself on the purchase, supposing[8] him to be one of the finest negroes on the island. The same evening this newly manufactured negro made[9] off[9] to his countryman, washed himself clean, and resumed his former appearance. Rewards were in vain offered in hand-bills, pursuit was eluded,[10] and discovery, by care and caution, was made impossible.

The two Irishmen commenced business with the money and succeeded[11] so well,[11] that they returned to England with a fortune of several thousand pounds. Previous,[12] however,[12] to their departure from the island, they went to the gentleman from whom they had received the money, recalled the circumstance of the negro to his recollection and made[13] amends[13] both for[19] principal and interest with thanks.

### 74.
### The Storks.

A tame stork lived quietly in the court-yard of the University of Tuebingen, in Suabia, till Count Victor Gravenitz, a student there, shot at[1] a stork's-nest adjacent to the college, and probably wounded the stork in it. This happened in autumn, when the storks begin their migrations. The next spring a stork was[2] observed on the roof of the college, and[3] by[4] its incessant chattering, seemed to wish the tame stork to understand[5] that it would be glad of its company. But as the wings of the other were clipped, the stranger was induced, with great precaution, to come down first to the upper gallery, the next day somewhat[6] lower, and at last after much ceremony, quite into the court. The tame stork, unconscious[7] of harm,[7] went to meet him with a cheerful note, when the other fell upon him with the utmost fury.

The spectators drove away the foreign stork, but he came again the next day to the charge, and during the whole summer skirmishes were exchanged between them.

M. Gravenitz had desired that the tame stork should not be assisted, as having[8] only a single antagonist, and thus[9] being obliged to shift for himself, he learned to be on his guard, and made such a defense that at the end of the campaign the stranger had obtained nothing.

Next spring, however, instead of one stork came four, which immediately attacked the tame stork, who, in the view[10] of several persons defended himself with great valor, till his strength began to fail, when auxiliaries came[11] to his assistance.[11] All the turkeys, geese, ducks, and fowls that were brought up in the court, probably attached by his mild behavior, formed a rampart round him, and permitted him a safe retreat. On this a stricter look-out[12] was kept[12] against the enemy[12] till at the beginning of the third spring, about twenty storks alighted in the college and deprived him of life. The only cause for this malevolence was the shot fired at the nest, which[13] they might have supposed to have been[13] instigated by the tame stork.

## 75.
### The Giant and the Dwarf.

Once a Giant and a Dwarf were friends, and kept together. They made a bargain that they would never forsake each other, but go and seek adventures. The first battle they fought[1] was with two Saracens; and the Dwarf, who was very courageous, dealt[2] one of the champions a most angry blow. It did the Saracen but very little injury, who lifted up his sword, and fairly struck off the poor Dwarf's arm. He was now in a woful plight; but the Giant, coming to his assistance,[3] in a short time left the two Saracens dead on the plain, and the Dwarf cut off the dead man's head out of spite.

They then traveled on to another adventure. This was against three bloody-minded Satyrs, who were carrying off a damsel in distress. The Dwarf was not quite so fierce now as before; but for[4] all that[4] struck the first blow, which was returned by another that knocked out his eye; but the Giant was soon up[5] with them,[5] and had they not fled, would certainly have killed them. They were all very joyful for this victory, and the damsel, who was relieved, fell[6] in love with[6] the Giant and married him.

They now traveled far, and farther than I can tell, till they met with[7] a gang of robbers. The Giant, for the first time, was the foremost now; but the Dwarf was not far behind. The battle was stout and long. Wherever[8] the Giant came, all fell before him; but the Dwarf had[9] like to have been killed[9] more than once. At last the victory declared[10] for the two adventurers; but the Dwarf lost his leg. The Dwarf had now lost an arm, a leg, and an eye, while the Giant was without a single wound: upon which he cried out to his little companion: "My little hero, this is a glorious sport; let us get one victory more, and then we shall have honor forever." "No," cries the Dwarf, who was by this time grown wiser, "no, I declare off,[12] I'll fight no more; for I find in every battle that you get all the honor and rewards, but all the blows fall upon me."

Unequal combinations are always disadvantageous to[13] the weaker side: the rich have the pleasure, and the poor the inconveniences that result[14] from them.[14]

## 76.
### Rotterdam in Winter.

Rotterdam presents a curious and entertaining scene in[1] frosty weather. The large windows, made of the clearest glass, and kept bright by the constant care of the housewives, sparkle in the sun with more than usual lustre; the fine trees, planted along the sides of the streets, are feathered with congealed snow; innumerable pleasure-boats and merchant-ships lie wedged together in the canals; their rigging, masts, and pendants[2] are candied over in the same manner as the branches of the trees; and multitudes[3] of men, women, and children, gliding in their sledges with incredible swiftness and dexterity along the streets and canals, render the whole prospect lively and amusing.

Indeed throughout[4] Holland, in winter, the whole country wears the appearance of a fair. The canals, from one town to another, are often frozen over for[5] three months together,[5] and form a solid floor of ice. The country-people skate to[6] market with milk and vegetables. Sometimes a party of twenty or thirty may be seen going together, young women as well as men, holding each other by the hand, and gliding away[7] with surprising swiftness. Booths are built upon the ice, with large fires in them; and every kind of sport[8] is to be seen on the frozen canals. Sledges drawn by the hand, others by horses, and all gayly decorated, and filled with ladies and children covered with warm furs, fly from one end of the streets to another.

These sledges have no wheels, but move on an iron shoe[9] rounded at the ends. The ladies of all the northern countries are[10] extremely fond[10] of riding[10] in "traineaux"[10] in the winter evenings. These carriages, prettily carved, painted and gilt, are made in the shape of lions, swans, dolphins, peacocks, or any other device, and are fixed on the sledge. The lady on these occasions is gayly dressed in velvet, sables, lace, and jewels, and her head is defended from[11] the cold by a velvet cap turned up with fur; the horse, too, is decorated with feathers and bells, and the horns of a stag are fixed on his head. Several pages on horseback, with flambeaux, attend the carriage to display[12] the equipage and prevent mischief, as they often drive at[13] full speed[13] through the streets in the darkest nights; but [it is] by moonlight [that] all this finery, contrasted with the snow, makes the most beautiful appearance.

## 77.
## A West-Indian Slave.

A negro in[1] one of the islands of [the] West Indies, who had been brought under the influence of religious instruction, became singularly valuable to his owner on account of his integrity and general good conduct, so that his master raised him to an important situation in the management of his estate. This owner wishing to purchase twenty additional[2] slaves, employed him to make the selection, and gave him instructions to choose those who were strong and likely[3] to make[4] good workmen.

The man went to the slave-market, and commenced his search. He had not long surveyed the multitudes offered[5] for[6] sale, before[7] he fixed his eye intently upon an old and decrepit slave, and told his master that he must[8] be one. The master seemed greatly surprised, and remonstrated[9] against it. The poor fellow begged that he might be indulged;[10] when the dealer remarked, that if they bought twenty, he would give[11] them the old man into[11] the bargain.[11]

The purchase was accordingly made, and the slaves were conducted to the plantation of their new master; but upon none did the selector bestow half the attention he did upon the poor old decrepit African. He took him to his own habitation, and laid him upon his own bed; he fed him at his own table, and gave[12] him drink[12] out of his own cup; when he was cold he carried him into the sunshine, and when he was hot he took him into the shade of the cocoa-nut trees.

Astonished at the attention which this confidential slave bestowed upon a fellow slave, his master interrogated him on the subject. He said: "You could not take so intense an interest in[13] the old man but for[14] some special reason; is he a relation of yours,[15] perhaps your father?" "No, massa,"[16] answered the poor fellow, "he is not my father."

"He is then an elder brother?" "No, massa, he is not my brother." "Then he is an uncle, or some other relation." "No, massa, he is not of my kindred at all, not even my friend." "Then," asked the master, "on what account does he excite your interest?" "He is my enemy, massa," replied the slave; "he sold me to the slave-dealer; and my Bible tells me: 'when my enemy hungers, feed him, and when he thirsts, give him drink, for in[17] so doing I shal heap coals[18] of fire[19] upon his head.'"

## 78.
### The Bishop and his Birds.

A worthy bishop, who died lately in a town on the continent, had for [his] arms two fieldfares with the motto: "Are not two sparrows sold for a farthing?" This strange coat of arms had often excited attention, and many persons had wished to know its origin, as it was generally reported that the bishop had chosen it for himself, and that it bore[1] reference to some event in his early life. One day an intimate friend asked him its[2] meaning, and the bishop related the following story: Fifty or sixty years ago, a little boy resided at[3] a small village on the banks of the Danube. His parents were very poor, and as soon as the boy was three or four years old, he was sent into the woods[4] to pick up sticks[5] for fuel.[6] When he grew older, his father taught him to pick the juniper berries, and carry them to a neighboring distiller, who wanted them for[7] making hollands.[8]

Day by day the poor boy went to his task, and on his way he passed by the open windows of the village school, where he saw the school-master teaching a number of boys of about the same age as himself. He looked at these boys with feelings almost of envy, so earnestly did he long to be among them. He was quite aware it was in vain to ask his father to send him to school, for his parents had no money to pay the school-master; and he often passed the whole day thinking, while he was gathering his juniper berries, what he could possibly do to please the school-master in the hope of getting some lessons.

One day, when he was walking sadly along, he saw two of the boys belonging to[9] the school, trying to set[10] a bird-trap, and he asked one of them what it was for. The boy told him that the school-master was very fond of fieldfares, and that they were setting the trap to catch some. This delighted the poor boy, for he recollected that he had often seen a great number of these birds in the juniper wood, where they came to eat the berries; and he had no doubt but[11] he could catch some.

## 79.
### The Same Subject Continued.

The (am) next day the little boy borrowed an old basket of his mother, went to the wood, and had the great delight to catch two fieldfares. He put them in the basket, and tying an old handkerchief over it, he took them to (in) the school-master's house. Just as he arrived at the door, he saw the two little boys, who had been setting the trap, and with some alarm he asked them if they had caught any birds. They answered in the negative[1], and the boy, his[2] heart beating with joy, was admitted into the school-master's presence. In a few words he told how he had seen the boys setting the trap, and how he had caught the birds, to bring them as a present to the master.

"A present, my good boy!" cried the school-master, "you do not look as if you could [afford to] make presents. Tell me your price, and I will pay it to you, and thank you besides."

"I would[3] rather[3] give[4] them to you, sir," said the boy.

The school-master looked at the boy as he stood before him, with[5] bare head and feet, and with ragged trousers that reached only half-way down[6] his naked legs. "You are a very singular boy!" said he; "but if you will take no money, you must tell me what I can do for you, as I cannot accept your present without doing something for it in return. Can I do anything for you?"

"Oh, yes!" said the boy, trembling with delight; "you can do for me what I should like[7] better[7] than anything else."[8]

"What is that?" asked the school-master, smiling.

"Teach me to read," cried the boy, falling on his knees; "oh, dear, kind sir, teach me to read."

The school-master complied. The boy came to him at all his leisure hours, and learned so rapidly that the school-master recommended him to a nobleman who resided in the neighborhood. This gentleman, who was as noble in mind as in his birth, patronized[9] the poor boy, and sent him to school. The boy profited by this opportunity, and when he rose, as[10] he soon did,[10] to wealth and honors, he adopted two fieldfares as his arms.

"What do you mean?" cried the bishop's friend.

"I mean," returned the bishop, with a smile, "that the poor boy was myself."

## 80.
### A Mystery Cleared Up.

A few years ago some persons were traveling in a stage-coach towards London, and at[1] the approach[1] of night they began to express their fears of being attacked by highwaymen. One gentleman said he had ten guineas about[2] him and did not know where to hide them for safety. A lady who sat next to him in the coach advised him to conceal them in his boots, which he immediately did. Soon after a highwayman came up[3] and demanded their purses: the lady told him that she had no money, but that if he would search that gentleman's boots, he would find ten guineas.

The astonished traveler was obliged to submit, and lost his money; but as soon as the robber was gone, he loaded⁴ the lady with abuse, declaring she was a confederate of the thief. She acknowledged that appearances⁵ were against her, but added that if the travelers would all do⁶ her the honor to dine with her on the following day, she would explain, to their satisfaction, her conduct, which appeared so mysterious.

They consented, and after partaking⁷ of⁷ a magnificent dinner, the lady conducted them to the drawing-room, where, showing a pocket-book, she said: "Here is an apology for my conduct of last night; it contains bank-notes for several hundred pounds." Then addressing herself to the gentleman, "Sir," said she, "if I had not directed the highwayman's attention to your ten guineas, I should have lost my bank-notes. I therefore beg that, to make⁸ you amends⁸ for your loss and vexation, you will accept one of a hundred pounds. No excuses, sir, for I consider⁹ myself fortunate in saving¹⁰ the others at that price." The travelers were highly pleased with the lady's generosity, and complimented her on¹¹ her presence of mind.

## 81.
### Dionysius the Tyrant.

Dionysius, the tyrant of Sicily, showed how far he was from¹ being happy¹ even whilst he was abounding² in³ riches, and all the pleasures which riches can procure. Damocles, one of his flatterers, was complimenting him upon his power, his treasures, and the magnificence of his royal state, and affirmed that no⁴ monarch ever⁴ was greater or happier than he. "Have⁵ you a mind,⁵ Damocles," says the king, "to taste this happiness, and know by experience what⁶ my enjoyments are, of which you have so high an idea?"

Damocles gladly accepted the offer; upon which⁷ the

king ordered that a royal banquet should be prepared, and a gilded couch placed[8] for him, covered with rich embroidery, and side-boards loaded with gold and silver plate[9] of immense value. Pages of extraordinary beauty were ordered[10] to wait[11] on him at table, and to obey his commands with the greatest readiness, and the most profound submission. Neither ointments, chaplets of flowers, nor rich perfumes were wanting.[12] The table was loaded with the most exquisite delicacies of every kind.

Damocles fancied[13] himself[13] amongst the gods. In the midst of all this happiness, he sees, let down[14] from the roof over his head, a glittering sword hung[15] by a single hair. The sight of destruction thus threatening him soon put a stop to his joy and reveling. The pomp of his attendants, and the glitter of the carved plate gave[16] him no[17] longer any[17] pleasure. He dreads to stretch forth his hand to the table. He throws off the chaplet of roses. He hastens to remove[18] from his dangerous situation, and at last begs the king to restore him to his former humble condition, having no desire to enjoy any longer such a dreadful kind of happiness.

## 82.
### Napoleon and the British Sailor.

Whilst the French troops were encamped at Boulogne, public attention was much excited by the daring attempt-at-escape made[1] by an English sailor. This person having escaped from the depot and gained the borders of the sea, the[2] woods near[2] which served[2] him for concealment,[2] constructed with no other instrument than a knife, a boat, entirely of[3] the bark-of-trees.

When the weather was fair, he mounted a tree and looked out for the English flag; and having at last observed a British cruiser, he ran to the shore with his boat on his back, and was about to trust himself in his frail vessel to the waves, when he was pursued, arrested, and loaded with chains.

Everybody in the army was anxious[4] to see the boat, and Napoleon having at length heard of the affair, sent for the sailor and interrogated[5] him. "You must,"[6] said Napoleon, "have had a great desire to see your country again, since you could resolve to trust yourself on the open sea in so frail a bark. I suppose you have left a sweetheart there?" "No," said the sailor; "but a poor infirm mother, whom I was anxious[7] to see." "And you shall see her," said Napoleon, giving at the same time orders to set him at[8] liberty, and to bestow upon him a considerable sum of money for his mother, observing that "she must be a good mother who had so good a son."

## 83.
## Avarice Punished.

An avaricious merchant in Turkey, having lost a purse containing two hundred pieces-of-gold, had[1] it cried by the public crier, offering half its contents to whoever[2] had found and would restore it. A sailor, who had picked it up, went to the crier and told him it was[3] in his possession, and that he was ready to restore it on[4] the proposed conditions. The owner, having thus learned where his purse was, thought he would endeavor to recover it without losing anything.

He therefore told the sailor that if he desired to receive the reward, he must[5] restore also a valuable emerald which was in the purse. The sailor declared that he had found nothing in the purse except the money, and refused to give[6] it up [6] without the recompense. The merchant went and complained[7] to[8] the cadi, who summoned the sailor to appear, and asked him why he detained the purse he had found. "Because," replied he, "the merchant has promised a reward of a hundred pieces, which he now refuses to give, under pretense⁹ that there was a valuable emerald in it, and I swear by Mahomet that in the purse which I found, there was nothing but gold."

The merchant was then desired¹⁰ to describe the emerald and to explain how it came¹¹ into his possession; he did so (es), but in (auf) a manner that convinced the cadi of¹² his dishonesty, and he immediately gave the following judgment: "You have lost a purse containing two hundred pieces of gold, and a valuable emerald; the sailor has found one containing¹³ only 200 pieces; therefore it cannot be yours; you must then have¹ yours cried again, with a description of the precious stone. You," said the cadi to the sailor, "will keep the purse during forty days without touching its contents, and if, at the expiration¹⁴ of that time, no person shall have justified a claim to¹⁵ it, you may justly consider it yours."

## 84.
### Pœtus and Arria.

In¹ the reign of Claudius, the Roman emperor, Arria, the wife of Cecinna Pœtus, was an illustrious pattern of magnanimity and conjugal affection.

It happened that her husband and her son were both, at the same time, attacked with (von) a dangerous illness. The son died. He was a youth endowed with every quality of mind and person² which could endear him to his parents. His mother's heart was torn with³ grief; yet she resolved to conceal⁴ the distressing event from her husband.⁴ She prepared and conducted his funeral so privately, that Pœtus did not know⁵ of his death. Whenever she came into her husband's bed-chamber she pretended her son was⁶ better, and as often as he inquired after his health, would answer that he had⁶ rested well, or had eaten with appetite. When she found that she could not longer retain her grief, and that her tears were gushing⁷ out,⁷ she would leave the room, and after having given[8] vent[8] to her passion, return again with dry eyes and a serene countenance, as if she had left her sorrow behind her at the door of the chamber.

Camillus Scribonianus, the governor of Dalmatia, having taken up arms against Claudius, Pœtus joined himself to[9] his party, and was soon after taken[10] prisoner, and brought to Rome. When the guards were going to put him on[11] board[11] the ship, Arria besought them that she might be permitted[12] to go with him. "Certainly," said she, "you cannot refuse a man of consular dignity, as he is, a few attendants to wait upon him; but, if you will take me, I alone will perform their office." This favor, however, was refused: upon which she hired a small fishing vessel, and boldly ventured to follow the ship.

## 85.
### The Same Subject Continued.

Returning[1] to Rome, Arria met the wife of Scribonianus in the emperor's palace, who pressed her to discover all that she knew of the insurrection. "What!" said she, "shall I regard thy advice, who[2] saw thy husband murdered in thy [very] arms, and yet survivest him?"

Pœtus being condemned to die, Arria formed[3] a deliberate resolution to share his fate, and made no secret of[4] her intention. Thrasea, who married her daughter, attempting to dissuade her from her purpose, among other arguments which he used, said to her: "Would you then, if my life were to be taken from me, advise your daughter to die with me?" "Most certainly I would," she replied, "if she had lived as long, and in as much harmony with you, as I [have lived] with Pœtus."

Persisting in her determination, she found means to provide herself with a dagger: and one day, when she observed a more than usual gloom on the countenance of Pœtus, and perceived that death by the hand of the executioner appeared to him more terrible than in the field of glory; perhaps, too, sensible[5] that it was chiefly for her sake that he wished to live, she drew the dagger from her side, and stabbed herself before his eyes. Then instantly plucking the weapon from her breast, she presented it to her husband, saying:[6] "My Pœtus, it is not painful."   PLINY.

## 86.
## Origin of the Chimney-Sweepers' Holiday in London.

There was formerly at London, on the first of May of every year, a superb feast given to the chimney-sweepers of the metropolis, at Montagu-House, Cavendish-Square, the town[1] residence[1] of the [2]Montagu [1]family. The custom is said[2] to have taken[3] its origin[3] from the following circumstances:

Lady Montagu, being at her country-seat as usual in the summer, used to send[4] her little boy Edward to walk[4] every day with the footman, who had strict orders never to lose[5] sight[5] of him. One day, however, the servant, meeting an old acquaintance, went into an ale-house to drink, and left the little boy running about by himself.[6] After staying some time drinking,[7] the footman came out to look for the child to take him home to dinner, but he could not find him. He wandered about till night,[8] inquiring at every cottage and at every house, but in vain; no Edward could be found. The poor mother, as may[9] well be imagined, was in the greatest anxiety about the absence of her dear boy; but it would be impossible to describe her grief and despair when the footman returned and told her he did not know what had become[10] of him. People were sent[11] to seek him in all directions; advertisements were put in all the newspapers; bills were stuck up in London, and in most of the great towns of England, offering a considerable reward to any[12] person[12] who would bring him, or give any news of him. All endeavors were, however, unsuccessful, and it was concluded that the poor child had fallen into some pond, or that he had been stolen by gypsies, who would not bring him back for[13] fear of being punished.

## 87.
### The Same Subject Continued.

Lady Montagu passed three long years in this miserable uncertainty: she did not return to London as usual in the winter, but passed her time in grief and solitude in the country. At length one of her sisters married; and after many refusals, Lady Montagu consented to give a ball and supper on the[1] occasion at her town-house. She arrived in London to superintend the preparations, and while the supper was cooking,[2] the whole house was alarmed by the cry of fire!

It appears that one of the cooks had overturned a saucepan, and set fire to the chimney. The chimney-sweepers were[3] sent for, and a little boy was sent up; but the smoke nearly suffocated him, and he fell into the fire-place. Lady Montagu came herself with some vinegar and a smelling-bottle; she began to bathe his temples and his neck, when suddenly she screamed out, "Oh! Edward!" and fell senseless on the floor. She soon recovered, and taking the little sweep in her arms, pressed him to her bosom, crying, "It is my dear Edward! It is my lost boy!"

It appears she had recognized him by[4] a mark on his neck. The master-chimney-sweeper, on[5] being asked[5] where he obtained the child, said he had bought him about a year before of a gypsy woman, who said he was her son. All that the boy could remember was, that some people had given him fruit, and told him they would take him home to his mamma; but that they took him a long[6] way[6] upon a donkey, and after keeping him a long while, they told him he must[7] go and live with the chimney-sweeper, who was his father : that they had[7] beaten him so much whenever[8] he spoke of his mamma and of his fine house, that he was almost afraid to think of it. But he said his master, the chimney-sweeper, had[7] treated him very well.

Lady Montagu rewarded the man handsomely, and from that time she gave a feast to all the chimney-sweepers of the metropolis on the first of May, the birthday of little Edward, who always presided at the table, which was covered with the good old English fare, roast beef, plum-pudding, and strong beer. This event happened many, many years ago, and Lady Montagu and Edward are both dead ; but the first of May is still celebrated as the chimney-sweepers' holiday, and you[9] may see them on that day in all parts of London, dressed[10] in ribbons and all sorts of finery,[11] dancing to music at[12] almost every door, and beating time with the implements of their trade.

## 88.
### Memory.

When Voltaire resided at the court of Frederic the Great, an English gentleman, it is said,[1] arrived at Berlin ; he had so extraordinary a memory that he could repeat a long composition without missing[2] a word, if once recited to him. The king had the curiosity to try him, and the gentleman exceeded all that[3] had been said of his powers.[4]

At this time Voltaire informed his Majesty that he had just finished a poem, which, with his permission, he would read to him. The king gave his consent, and immediately determined to divert himself at the expense of the poet. He ordered[5] the Englishman to be placed[5] behind a screen, and desired him to pay[6] particular attention to[6] what Voltaire was about to read. The author came and read his poem with great emphasis, in hopes of obtaining the king's warm approbation. But, to his great astonishment, the monarch seemed perfectly indifferent all[7] the time[7] he was reading.

When the poem was finished, Voltaire asked his Majesty's opinion about it, and received for[6] answer that of late he observed that M. Voltaire fathered[9] the works of others, and gave them to the world as his own; that he knew this was the case in the present circumstance, as he had once already heard the same poem, and that he therefore could[10] not but[10] feel[10] greatly displeased at the deception attempted[11] to be put upon him. The Frenchman was highly astonished, and complained how grievously he was abused, having just the day before ended the poem. "Well then," said the king, "we will put the matter to the proof." On this he called the gentleman forward and desired him to repeat the verses of which M. Voltaire pretended to be the author.

The Englishman, after a little pause and with great composure, went through the whole poem without missing a single word. "Now," said the king, "must you not confess that my accusation is just?"

"Heavens!" exclaimed the poet, "what have I done to deserve this wrong? Here must be sorcery employed to rob me of my reputation and to drive me to despair."

The king laughed heartily on seeing the poet in such a rage, and, having sufficiently sported with his passion, he told him the artifice which had been employed, and liberally rewarded the Englishman for the amusement he had procured him.

## 89.
## Accident at Prince Schwartzenberg's Hotel at Paris.

On[1] the marriage of Napoleon and Marie Louise, Prince Schwartzenberg gave a splendid festival in honor[2] of his master, the Emperor of Austria, father of the royal bride. For this purpose he caused[3] a sort of hall to be[3] constructed, in the garden of his hotel, in the Chaussée d'Antin. In the midst of the festival the curtains took[4] fire, and in a moment the whole room was⁵ in flames. Napoleon, taking his wife in his arms, retired⁶ with Prince Schwartzenberg to a short distance. Marie Louise returned to St. Cloud, and Napoleon remained in the garden until morning.

The building was entirely consumed and Prince Schwartzenberg's sister-in-law, who had effected her escape from the hall, being uneasy about⁷ one of her children, had entered again, when, in endeavoring to return by a little door which led to the interior of the hotel, she was suffocated and nearly consumed by the flames. Great concern and uneasiness was manifested during the night about her fate, when in the morning her remains were discovered among the ruins. Prince Kourakin, the Russian ambassador, was also severely burned, and about twenty ladies and gentlemen fell victims⁸ to⁹ this shocking accident.⁹

All those who in 1771 had witnessed the festivals given by the city of Paris on the occasion of the marriage between Louis XVI. and Marie Antoinette, were reminded of¹⁰ the catastrophe which took place in the Champs-Elysées and the Place Louis XV., where nearly two thousand persons perished, and saw a melancholy omen in the present occasion.

Although Napoleon is said not to have been superstitious, he was much affected by it, and long after, on the morning before the battle of Dresden, when he was informed that Prince Schwartzenberg had been killed, he said: "He was a brave man, but nevertheless there is something consoling in his death. It was against him, then,¹¹ that the fatal omen, which occurred at that ball on the wedding-day, was directed. We are clear¹² of it."

Two hours afterwards, however, he was informed that Moreau, not Schwartzenberg, had been killed.

## 90.
### Ingratitude and Avarice Punished.

A gentleman, who had acquired a considerable fortune

by care and industry in trade, finding himself at an advanced age, became desirous[1] of quitting the bustle of business,[2] and of passing the remainder of his days in tranquillity. He had a son, newly married, whom he had taken into partnership,[3] and he now gave up the whole business and stock to him. The son and his wife expressed their gratitude for his kindness, and assured him that their greatest attention should be to make him happy.

During some time the old gentleman found himself very comfortable with[4] his son and daughter-in-law and hoped that his worldly cares were over. At length, however, he began to perceive a little inattention, which grew[5] by degrees into[5] absolute neglect. Stung by such base ingratitude, he communicated his affliction to one of his old friends, who consoled him by assuring him that he should soon receive the usual attention from his children if he would follow his advice. "What would you have me[6] do?" said the old gentleman. "You must lend me £500, and it must be done in presence of your son." "Five hundred pounds! I have not so many shillings at[7] my disposal." "Never mind," replied the friend, "I will furnish[8] you, come with me." He gave him the sum and appointed the next day for the experiment.

He called on him in the morning about breakfast-time, and told him before his son and daughter that he had an opportunity of making an excellent speculation, but was[9] rather short[9] of ready money. "Don't let that be an obstacle," said the old gentleman, "how much do you want?" "About £500," replied he. "Oh, if that is all, it is at your service, and twice the sum if necessary." The old gentleman went to his desk, counted [out] the money, and told his friend to take his own time for payment. The son and his wife could but ill[10] conceal their astonishment. On finding (as[11] they imagined) that their father had reserved a considerable sum of money, their conduct changed, and from that day to his death the old gentleman had no reason to complain of want of[12] attention.

He died some years after, having previously made his will, which he deposited in the hands of his old friend. It is the custom in England, on the day of funeral, to read the will of the deceased in presence of the family. It was opened and read; the son and daughter listened with great attention and hopeful anxiety. Judge what was their surprise on finding[15] that the only legacy their father had bequeathed them was a recipe how to[13] reward ungrateful children.

# LETTERS.

### 91.
### Returning[1] Some Books.
*Monday Morning.*

DEAR COUSIN:

I send you the books that you were so good [as] to lend me, and thank you very much for the amusement they have afforded me. I hope I have not put[2] you to[2] any inconvenience[2] by keeping them so long, but I assure you that you are[3] at liberty[3] to do the same with any[4] of mine, and to give you an opportunity, I send you some which I think will interest you; keep them as long as you please.

Adieu, my dear; remember[5] me to my aunt.

*Yours ever truly.*

### 92.
### From an Uncle to His Nephew.
*London*, May 6th, 1865.

MY DEAR NEPHEW:

Having heard that you are very attentive[1] to your studies, and that you are making great progress, I send you a trifling present as a reward for your perseverance. It is a set of Chesterfield's letters elegantly bound; but [it is] not to[2] the binding I wish to draw[3] your attention; the contents[4] of the book, my dear nephew, are[5] what I strongly recommend to your notice.[6]

Read, study, and put[7] in practice[7] the precepts you will there find, and you will become a good man, an ornament of society, and a pattern for mankind to follow.[8] I present you the book in the full reliance that you will profit by it, and that you will receive it as an additional proof that I am ever,

*Your*[9] *affectionate*[9] *uncle.*

## 93.
Answer.

*Cambridge*, May 10th, 1865.

My Very Dear Uncle:

Believe me, I feel highly flattered and honored by your kind attention, and I am delighted with the valuable present you have sent me.

I am happy to have merited your esteem, and will endeavor to convince you how desirous[1] I am to follow your advice, by[2] attentively perusing and scrupulously adhering to the valuable precepts which Lord Chesterfield has bequeathed to the British youth.

Adieu, my dear uncle, accept my grateful thanks[3] and believe me,[4]

Your affectionate nephew,
Charles R.

## 94.

Dear Sir:

A young friend of mine,[1] Mr. Williams, is going to London for a year, to perfect himself in drawing and painting, for which he has great talents. I think he will prove[2] a very pleasant acquisition³ to⁴ the circle of your acquaintance, as he is a young man of good information and agreeable manners. He is quite a stranger⁵ in London, and should there be⁶ any opening for the lucrative exercise of his art, you will much oblige me by⁷ forwarding his views; for although highly respectable in his connections and family, some late⁸ misfortunes which have overtaken them, compel him to rely on the productions of his pencil as a means of subsistence. I have given him a letter to you which he will deliver on⁹ arrival, and I do not doubt that any¹⁰ favor shown him will be amply justified, not only by his merits in his profession, but also by the pleasure to be derived¹¹ from his acquaintance.¹¹

I remain, dear sir,
Your obliged¹² and sincere friend,
MATTHEW SMITH.

## 95.

*Paris.*

DEAR RICHARD:

In consequence of the dullness of every¹ thing here, and of some severe losses that my father has lately experienced, I have determined to seek a situation, and to endeavor to provide for myself. Knowing you are so much in the world at London, I thought it probable that you might hear of² something to suit³ me. I will tell you my idea⁴ of⁴ the subject.

You know that I have always kept⁵ my father's books, by which means I have acquired much useful knowledge.⁶ I have also studied English during two years and made considerable progress.⁶ Now if it were possible to obtain a situation in an English counting-house, I would willingly give⁷ my services during the first twelvemonth, in consideration⁸ of my board.⁸ I should, of course, prefer a house that has French correspondence, as I should be able to undertake⁹ that branch entirely.

I have not mentioned my intention to my father, because I know he would wish to keep me at home; but he has a large family to support, and I wish to lighten his burden; besides, my brother William is now capable of taking[10] my place. When you write, address to[11] me at the post-office, as I shall not communicate it to my father till I have procured something.

Yours[12] sincerely,[12]<br>
CHARLES OLIVIER.

## 96.

DEAR FATHER:

The fear of offending you, and the hope that things[1] would mend, have hitherto prevented me from[2] addressing[2] you on the subject of my situation at Mr. C—'s. I have[3] now been two years with[4] him, and I am sorry to say without much benefit. It is true, I am treated very well as far as regards living, but I am convinced I shall never learn my trade sufficently well to be able to obtain a more lucrative situation. Mr. C— is frequently out-of-town[5] during a fortnight, leaving the business under the direction of his son, who knows very little more of it than I [do].

I think, therefore, dear father, it is a pity to waste my time, and should be much obliged if you would take an opportunity of speaking to Mr. C— on the subject. I have no doubt but[6] a situation might be found which would prove more advantageous in many respects; but I would avoid, if possible, giving[7] offense[7] to my employer.[8] I leave the whole, however, to your judgment and decision, being fully convinced that whatever you do will be for my good.[9] Adieu, dear father; believe me

Your obedient and affectionate son,<br>
JOSEPH WILSON.

## 97.
### Information on Going¹ to London.

*Lyons*, June 3d, 1862.

DEAR SIR:

An opportunity of going to London has just presented itself to me. As you have been there several times, and are no doubt acquainted with the different modes² of traveling and of living there, I will thank³ you for a little advice on these subjects.

I intend to be as economical as possible, but at the same time to see all I can. I shall stay perhaps six weeks or two months, and should like to know in what part of the town it would be most convenient for me to lodge. I hear that there are many furnished rooms in Leicester-square and Covent-Garden ; tell me what you think of them. Perhaps you could also give me an idea how much the journey would cost me, and whether⁴ I had better⁵ procure English money before my departure. I should like also to take a few trifling presents for some friends to whom I am recommended ; tell me what would be most acceptable. I intend to set off in about a week, and will thank you³ for an answer as⁶ soon as convenient.⁶

*I am yours.*

P.S.⁷ If I can execute⁸ any commissions for you, you have only to command me.

## 98.
### Answer.

*Lyons*, June 4th, 1862.

MY DEAR FRIEND :

I am very happy to be able to be of service¹ to you, and I flatter myself you could not apply to any one more capable of giving you the necessary information.

In the first place I advise you to go by the mail to Calais, and then by the steam-packet direct to London. It is the best method for several reasons : first, it is the cheapest ; next,² you avoid the unpleasant examination of your trunks at Dover by the custom-house officers ; it is true they will be examined on your arrival at London, but it will not give³ you so much trouble. Another reason why I recommend you to go direct to London, is the beautiful scenery you will view on each side of that magnificent river (the Thames) which⁴ you will ascend⁴ sixty miles. On your arrival at London, I advise you to take a lodging in a private house where you can board with the family; it will give you an opportunity of perfecting yourself in the language. With respect⁵ to⁵ money, the best method is to procure a letter of credit; and for your presents, if they are for ladies, you can offer nothing more acceptable than lace or gloves.

If you wish any further information, take⁶ the trouble to call on me before your departure, and I will give you all I can. *Yours truly.*

P.S. I open my letter to say⁷ I have just seen a friend who is on the point of going to London, and will be very happy to accompany you; he cannot, however, fix a day for his departure, as he awaits the arrival of letters from Bordeaux.

If your business is not very pressing, I think you would do well⁸ to wait for⁹ him; you would find his company very valuable, as he not only speaks English with great facility, but is also acquainted with London and with several families of-distinction.¹⁰

He dines with me to-morrow; if you can do the same, you will have an opportunity of making his acquaintance; if not, let me hear from you as soon as possible.

## 99.

MADAM:
I am extremely sorry to be under¹ the necessity of giving

you unpleasant and afflicting news concerning your son William. He took cold about a fortnight ago, and in spite of every attention, it has increased[2] and brought on a violent fever, under which he is now suffering severely. He has the best medical advice that can be procured; but I am sorry to say, he grows daily worse, and the physician has this morning declared him[3] to be in a dangerous state. Do not, my dear madam, be displeased[4] that I did not inform you sooner. I hoped it would have passed away, and that he would have recovered before you knew he had been ill. My hopes are, however, disappointed, and I am compelled to give you the distressing intelligence.

I beg[5] to assure you that nothing has been neglected, and that he is treated as if he was my own son. He wishes very much to see you, and says he has something to communicate. If you can come, we will accommodate[6] you with a room as long as you please[7] to stay.

The doctor has this moment paid another visit and says he observes a favorable change since morning. If my hopes had not been so often deceived, I would not send this; my anxiety, however, prompts me not to delay any longer. I earnestly hope that you may find him much better on your arrival. Believe me, madam,

Yours respectfully,<br>
JOHN BRITCHARD.

### 100.
### On a Journey to Marseilles.

*Marseilles*, May 10th, 1865.

MY DEAR SISTER:

When I last[1] wrote to you, I was on the point of setting off for Marseilles, where I arrived the day before yesterday. I did not find the journey so agreeable as that from Paris to Lyons. The roads are excessively dusty, and the country rocky and mountainous; the weather, however, is very fine, though somewhat hot.

I have already paid several visits, and seen a great part of the town, which I like[2] very much, particularly that called the New Town; the streets are very clean and well paved; the principal one is elegant, and leads directly to the port, which is very capacious, and frequented by ships of all nations.

You will perhaps ask how I can be so well acquainted with these things, after a residence of two days; I will tell you. Our excellent friend, Mr. H., has been kind enough to conduct me about[3] the town, and to describe everything[4] worthy of notice;[4] he has also invited me to dine with his family, at his country-house, on Sunday next.

You do not say in your last whether you have received a little parcel I sent you from Lyons; do not fail to let me know it in your next. If I continue[5] to like Marseilles, I shall stay some time; therefore your next letter will, in all[6] probability, find me at No. 45, rue Beauveau. Pray send me all the news you can, and present[7] my kind remembrances[8] to our dear friends. Farewell, dear Anna; accept the best wishes of

*Your affectionate sister.*

## 101.
### From Lord Byron to His Mother.
*Constantinople*, May 18th, 1810.

DEAR MADAM:

I arrived here in an English frigate from Smyrna a few days ago, without any events worth[1] mentioning, except landing[2] to view the plains of Troy, and afterwards, when we were at anchor[3] in the Dardanelles, swimming[4] from Sestos to Abydos, in imitation[5] of Monsieur Leander, whose story you no doubt know too well for[6] me to add[6] anything on the subject,[7] except that I crossed[8] the Hellespont without having so good a motive for the undertaking. As I am just going to visit the Captain-Pacha, you will excuse the brevity of my letter.

When Mr. Adair takes leave, I am to see the Sultan and the mosques, etc.
Believe me yours ever,
BYRON.

## 102.
### Mr. Sterne to Mr. Panchard.
*Turin,* November 15th, 1765.

DEAR SIR:

After many difficulties I have got[1] here safe and sound, though I spent eight days in passing the mountains of Savoy. I am stopped here for ten days, the[2] whole country betwixt here and Milan being[2] laid under water[2] by continued rains; but I am very happy, and have found my way into a dozen houses already. To-morrow I am to be presented to the king; and when the ceremony is over, I shall have my hands full of engagements. There are no English here but Sir James Macdonald, who meets[3] with much respect, and Mr. Ogilby. We are all together. My kind regards[4] to all. Pray forward the inclosed.
Yours[5] most truly,[5]
L. STERNE.

## 103.

HONORED SIR:

After the many occasions[1] I have given you for[2] displeasure, permit me to ask your advice in an affair which may render my life comfortable or miserable. You know, sir, to what low ebb my folly and extravagance have reduced[3] me. Your generous indulgence has made[4] you stretch your kindness, to my shame I say it, even beyond[5] the bounds which wisdom[6] and a necessary regard to[7] the rest of your family would permit; therefore I cannot hope for[7] further assistance from you. Something,[8] however, I must resolve upon to gain a maintenance, and with this view I cannot[9] but[9] rejoice at the offer that was made me

yesterday by Mr. Rich, manager of one of our theatres. He happened¹⁰ to dine at my uncle's when I was there. After dinner, the subject of discourse was the art of an actor, on which my uncle took occasion to mention the little flights¹¹ in that way with which I have diverted myself in my gayer moments, and partly compelled me to give an instance¹² of my abilities. Mr. Rich was pleased to declare his approbation of my manner¹³ and voice, and on being told my circumstances, offered at once to engage me, with an allowance sufficient for present subsistence, and additional encouragement if I should be found to deserve it. Half a benefit¹⁴ he promised me in the first season, which by my numerous acquaintances might, I believe, be turned¹⁵ to pretty good account.¹⁵ I am not fond of this life; but I see no other means of supporting myself like¹⁶ a gentleman.¹⁶ Your speedy answer, honored sir, will be ever gratefully acknowledged by
  Your dutiful, though unhappy son,
        DAVID GARRICK.

## 104.
## Mary Stuart to Queen Elizabeth.

MADAM!

 I am undeceived; I relied on your clemency and generosity. Why will you not see me? Why, instead of offering me a palace, do you throw me into a prison? Why have I incurred your hatred rather than your friendship? By¹ what right does your council and your parliament condemn me to a prison and to chains? Do you persecute me, madam, because my faith differs² from yours, and that we are not daughters of the same church? Is that a political reason why I must support your injustice? However, madam, if you have no regard for my rank and misfortune, condescend at least to have a little consideration³ for my situation; . . . You wish to terrify me, I know it . . . and I know why! Know therefore that I fear nothing. Elizabeth does not yet know Mary Stuart's greatness of soul. I will be silent then under affliction, because I have to console me one who giveth and who taketh away empires, who establishes and who overthrows thrones. Reign, Elizabeth, reign in peace and glory, but remember[4] to govern with justice and humanity.

## 105.

MY DEAR SON:

A bill for[1] ninety pounds sterling was brought to me the other day, said[2] to be drawn upon me by you. I scrupled paying it at first, not on account of the sum, but because you had sent me no letter of advice, which is always done in those transactions; and still more because I did not perceive that you had signed it. The person who presented it desired me to look again, and said that I should discover your name at the bottom. Accordingly I looked again, and with the help of my magnifying-glass, I perceived that what[3] I had first taken only for somebody's mark, was, in truth, your name, written in the worst and smallest hand I ever saw in my life. I cannot write quite so ill, but it was something like this: *Philip Stanhope.*

However, I paid the bill at a venture,[4] though I would almost rather lose the money than that such a signature should be yours. If you were to write in such a character to the secretary's-office,[5] your letter would immediately be sent to the decipherer as[6] containing matters of the utmost secrecy, not fit[7] to be trusted to the common character; whereas an antiquarian would certainly try it by[8] the Runic, Celtic or Sclavonian alphabet, never suspecting it to be[9] a modern character. I have often told you that every man, who has the use of his eyes and of his hand, can write whatever hand he pleases.

You will perhaps say, that when you write so very ill, it is because you are in a hurry, to which I answer: "Why are you ever in a hurry?" I own, your time is much taken up,¹⁰ and you have a great many different things to do; but remember that you had much better¹¹ do half of them well, and leave the other half undone, than do them all indifferently. I hope you won't let me see such a bad hard again, in which expectation I remain,

Yours affectionately,<br>
CHESTERFIELD.

## 106.

DEAR COUSIN:

I am just setting out for Wells, and have not time to say as much as I would on¹ the occasion upon which² I now write to you. I hear that Mr. Dandy and you have lately contracted such an intimacy that you are hardly³ ever³ asunder, and as I know his morals⁴ are not the best, nor his circumstances⁵ the most happy, I fear he will, if he has not already done it, let you see⁶ that he better knows what he does in seeking your acquaintance, than you do in cultivating his.

I am far⁷ from desiring⁷ to abridge you in any necessary or innocent liberty, or to prescribe too much to your choice of a friend; nor⁸ am I against your being complaisant to strangers; for this gentleman's acquaintance is not yet a month old with you; but you must not think that every man, whose conversation is agreeable, is fit⁹ to be immediately treated as a friend. Of all sorts of friendship, hastily contracted ones promise the least duration or satisfaction, as they commonly arise from design on one side, and weakness on the other. True friendship must be the effect of long and mutual esteem and knowledge. It ought to have for its cement an equality of years, a similarity of manners and pretty much a parity in circumstances⁵ and degree (Rang).

But, generally speaking,¹⁰ an openness to a stranger carries with it strong marks of indiscretion and not seldom ends in repentance. For¹¹ these reasons, I recommend you to be upon your guard and proceed cautiously in this new alliance. Mr. Dandy has vivacity and humor enough to please any man[12] of a light turn,[12] but were I to give my judgment of him, I should pronounce[13] him fitter for the tea-table than the cabinet. He is smart, but very superficial, and treats all serious subjects with a contempt too natural to bad minds; and I know more young men than one of whose good opinion he has taken advantage, and has made them wiser, though at their own expense, than he found them.

The caution I here give you is the pure effect of my experience in life, some knowledge of your new associate, and my affection for you. The use you make of it will determine whether you merit this concern from

Your affectionate kinsman,

HARRY CHESTER.

## 107.
## Dr. Johnson to Mr. Elphinstone.

July 27th, 1778.

DEAR SIR:

Having myself suffered what you are now suffering, I well know the weight of your distress, how much need[1] you have of comfort, and how little comfort can be given. A loss such as yours lacerates the mind, and breaks the whole system of purposes and hopes. It leaves a dismal vacuity in life, which affords nothing on which the affections can fix, or to which[2] endeavor[3] may be directed. All this I have known, and it is now, in the vicissitude of things, your turn to know it. But in the condition of mortal beings one must lose one another.[4] What[5] would be the wretchedness of life if there was not always something in view,[6] some Being immutable and unfailing, to whose mercy man must have recourse!

Here we must rest. The greatest Being is the most benevolent. "We must not grieve[7] for the dead, as men without hope," because we know that they are in His hand. We have not indeed leisure to grieve long, because we are hastening to follow them. Your race[8] and mine have been interrupted by many obstacles, but we must humbly hope for[9] a happy end.

I am, sir, etc.

## 108.

My Dear Friend:

I understand[1] that you are in the habit of going to bed early, and that you don't get up till breakfast is ready. Is that true? I can hardly believe it, because I should think you know better how to employ[2] your time.

Man lives but[3] as long as he is awake and does something useful. If you snore away twelve hours out[4] of[4] every twenty-four, you live but one-half of your life, and he[5] who reaches the age of fifty, of which he has passed one-half in bed, cannot be[5] said to have lived more than fifteen years, because he spent the rest of his time in[6] eating, drinking, playing, dressing and other more or less useless things.

What shall we be able to say in[7] justification of such an abuse of our time?

You will find that six or seven hours out of twenty-four are quite sufficient to recover strength against[8] the fatigues of the following day.

The less you sleep, the longer you live, and in employing your time usefully consists the great art of prolonging life.

Take[9] my advice: try to get rid[10] of that bad habit. It can but[3] be conducive to your health and promote your own interest.

Your well-wisher,[11]
John Bennet.

## 109.

HONORED SIR:

I wrote to you by Mr. Bright, but not having received any answer makes me very uneasy. Although I have been as economical as possible, yet I find the pocket-money you allowed me to take monthly from Mr. Walter is not sufficient to defray my necessary expenses, though it was so at first. London is such a place that unless one maintains[1] something[1] of a character,[1] one is sure[2] to be treated with contempt and pointed at as an object of[3] ridicule.

I assure you, sir, that I detest extravagance as much as you can desire, and the small sum which I ask as an addition to your former allowance is only to promote my own interest, which I[4] am sure[4] you have[5] as much at heart[5] as any parent possibly can.

My employer will testify that my conduct has been consistent with the strictest rules of morality. I submit to your judgment what you think proper to allow me in future.[6] I did not choose[7] to mention my want of money to Mr. W—, and for that reason have not taken anything more than what you ordered. I hope you will not be offended with[8] what I have written, as I shall always consider myself happy in performing my duty and securing to myself the favor of my honored parents.

I am, honored sir, your affectionate son,

ALBERT.

## 110.
### Lord Chesterfield to his Son.

DEAR BOY:

People of your age have commonly an unguarded frankness about[1] them, which makes them the easy prey[2] and bubble of the artful and the experienced; they look upon every knave or fool who tells them that he is their friend, to be[3] really so; and pay that profession of simulated friendship with an indiscreet and unbounded confidence, always to[4] their loss, often to their ruin. Beware, therefore, now that[5] you are coming into the world, of these false friendships. Receive them with great civility, but with great incredulity too ; and pay them with compliments, but not with confidence. Do not let[6] your vanity and self-love make you suppose that people become your friends at[7] first sight, or even upon[8] a short acquaintance. Real friendship is[9] a slow grower,[9] and never thrives unless ingrafted upon a stock of known and reciprocal merit.

There is another kind of nominal friendship among young people, which is warm for the time,[10] but, by[11] good luck, of short duration. This friendship is hastily produced by[12] their being accidentally thrown together and pursuing the same course of riot and debauchery. A fine friendship, truly ! and well cemented by levity and drunkenness. It should rather be called a conspiracy against morals and good manners, and be punished as such by the civil magistrate.[13] However, they have the impudence and the folly to call this confederacy a friendship. They lend one another money for bad purposes ; they engage[14] in quarrels,[15] offensive[15] and defensive,[15] for their accomplices; they tell one another all they know, and often more too, when of a[16] sudden some[17] accident disperses them, and they think no more of[18] each other, unless[19] it be[19] to betray their imprudent confidence and laugh at it.[20] Remember to make a great difference between companions and friends; for a very complaisant and agreeable companion may[21] be a very improper and a very dangerous friend. . . .

I long to hear from my several correspondents at Leipsic of your arrival there, and what impression you make on them at first; for I have Arguses with a hundred eyes each, who will watch you narrowly, and relate to me faithfully. My accounts[22] will certainly be true ; it depends upon you entirely of what kind they shall be. Adieu.

# HISTORICAL EXTRACTS.

## 111.
### Franklin.

Benjamin Franklin was ₂a ₃remarkable ₁rather than an accomplished¹ man, and his name in England is connected with the idea² of worldly prudence and strong common sense; while in the United States of America he is almost adored³ as one of the directors⁴ of their struggle for independence. He has attracted also some attention by his experiments on⁵ lightning. The ancestors of his family had been Englishmen, of Eaton, in Northamptonshire; but at the time when the colonies of North America afforded an easy retreat for all who were dissatisfied with the government at home, his father and his uncle changed their religious⁶ sentiments,⁶ became dissenters, and crossed the Atlantic, to settle in New England.

Here his father set up⁷ the business of soap-boiler and tallow-chandler. Benjamin Franklin was born 1705, and was one⁸ of a family of thirteen children. He was tried⁹ at several trades, none¹⁰ of which he liked. Finally he settled¹¹ to the business of printer, one not much practiced¹² at that time in the new settlement. His father seems to have contributed much to form the young character of his son; by his example he taught him to aim¹³ at high and honorable¹⁴ objects; by the severity of his remarks he urged him to bestow pains upon the cultivation of an accurate and just taste-in-¹⁵composition; and by his own necessities,¹⁶ taught him to earn his daily bread with industry and honor.

At seventeen Benjamin disagreed¹⁷ with his elder brother,

to whom he had been articled[18] as apprentice, and set off to seek his fortune in New-York. After several months of labor, he went to England, where he entered a printing-office, and worked for a year and a half. This visit proved of great advantage to him, both directly in his business of printer, and indirectly in expanding his mind. His energy and perseverance made him finally a successful tradesman, as was reasonably to be expected.

When the differences between the American colonies and the mother country arose, Franklin was engaged[19] as an agent in England, Canada, and France; and the art of composition,[15] in which he had become a master, was now employed in[20] drawing up[20] addresses, manifestoes, and declarations, in[21] defense of the politics of the new republic. He was elected one of the delegates to the congress, or temporary government, which took the first steps towards[22] cutting[22] off the ties binding America to the British empire; and after enjoying many honors, he died at Philadelphia, in 1790.

### 112.
### Patriotism of Regulus.

The Carthaginians resolved to send to Rome to negotiate[1] a peace, or at least to procure an exchange of prisoners. For this purpose they supposed that Regulus, the Roman general, whom they had now for[2] four years kept in prison would be a proper solicitor. It was[3] expected that,[4] being[4] wearied with imprisonment and bondage, he would gladly endeavor to persuade his countrymen to discontinue[5] the war, which only prolonged his captivity. He was accordingly sent with their ambassadors to Rome, but with a promise, previously[6] exacted[7] from him, to return in case[8] of being unsuccessful.[8] He[9] was even given to understand[9] that his life depended upon[10] the success of his expedition.

When this old general, together with the ambassadors

of Carthage, approached Rome, many of his friends came out[11] to see[11] him and congratulate him on[12] his return. Their acclamations resounded through the city; but Regulus refused to enter the gates. It was in vain that he was entreated on every side to visit once more his little dwelling, and share in[13] that joy which his return had inspired. He persisted in saying that he was now but a slave belonging to the Carthaginians, and unfit to partake[13] in the honors of his country. The senate assembling without the walls, as usual, to give audience to the ambassadors, Regulus opened his commission, as he had been directed[14] by the Carthaginian council, and their ambassadors seconded his proposals. The senate was by this time weary of a war which had been protracted above eight years, and was no way[15] disinclined[16] to a peace. It seemed the general opinion that the enmity between the two states had continued too long; and that no terms should be refused which might not only give rest to the two nations, but liberty to an old brave general whom the people reverenced and loved.

### 113.
### The Same Subject Continued.

It[1] only remained for Regulus to give his opinion, who, when it came to[2] his turn to speak, to[3] the surprise of[4] every person present[4] gave his voice for continuing[5] the war. He assured the senate that the Carthaginian[6] resources were now almost exhausted; their populace[7] harassed out[8] with fatigues, and their nobles with contention; that all their best generals were prisoners with[9] the Romans, while Carthage had none[10] but the refuse of the Roman army; that not only the interest of Rome, but its honor also was concerned[11] in continuing the war; for their ancestors had never made peace till they were victorious.

So unexpected an advice not [a] little disturbed[12] the senate; they saw the justice of his opinion, but they also saw the dangers he incurred[13] by giving it; they seemed entirely satisfied with the expediency of prolonging the war; their only obstacle was how[14] to secure the safety of *him* who had advised its continuance; they pitied and admired a man who had used such eloquence against his private interest, and could not conclude[15] upon a measure which was to terminate in[16] his ruin. Regulus, however, soon relieved[17] their embarrassment by breaking off the treaty and by rising in order to return to his bonds and confinement. It was in vain that the senate and all his dearest friends entreated him to stay; he still repressed their solicitations. Marcia, his wife, with her little children, filled the city with her lamentations, and vainly entreated to be[18] permitted to see him; he still obstinately persisted in keeping his promise; and though sufficiently apprised of the tortures that awaited him on (bei) his return, without embracing his family or taking leave of his friends, he departed with the ambassadors for Carthage.

Nothing could equal[19] the fury and the disappointment of the Carthaginians when they were informed by their ambassadors that Regulus, instead of promoting a peace, had given his opinion for continuing the war. They accordingly prepared to punish his conduct with the most studied[19] tortures. . . . At last, when malice was fatigued with[20] studying all the arts of torture, he was put into a barrel[21] stuck full[21] of nails that pointed[22] inwards, and in this painful position he continued till he died.

GOLDSMITH.

### 114.
### Copernicus.

Copernicus derives his celebrity from his researches into[1] the laws which regulate the solar system. This system comprehends a number of the heavenly bodies depending[2] on the sun. In early times, it had been observed that some of the stars varied their place with[3] regard to other stars, and these were therefore called *planets*, from a Greek word signifying *to wander*. The sun, the moon, the earth, and the planets, form altogether the solar system.

It was[4] required of astronomy to account[5] for all the appearances which may be seen in these heavenly bodies; for the seasons, for the months, for the movements of the planet Venus, for those of Jupiter, and all the others. It had been supposed, by those who considered the subject in ancient times, that the earth was the principal body amongst all these, and that the others rolled[6] round it. Various alterations had been made in this supposition, as observation pointed out things which were quite contrary to it. And the opinion of the central position of the earth, and the dependence of the rest upon it,[7] continued[8] till the time of Copernicus. He showed that the truth is, that the sun is the chief body of all these which belong to the solar system, and that the rest turn round it. This was a very considerable alteration.

The ancient supposition[9] had been assisted by the most ingenious conjectures with regard[10] to the motions of the planets. But by all these conjectures and alterations, it had become a most complicated and difficult system, and what remained unaccounted for was a strong objection to its truth.

When Copernicus substituted[11] a number of the heavenly bodies revolving[12] round the sun, and showed that the earth is one of them, he abolished all the ingenious errors of the ancient method, and gave us a system clear and simple. His merits consist in this: he showed that the various places, movements, and appearances of the planets can be fully explained and accounted for, by imagining[13] them to move round the sun as a centre: Mercury in eighty-seven days, Venus in two hundred and twenty-four, the earth in one year, Mars in nearly two, Jupiter in eleven, Saturn in twenty-nine.

It is to be[14] remarked, also, that these discoveries were made by him with very poor instruments for his observations, and without any telescopes. But in spite of all difficulties, he made known to mankind the true system of the universe, and has left behind him an everlasting memorial of his industry and genius. He was born at Thorn in Prussia, and studied in Italy at Bologna. His new doctrines gave offense to the Pope, Urban VIII., and for a time he was thrown into prison. He died 1543, in his seventy-first year.

## 115.
### History of Catharine I., Empress of Russia.

Catharine, born near Derpat, a little city in Livonia, was[1] heiress to no other inheritance than the virtues and frugality of her parents. Her father being dead, she lived with her aged mother in their cottage covered with straw ; and both, though very poor, were very contented. Here, retired from the gaze of the world, by the labor of her hands she supported her parent, who was now incapable of supporting herself. While Catharine spun, the old woman would[2] sit by[3] and read some book of devotion ;[4] thus, when the fatigues of the day were over, both would[5] sit down contentedly by[6] their fireside, and enjoy the frugal meal.

Though her face and person were models of perfection, yet her whole attention seemed bestowed upon her mind ; her mother taught her to read, and an old Lutheran minister instructed her in the maxims and duties of religion. Nature had furnished her with a ready and a solid turn-of-thought[7] and with a strong understanding. Such truly female accomplishments procured her several solicitations[8]-of-marriage from the peasants of the country ; but their offers were refused ; for she loved her mother too[9] tenderly to[9] think of a separation.

Catharine was fifteen years old when her mother died : she now therefore left her cottage and went to live with[10] the

Lutheran minister by whom she had been instructed from her childhood. In his house she resided in-quality[11]-of governess to[12] his children, at once reconciling in her character unerring prudence with surprising vivacity.

The old man, who regarded her as one of his children, had[13] her instructed in dancing and music by the masters who attended the rest of his family; thus she continued to improve till he died, by which accident she was once more reduced[14] to pristine[15] poverty. The country of Livonia was at this time wasted by war, and lay in a most[16] miserable state of desolation. Those calamities are ever most heavy upon the poor; wherefore Catharine, though possessed[17] of so many accomplishments, experienced all the miseries of hopeless indigence. Provisions becoming every day more scarce, and her private stock being exhausted, she resolved at last to travel to Marienburgh, a city of greater plenty.

With her scanty wardrobe packed up in a wallet, she set[18] out on her journey on[19] foot: she was to[20] walk through a region miserable by nature; but rendered still more hideous by the Swedes and Russians, who, as[21] each happened to become master, plundered it at[22] discretion: but hunger had taught her to despise the dangers and fatigues of the way.

## 116.
### The Same Subject Continued.

One evening upon her journey, as she entered a cottage by[1] the way-side, to take up her lodging for the night, she was insulted by two Swedish soldiers, who might probably have carried[2] their insults into[2] violence had not a subaltern[3]-officer, accidentally passing by, come in to her assistance; upon[4] his appearing, the soldiers immediately desisted; but her thankfulness was hardly greater than her surprise when she instantly recognized in her deliverer the son of the Lutheran minister, her former instructor, benefactor and friend.

This was a happy interview for Catharine; the little stock of money she had brought from home was by[5] this time quite exhausted, her clothes were gone, piece by piece, in order to satisfy those who had entertained her in their houses; her generous countryman, therefore, parted[6] with what he could spare,[7] to buy her clothes, furnished her with a horse, and gave her letters of recommendation to Mr. Gluck, a faithful friend of his father's, and superintendent at Marienburgh.

Our beautiful stranger had[8] only to appear to be well received; she was immediately admitted into the superintendent's family, as governess to his two daughters; and though yet[9] but[9] seventeen, showed herself capable of instructing her sex, not only in virtue, but in politeness. Such[10] was her good sense and beauty, that her master himself in a short time offered her his hand, which to his great surprise she thought[11] proper to refuse. Actuated by a sentiment of gratitude, she was resolved[12] to marry her deliverer only, even[13] though[13] he had lost an arm, and was otherwise disfigured by wounds in the service.

In order, therefore, to prevent[14] further solicitations from others, as soon as the officer came to town upon duty,[15] she offered him her person, which he accepted with transport, and their nuptials were solemnized as usual. But all the lines of her fortune were[16] to be striking; the very day on which they were married, the Russians laid[17] siege to Marienburgh. The unhappy soldier had now no time to enjoy the well-earned pleasures of matrimony; he was called off to an attack from which he never after returned.

## 117.
### Continuation.

In the mean time the siege went on with fury, aggravated on one side by obstinacy, on the other by revenge.

This war between the two northern powers was, at that time, truly barbarous; the innocent peasant and the harmless virgin often shared the fate of the soldier in arms. Marienburgh was then taken by[1] assault; and such was the fury of the assailants, that not only the garrison, but almost all the inhabitants, men, women, and children, were put[2] to the sword.[2] At length, when the carnage was pretty[3] well over,[3] Catharine was found hid in an oven.

She had been hitherto poor, but still was free; she was[4] now to conform[5] to her hard fate, and to learn what it was to be a slave; in this situation, however, she behaved with piety and humility; and though misfortune had abated her vivacity, yet she was cheerful. The fame of her beauty and resignation reached Prince Menzikoff, the Russian general; he desired to see her, was struck with[6] her beauty, bought her of the soldier, her master, and placed her under the direction of his own sister. Here she was treated with all the respect which her merit deserved, while her beauty every day improved with her good fortune.

She had not been long in this situation when Peter the Great paid the prince a visit, and Catharine happened to come in with some dry fruits which she served round with peculiar modesty. The mighty monarch saw her, and was struck with her beauty. He returned the next day, called for[7] the beautiful slave, asked[8] her several questions, and found her understanding even more perfect than her person.

He had been forced, when young, to marry from motives of interest; he was now resolved to marry according to his own inclination. He immediately inquired[9] the history of the fair Livonian, who was not yet eighteen. He traced[10] her through the veil of obscurity, through all the vicissitudes of her fortune, and found her truly great in them all. The meanness of her birth was no obstacle to his design : their nuptials were solemnized in private; the prince assuring his courtiers that virtue alone was the most proper ladder to a throne.

We now see Catharine, from the low mud-walled cottage, empress of the greatest kingdom upon earth. The poor solitary wanderer is now surrounded by thousands, who find happiness in her smile. She who formerly wanted[11] a meal, is now capable of diffusing plenty upon whole nations. To her fortune she owed a part of this pre-eminence, but to her virtues more.

She ever after retained those great qualities which first placed her on a throne; and while the extraordinary prince, her husband, labored for[12] the reformation of his male subjects, she studied in[13] her turn[13] the improvement of her own sex. She altered their dresses, introduced mixed assemblies, instituted an order of female knighthood; and at length, when she had greatly filled[14] all the stations[15] of[15] empress, friend, wife, and mother, bravely died without regret, regretted by all. GOLDSMITH.

### 118.
### Combat between the Horatii and Curiatii.

After the death of Numa, the Roman people elected Tullus Hostilius for[1] their king. This monarch was every way[2] unlike his predecessor, being entirely devoted to war, so that he only sought a pretext for[3] leading his forces to the field. The Albans were the first people who gave him an opportunity of[3] indulging his favorite inclination. The Roman and Alban forces met[4] about five miles from Rome, prepared to decide the fate of their respective kingdoms· for almost every battle in these barbarous times was de cisive. The two armies were for some time drawn out ir array, awaiting the signal to begin, both chiding[4] the lengtl of that dreadful suspense which kept them from death or victory. But an unexpected proposal from the Alban gen eral put[5] a stop[5] to the onset: he stepped in between botl armies, and by[6] single-combat offered the Romans a choice of deciding the dispute; adding, that the side whose cham pion was overcome, should submit to the conqueror.

A proposal like this suited[7] the impetuous temper of the Roman king, and was embraced[8] with joy by his subjects, each[9] of whom[9] hoped that himself should be chosen to fight[10] the cause of his country. Many valiant men offered themselves, but could not be accepted to the exclusion of others, till at last, chance suggested a remedy. There were at that time three brothers in each army; those of the Romans were called Horatii, and the Albans, Curiatii; all were remarkable for their courage, strength and activity; to[11] them it was resolved[11] to commit the management of the combat.

## 119.
### Continuation.

When the previous ceremony of oaths and protestations binding[1] the army of the vanquished party to submit to that of the victorious was over,[2] the combatants were led forth, amidst the encouragements, the prayers, and the shouts of their country. They were reminded of[3] their former achievements; they were admonished that their fathers, their countrymen, and even the gods, were spectators of their behavior. When the people expected to see them rush to combat, they quitted[4] their arms, and embraced each other with all the marks of the most tender friendship; but, at length warned[5] of the importance of the trial, the champions engaged;[6] and each, totally re gardless of his own safety, sought only the destruction of his opponent.

The spectators, in horrid silence, trembled at[7] every blow, and wished to share the danger, till at length victory, which had hitherto been doubtful, appeared to declare against the Romans; they beheld[8] two of their champions lying[8] dead upon the plain, and the three Curiatii, being all wounded, slowly endeavoring to pursue the survivor, who seemed by flight to beg for mercy. The Alban army, unable to suppress their joy, raised a loud acclamation, while the Romans inwardly cursed and repined[9] at the cowardice of him whom they saw in circumstances of such baseness. Soon, however, they began to alter their sentiments, when they perceived that his flight was only pretended in order to separate his antagonists, whom he was unable to oppose united.

## 120.
## Conclusion.

The Roman champion quickly after stopped his course, and turning[1] upon him who followed most closely behind him, laid him dead at his feet. The second brother, advancing to assist[2] him who was fallen, soon shared the same fate; and now there remained but the last Curiatius to conquer, who, fatigued and quite disabled[3] with[3] his wounds, slowly came up to offer easy victory. He was killed, almost unresisting,[4] while the conqueror exulting, offered him as a victim to the superiority of the Romans, whom now the Alban army consented to obey.

A victory so great, and attended with such signal effects, deserved every honor Rome could bestow; but as if none of the virtues of that age were to be without alloy,[5] the hand which in the morning was exerted to[6] save his country, was before night imbrued in the blood of a sister. Returning triumphant from the field, it raised his indignation to behold her bathed[7] in tears and lamenting the loss of her lover, one of the Curiatii, to whom she was betrothed; but, upon seeing the vest which she had made for her lover among the number of his spoils, and hearing her upbraidings, it provoked him beyond[8] the power of sufferance,[8] so that he slew her in a rage. This action greatly displeased the senate, and drew on himself[9] the condemnation of the magistrates; but he was[10] pardoned by making[11] his appeal to the people.

GOLDSMITH.

## 121.
### Captain Cook.

James Cook, one of the most celebrated circumnavigators ever produced by Britain or any other country, was a native[1] of Yorkshire,[1] and born in 1728. Before the age of thirteen he was bound[2] apprentice to a shop-keeper near Whitby; but some disagreement taking place between himself and his master, he indulged[3] his own inclination in binding[4] himself to some owners of coal vessels at Whitby, and after serving for some years as a common sailor, he was raised to be[5] mate in one of these ships. By-and-by he entered the king's service, and by distinguishing himself as a nautical surveyor and a good calculator and mathematician, he raised[6] himself to notice.

It having been calculated that a transit of Venus over the sun's disk would happen in 1769, a memorial to His Majesty was presented by the Royal Society, in which they stated the importance of making proper observations of this transit, and the attention which had been paid[7] to it in other countries; and entreated that persons might be sent out, at the government's expense, to the Friendly Islands, for[8] the sake[8] of making the proper observation. Alexander Dalrymple was selected, but when the appointment of this gentleman to the command was brought before the Admiralty, Sir Edward Hawke refused to sign the commission of a man not[9] brought up at[10] sea, and unacquainted with the management of a ship; for Mr. Dalrymple's qualifications[11] were those of an astronomer. On the other hand Dalrymple would not go without the commission, and the difficulty ended in[12] the appointment of Cook.

Captain Wallis, who had already been round the world (1766-1768), pitched[13] upon Otaheite as the proper island for the astronomical observations. Cook was made a[14] lieutenant, and sailed July 30th, 1768, with Mr. Banks, afterwards the famous Sir Joseph Banks, Dr. Solander, and others. The countries discovered during this voyage and those that followed are now familiar to us, and need not be mentioned here; but to give a more distinct notion of Cook's character, we will sketch[15] a few of his adventures, and relate the manner of his death.

## 122.
### Continuation.

When they got[1] to Otaheite, the whole affair of the transit of Venus was nearly frustrated by a single savage, who stole the quadrant; by[2] judicious exertions, however, it was regained. The day of the transit was clear, and the observations were successfully made. When the ship first arrived at Otaheite, provisions were obtained by the exchange of beads and other trifles; but these ornaments became no longer matters[3] of request,[3] and the nails were next produced; dealing with this new article, a nail[4] four inches long would purchase[4] twenty cocoanuts, and bread fruit in proportion. June 26th, Cook made a circuit in the pinnace round the island; he also took on board a principal man of the island, Tupia, with a boy of about thirteen. They left Otaheite, and touched[5] at Huaheine, where the king Oree was so pleased with the English, that he desired to exchange names with Cook, and the lieutenant, therefore, was called Oree, while the king took the title of Cookee.

Soon afterwards they reached New Zealand, which had been discovered by Tasman, a Dutch navigator, a hundred years before. The New Zealanders were very thievish and unfriendly, and many lives were lost in the quarrels that took place. On one occasion, Tayeto, the Otaheitan boy, was leaning over the side to hand up some fish, when one of the Zealanders dragged[6] him into the canoe, and paddled[7] off as fast as possible. The marines, on this violent aggression, fired with effect, and Tayeto sprang into the sea and swam back to the ship. In this island, or rather these two islands, were seen certain proofs of the prevalence of the practice of eating human-flesh.

At[8] great risk Cook explored the strait which separates New Zealand into two islands, nearly equal to one another; a current of much violence ran through it, and the ship was scarcely saved from the rocks. This strait is four or five leagues broad at the narrowest part. The adventurers took in a store of fresh water and of wood, and sailed for[9] the Indian seas,[9] intending to return by the Cape of Good Hope to England. They explored a part of the coast of New Holland, or New South Wales, and anchored in a bay, which from the numerous unknown plants found near it (nabe babei) was called Botany Bay. As the sea on this coast was altogether unknown, they were in constant danger from[10] the coral reefs and rocks with[11] which the waters abound.[12]

## 123.
### Continuation.

On one occasion the ship grounded and was lifted over the ledge of a rock, and lay in a hollow within it, while the bumping[1] and grating of the bottom tore away the sheathing-boards and the false keel, and parts of her planking were floating about.[2] When they extricated the ship from this peril, she drew[3] so much water that three pumps could hardly keep it down; they then took a sail, and mixing a large quantity of oakum and wool together, stitched[4] them down[4] by handfuls,[5] and then spread[6] the whole with sheep's-dung. The sail was then hauled[7] under the ship's bottom; and when it came to the leak, the wool and oakum with a part of the sail, were forced[8] inwards[8] by the pressure of the water, so that one pump, instead of three, now now sufficed to keep it under.[9] But they afterwards discovered that the rock itself had contributed to their preservation, for a large piece of it had stuck in one of the holes, and so had kept out the water.

Cook returned home after losing the astronomer who had taken the transit, the midshipman who had suggested the method of patching up the damaged bottom by a sail, and several others, by sickness, and arrived in England on the 11th June, 1771. The circumstances here mentioned, induced him to pay so much attention to the health of his men, that on his second voyage, which lasted more than three years, he lost only one man, and that[10] by consumption.

In 1776 he left on a third voyage, going by the Cape of Good Hope, New Zealand, the Sandwich Islands, to the point where the great continents of America and Asia approach most nearly to each other. In February, 1779, he left the island of Owhyhee, or Ooui, well provided with stores of fresh meat, but unhappily a storm brought him back again. Quarrels began by[11] the natives stealing the tongs and chisel from the armorer's forge; and the day that[12] this happened, there were blows struck and stones thrown in[13] attempts[13] to recover them and punish the thief. The next night the large cutter of one of his vessels was carried off, and Cook set out[14] with armed men to the king's residence.

## 124.
### Conclusion.

All was very quiet, and there was every show[1] of sub mission, till the news came in that one of the native chiefs had been killed by the people in the boats. Now the savages began to arm themselves with long spears, clubs, knives, and mats, and the women, who had been sitting on the shore chatting and eating, removed themselves; while a low murmur ran through the multitude. An old priest came with a cocoanut, and by singing and making a noise, endeavored to distract Captain Cook's attention. He began to think that there[2] was danger, and retired with the marines to the shore, holding the king by the hand, who went very quietly and willingly with him. The natives made a lane for them [to pass], and as they had only fifty or sixty yards to go, and as the boats lay about their own length from the shore, there was no apprehension of[3] the fatal result.

The king's youngest son entered the pinnace without hesitation, and the king himself was doing[4] the same, when his wife threw her arms round his neck, and with one or two chiefs detained him. Cook was desirous of getting the king on board, but after ineffectual attempts was ready to give it up, when one of the natives threw a stone at[5] him. Cook fired at[5] him with small shot, but the fellow had a thick mat, and the charge had little effect; another brandished his spear, when Cook leveled the second barrel, and missing him, shot the next; the sergeant then aimed, and killed him on the spot. When the man fell, the natives retired, but urged by those behind, advanced again and threw a volley of stones. On this the marines fired, and so[6] did[6] the people in the boats. Captain Cook did not approve of this firing and waved[7] his hand to stop it, desiring also the boats to come closer to receive the marines. Unfortunately this waving of the hand was mistaken by one of the officers for a signal to go further[8] off shore;[8] the natives made a rush, the marines hastened to the boats, and Cook was left alone.

He went towards the boat with one hand on the back-of-his-head, to protect it from stones, and with his musket under his arm. One native, with great marks of fear, followed, and struck him on the back of the head with a club. Cook staggered and fell; then another stabbed him in the neck with a dagger. Cook staggered knee-deep into the water, being within five or six yards, all this time, of his own boat. The savages crowded around him and struggled with him in the water, and finally dispatched[9] him, while the men in the boat, as it were within arm's length of him, were so confused and crowded that they could do nothing. Under these circumstances blame has been laid[10] on one or two individuals concerned, imputing either carelessness or stupidity, but it seems no wonder that in such a crowd of assailants the result was thus fatal. Cook's body was devoured by the savages, and only some bones and the hands, already salted, were obtained by burning a village, and other acts of war.

The peculiar excellence[11] of Cook's voyages consists in this,[12] that everything is seen with an accurate and observing eye. He describes the productions, habits of the natives, appearances of the seas, water-spouts in the air, oyster-beds, [in] short everything, in a way[13] that interests and delights us.

## 125.
### Discovery of America.

On the third of August, in the year 1492, Columbus set sail a little before sunrise, in presence of a vast crowd of spectators, who sent [up] their supplications to heaven for the prosperous issue of the voyage, which they wished rather than expected. Columbus steered directly for the Canary Islands, and arrived there without any occurrence that would have deserved notice on any other occasion. But in a voyage of such expectation and importance, every circumstance was the object of attention.

On the first of October they were, according to the admiral's reckoning, seven hundred and seventy leagues to the west of the Canaries; but lest[2] his men should be intimidated by the prodigious length of the navigation, he gave[3] out that they had proceeded only five hundred and eighty-four leagues; and fortunately for Columbus, neither his own pilot nor those of the other ships had skill enough to correct this error and discover the deceit. They had now been above three weeks at sea; they had proceeded far[4] beyond[4] what former navigators had attempted or deemed[5] possible; all their prognostics of discovery, drawn from the flight of birds and other circumstances, had proved fallacious; the appearances of land, with which their own credulity or the artifice of their commander had from time to time flattered and amused them, had been altogether illusive, and their prospect of[6] success seemed now to be as distant as ever.

These reflections occurred often to men who had no other object or occupation than to reason and discourse concerning[7] the intention and circumstances of their expedition. They made impression at first upon the ignorant and timid, and[8] extending by degrees to such[9] as were better informed or more resolute, the contagion spread at length from ship to ship. From secret whispers or murmuring they proceeded to open cabals and public complaints. They taxed[10] their sovereign with inconsiderate credulity in paying such[11] regard to the vain promises and rash conjectures of an indigent foreigner, as[11] to hazard[12] the lives of so many of her own subjects in prosecuting a chimerical scheme. They affirmed that they had fully performed their duty by venturing so far in an unknown and hopeless course, and could incur no blame for[13] refusing to follow any longer a desperate adventurer to certain destruction. They contended that it was necessary to think of returning[14] to Spain while their crazy vessels were still in a condition to keep the sea, but expressed their fears that the attempt would prove vain, as the wind, which had hitherto been so favorable to their course, must render it impossible to sail in the opposite direction.

## 126.
### Continuation.

All agreed that Columbus should be compelled by force to adopt a measure on which their common safety depended. Some of the more audacious proposed as the most expeditious and certain method for[1] getting[1] rid at once of his remonstrances, to throw him into the sea, being persuaded that on their return to Spain, the death of an unsuccessful projector would excite little concern, and be[2] inquired into with[3] no curiosity.[3]

Columbus was[4] fully sensible[4] of his perilous situation. He had observed, with great uneasiness, the fatal operation of ignorance and of fear in[5] producing[5] disaffection among his crew, and saw that it was now ready to burst out into open mutiny. He retained, however, perfect presence of mind. He affected to seem ignorant of their machinations. Notwithstanding the agitation and solicitude of his own mind, he appeared with cheerful countenance, like a man satisfied with the progress he had made, and confident of success. Sometimes he employed all the arts of insinuation to soothe his men; sometimes he endeavored to work upon their ambition or avarice by magnificent descriptions of the fame and wealth they were about to acquire. On other occasions he assumed a tone of authority, and threatened them with vengeance from their sovereign if, by their dastardly behavior, they should defeat this noble effort to promote the glory of God, and to exalt the Spanish name above that of every other nation. Even with[6] seditious sailors, the words of a man whom they had been accustomed to reverence were weighty and persuasive, and not only restrained them from those violent excesses which they meditated, but prevailed[7] with them to accompany their admiral for[8] some time longer.[8]

## 127.
### Continuation.

As they proceeded, the indications of approaching land seemed to be more certain, and excited hope in proportion The birds began to appear in flocks flying towards the[1] south-west. Columbus, imitating the Portuguese navigators, who had been guided in several of their discoveries by the motion[2] of birds, altered his course from due west towards that quarter whither they pointed their flight. But after holding on for several days in this new direction without any better success than formerly, having seen no object during thirty days but the sea and the sky, the hopes of his companions subsided faster than they had risen; their fears revived[3] with additional force;[3] impatience, rage and despair, appeared in every countenance. All sense of subordination was lost. The officers, who had hitherto concurred[4] with Columbus in opinion[4] and supported his authority, now took part with the private men; they assembled tumultuously on the deck, expostulated with their commander, mingled threats with their expostulation, and required him instantly to tack[5] about and return to Europe.

Columbus perceived that it would be of no[6] avail to have recourse to any of his former arts, which having been tried so often, had lost their effect; and that it was impossible to rekindle any zeal for the success of the expedition among men in whose breasts fear had extinguished every generous sentiment. He saw that it was no less[7] vain to think of employing either gentle or severe measures to quell a mutiny so general and so violent. It was necessary, on[8] all these accounts,[8] to soothe passions which he could no longer command, and to give way to a torrent too[9] impetuous to be[9] checked. He promised solemnly to his men that he would comply with their request, provided they would accompany him and obey his command for three days longer; and if, during that time, land were not discovered, he would abandon then the enterprise, and direct his course towards Spain.

## 128.
### Continuation.

Enraged as[1] the sailors were, and impatient to turn their faces again towards their native country, this proposition did not appear to them unreasonable; nor[2] did Columbus hazard much in confining[3] himself to a term so short. The presages of discovering land were now so numerous and promising that he deemed them infallible. For some days the sounding-line reached the bottom, and the soil which it brought up, indicated land[4] to be[4] at no great distance.[4] The flocks of birds increased, and were composed not only of sea-fowl, but of such land-birds as could not be supposed to fly far from the shore. The crew of the Pinta observed a cane floating, which seemed to have been newly cut, and likewise a piece of timber artificially carved. The sailors on board the Nina took[5] up the branch of a tree with red berries perfectly fresh. The clouds around the setting sun assumed a new appearance; the air was more mild and warm, and during night the wind became unequal and variable.

From all these symptoms Columbus was so confident of being near land, that on the evening of the eleventh of October, after public prayers for success, he ordered[6] the sails to be[6] furled and the ships to lie to, keeping[7] strict watch[7] lest they should be driven ashore in the night. During this interval of suspense and expectation, no man shut his eyes, all kept[8] upon deck; gazing intently towards that quarter where they expected to discover the land which had so long been the object of their wishes.

## 129.
### Continuation.

About two hours before midnight, Columbus, standing on the forecastle, observed a light at a distance, and privately pointed it out to Pedro Guttierez, a page of the queen's wardrobe. Guttierez perceived it, and calling to Salcedo, comptroller of the fleet, all three saw it in motion, as if it were carried from place to place. A little after midnight, the joyful sound of *land! land!* was heard from the Pinta, which kept[1] always ahead[1] of the other ships. But having been so often deceived by fallacious appearances, every man was now become slow of belief, and waited in all the anguish of uncertainty and impatience for[2] the return of day.

As soon as the morning dawned, all doubts and fears were dispelled. From every ship an island was seen[3] about two leagues to the north, whose flat and verdant fields, well stored with wood and watered with many rivulets, presented the aspect of a delightful country. The crew of the Pinta instantly began the *Te Deum*, as a hymn of thanksgiving to God, and were joined[4] by those of the other ships with tears of joy and transports of congratulation. This office[5] of gratitude to Heaven[5] was followed[5] by an act of justice to their commander. They threw themselves at the feet of Columbus, with feelings of self-condemnation mingled with reverence. They implored him to pardon their ignorance, incredulity, and insolence, which had caused him so much unnecessary disquiet, and had so often obstructed the prosecution of his well-concerted plan: and, passing in the warmth of their admiration from one extreme to another, they now pronounced the man whom they had so lately reviled and threatened, to be[6] a person[6] inspired by Heaven with sagacity and fortitude more[7] than human,[7] in order to accomplish a design so far beyond the ideas and conception of all former ages.

As soon as the sun rose, all their boats were manned and armed. They rowed towards the island with their colors displayed, with warlike music, and other martial pomp. As they approached[8] the coast, they saw it covered with a multitude of people, whom the novelty of the spectacle had drawn together, whose attitudes and gestures expressed wonder and astonishment at the strange objects which presented themselves to their view.

## 130.
## Conclusion.

Columbus was the first European who set foot[1] on the new world which he had discovered. He landed in a rich dress, and with a naked[2] sword in his hand. His men followed, and kneeling down, they all kissed the ground which they had so long desired to see. They next[3] erected a crucifix, and prostrating themselves before it, returned thanks to God for[4] conducting their voyage to such a happy issue. They then took solemn possession of the country for the crown of Castile and Leon, with all the formalities which the Portuguese were accustomed to observe in acts of this kind in their new discoveries.

The Spaniards while thus employed were surrounded by many of the natives, who gazed in silent admiration upon actions which they could not comprehend, and of which[5] they could not foresee the consequence. The dress of the Spaniards, the whiteness of their skins, their beards, their arms, appeared strange and surprising. The vast machines in which they had traversed the ocean, that seemed to move upon the waters with wings, and uttered a dreadful ound resembling thunder, accompanied with lightning and moke, struck[6] them with such terror that they began to respect their new guests as a superior order of beings, and concluded they were children of the sun who had descended to visit the earth.

The Europeans were hardly less amazed at the scene now[7] before them. Every herb and shrub and tree was different from those which flourished in Europe. The soil seemed to be rich, but bore few marks of cultivation. The climate, even to the Spaniards, felt warm, though extremely delightful. The inhabitants appeared in the simple innocence of nature. Their black hair, long and uncurled, floated upon their shoulders, or was bound in tresses on their head. They had no beards, and their bodies[8] were perfectly smooth. Their complexion was of a dusky copper color, their features singular rather than disagreeable, their aspect gentle and timid. Though not tall, they were well-shaped and active. Their faces[8] and several parts of their bodies,[8] were fantastically painted with glaring colors. They were shy at first through fear, but soon became familiar with the Spaniards, and with transports of joy received from them hawk-bells, glass beads, or other baubles; in return for which they gave such provisions as they had, and some cotton yarn, the only commodity of value which they could produce.

Towards evening Columbus returned to his ship, accompanied by many of the islanders in their boats, which they called canoes, and though rudely formed out of the trunk of a single tree, they rowed them with surprising dexterity. Thus in[10] the first interview between the inhabitants of the old and new worlds everything was conducted amicably and to their mutual satisfaction. The former enlightened and ambitious, formed[11] already vast ideas with respect to the advantages which they might derive from the regions that began to open to their view. The latter, simple and undiscerning, had no foresight of the calamities and desolation which were approaching[12] their country!

ROBERTSON.

### 131.
### Columbus's First Return to Europe.

The voyage was prosperous till the fourteenth of February, and he had advanced near five hundred leagues across the Atlantic ocean, when the wind began to rise, and continued to blow with increasing rage, which terminated in a furious hurricane. Everything that the naval skill and experience of Columbus could devise was employed, in in order to save the ships. But it was impossible to withstand the violence of the storm, and as they were still far from any land, destruction seemed inevitable. The sailors had recourse to prayers to Almighty God, to the invocation of Saints, to vows and charms, to everything that religion dictates or superstition suggests to the affrighted mind of man. No prospect of deliverance appearing, they abandoned themselves to despair, and expected every moment to be swallowed up in the waves.

Besides the passions which naturally agitate and alarm the human mind in such awful situations, when certain death in one of his most terrible forms is before it, Columbus had to endure feelings[1] of distress peculiar to himself.[1] He dreaded that all knowledge of the amazing discoveries which he had made was now to perish; mankind were to be deprived of every benefit that might[2] have been derived from the happy success of his schemes, and his own name would descend to posterity as that of a rash, deluded adventurer, instead of being transmitted with the honor due[3] to the author and conductor of the most noble enterprise that had ever been undertaken.

These reflections extinguished all sense of his own personal danger. Less affected[4] with the loss of life than solicitous to preserve the memory of[5] what he had attempted and achieved, he retired to his cabin, and wrote upon parchment a short account of the voyage which he had made, of the course which he had taken, of the situation and riches of the countries which he had discovered, and of the colony that he had left there. Having wrapped up this in an oiled-cloth, which he inclosed in a cake of wax, he put it into a cask carefully stopped up, and threw it into the sea, in hopes that some fortunate accident might preserve a deposit of so much importance to[6] the world. At length Providence interposed[7] to save a life reserved for other services. The wind abated, the sea became calm, and on the evening of the fifteenth, Columbus and his companions discovered land. They found it to be[8] St. Mary, one of the Azores.  ROBERTSON.

## 132.
### Life and Writings of Oliver Goldsmith.

Oliver Goldsmith was a native of Ireland, and was born on the 29th of November, 1728. Two villages claim the honor of having given him birth; Pallas, in the county of Longford, and Elphin, in the county of Roscommon. The former is named as the place in the epitaph by Dr. Johnson, inscribed on his monument in Westminster Abbey, but later investigations have decided in favor of Elphin.

He was the second son of the Rev. C. Goldsmith, a clergyman of the established church, but without any patrimony. He was equally distinguished for his literary attainments and for his benevolence. His family consisted of five sons and two daughters, and from this little world at home, Goldsmith has drawn many of his domestic scenes, both[1] whimsical and[1] touching; his father's fireside furnished many of the family scenes of the *Vicar of Wakefield*, and it is said that the learned simplicity and amiable peculiarities of that worthy divine have been happily illustrated in the character of Dr. Primrose.

After being instructed in the classics, to qualify him for the university, on the 11th of June, 1744, Goldsmith, then fifteen years of age, was placed[2] in Trinity College, Dublin, and was admitted to[3] the degree[3] of Master of Arts[3] in February, 1749. After various consultations respecting his future pursuits,[4] it was at last determined that he should study physic, and accordingly he proceeded to Edinburgh in 1752, and there studied medicine under the professors of that university.

After he had attended some courses of lectures, it was[5]

thought[6] advisable that he should complete his medical studies at the University of Leyden, then celebrated as a great medical school; and being from[7] his benevolent disposition involved in difficulties, augmented by an engagement to pay a considerable sum for a fellow student, he was obliged to leave Scotland precipitately. In the beginning of 1754 he arrived at Leith, where he was arrested at[8] the suit[8] of a tailor in Edinburgh, to whom he had given security for his friend. By the good offices of Lachlan Maclane, Esq.,[9] and Dr. Sleigh, then in college, he was delivered out of the hands of the bailiff, and took his passage on board[10] a Dutch ship to Rotterdam, from whence after a short stay he proceeded to Leyden.

### 133.
### Continuation.

His passion[1] for travel,[1] which had long lain dormant, was now thoroughly awakened; he visited a great part of Flanders, and after passing some time at Strasbourg and Louvain, where he took the degree of M.B.,[2] he accompanied an English gentleman to Berne and Geneva. He traveled on foot during the greatest part of his tour, having left England with very little money. Being capable of sustaining fatigue, and not easily terrified at danger, he became enthusiastically fond of visiting different countries. He had some knowledge of French and of music, and played tolerably well on the German flute; which from an amusement, became at times[3] the means of subsistence. His learning procured him a hospitable reception at most of the religious houses, and his music made him welcome to the peasants of Flanders and other parts of Germany. "Whenever I approached," he said, "a peasant's house toward night-fall,[4] I played one of my most merry tunes, and that procured me not only a lodging, but subsistence for the next day; but in truth, I must own, whenever I attempted to entertain persons of a higher rank, they always thought my performances[5] odious, and never made any return for my endeavor to please them."

On his arrival at Geneva, he was recommended as a traveling tutor to a young man to whom a considerable sum of money had been left by his uncle, a pawn-broker near Holborn. During Goldsmith's continuance in Switzerland, he assiduously cultivated his poetical talents, of which he had given some proof while[6] at the college of Edinburgh. It was from hence he sent the first sketch of his delightful poem, *The Traveler*, to his brother, the clergyman in Ireland, who lived with an amiable wife on[7] an[7] income of only £40 a year. From Geneva, Goldsmith and his pupil visited the south of France, where the young man, upon some disagreement with his preceptor, paid him the small part of his salary which was due, and embarked at Marseilles for England.

Our wanderer was left once more on the world[8] at large.[8] He set out from hence on foot, and in that manner traveled through various districts of France. He finally pursued his journey into Italy, visiting Venice, Verona, Florence, and other celebrated places. At Padua, where he stayed six months, he is said[9] to have taken[10] a medical degree.[10] In Italy, Goldsmith found his talent for[11] music almost useless, for every peasant was a better musician than himself; but his skill[12] for disputation still served his purpose, and the religious-establishments were equally hospitable. At length, his curiosity being fully gratified, he resolved to trace[13] his steps towards his native home. He returned through France, as the shorter route and as affording greater facilities to a pedestrian. He was lodged and entertained as formerly, sometimes at religious and learned establishments, and sometimes at the cottages of the peasantry,[14] and thus, with the aid of his philosophy and his flute, he disputed and piped his way homewards.

## 134.
### Continuation.

He arrived at Dover in the beginning of the winter of 1756. His whole stock¹ of cash¹ could not defray the expense of the ordinary conveyance, and neither flute nor logic could help him to a supper or a bed. He however contrived² to reach London in safety, where, to use his own words, he found himself "without friends, money, or impudence;" his mind, too, was filled with the gloomiest apprehensions. By the kind recommendation of Dr. Radcliffe, one of his tutors at Trinity College, he obtained a situation as assistant to³ a boarding-school or academy. But to⁴ a person of his temper and habits, this employment was peculiarly distasteful.⁵

How long he remained in this situation is not known, but he left it to take that of assistant⁶ to⁶ a chemist, near Fish-street Hill. While he was here, he discovered that his old friend and fellow-student, Dr. Sleigh, was in London, and he soon found him out. By his advice and friendly assistance, Goldsmith commenced as medical⁷ practitioner⁷ at Bankside, in Southwark, whence he afterwards removed⁸ to the Temple. His practice was not very productive; he was obliged to have recourse also to his pen, and thus, as he says, "with very little practice as a physician, and very little reputation as a poet, I made a shift⁹ to live."⁹

A rapid change now took place in his circumstances, in consequence of the increased patronage of the book-sellers. The late Mr. Newberry, who gave encouragement to men of literary abilities, became his patron, and introduced him as one of the writers in the *Public Ledger*, in which his *Citizen of the World* originally appeared, under the title of¹⁰ *Chinese Letters*. At this time also he wrote occasionally for the *British Magazine and Critical Review*, conducted¹¹ by Dr. Smollett, from which connection Goldsmith is said to have derived important advantages. The liberal soul of Smollett made him the[12] friend of every author in distress, and he warmly interested himself in Goldsmith's success. He not only recommended him to the patronage of the most eminent book-sellers, but introduced him to the notice of the first literary characters; but the most remarkable in point of[13] eminence to whom he was introduced at this time was Dr. Johnson, with whom he now regularly associated, either from similarity of dispositions or pursuits.

### 135.
### Continuation.

He now removed to Wine Office Court, in Fleet-street, where he occupied genteel apartments, received visits of ceremony, and sometimes gave entertainments to his literary friends. But his improvidence and generosity soon produced embarrassments in his circumstances, notwithstanding the sums which he received for his writings, which ought[1] to have more than sufficed to keep him out of debt; and we find him under arrest[2] for his rent just as he was finishing for the press his *Vicar of Wakefield*. In this dilemma he sent for his friend Johnson, who sold the work to Mr. Newberry for sixty pounds, and paid his landlady.

This price was certainly little for a work of such merit, but the author's name was not then well known to the public, and the purchaser took the whole risk on himself, by paying[3] the money down.[3] · It was not till after the publication of his *Traveler*, which met with great success, that Mr. Newberry ventured to put the *Vicar of Wakefield* to the press, and he then reaped the two-fold advantage arising from the intrinsic merit of the work, and the rising character[4] of its author.

After the sale of this novel, Goldsmith worked assiduously for Mr. Newberry. He revised and corrected several publications; among others, *The Art of Poetry*, a *Life of*

*Beau Nash*, and a re-publication[5] of his own letters, originally contributed to the *Public Ledger*, under the title of *The Citizen of the World*, a work entitled[6] to the praise of supereminent merit, and which is still[7] ranked among the classical productions of the British muse. He also published, for his own benefit, a selection of all his fugitive pieces, in one volume, under the title of *Essays*. Goldsmith about this time fixed[8] his abode in the Temple, where he ever after resided.

## 136.
### Continuation.

In the number of literary friends who visited him there, and with whom he now associated,[1] were Burke, Fox, Johnson, Percy, Reynolds, Garrick, Colman, Boswell, Beauclerk, with the lords Nugent and Charlemont, and with whom he formed the celebrated literary club, so renowned at the time, and so often mentioned in the *Life of Johnson*. He now published his *History of England in a series of Letters from a Nobleman to his Son*. This little work was at first published anonymously, and was very generally attributed to Lord Littleton, who then held[2] some rank in the world of letters,[3] from its easy elegance of language. That it was really the production of Goldsmith was soon afterwards known, and few works have had a more extensive circulation.

The fame he had now acquired as a critic, novelist, and poet, prompted him to try his talent in the drama, and he produced the *Good-natured Man*, at Covent-Garden Theatre. Dr. Johnson wrote the prologue; but it was withdrawn after nine representations. He* next published a series of histories for the instruction of young readers; these were his *History of England* in four volumes; the *History of Rome* in two volumes; and the *History of Greece* in two volumes. For the *History of England* he received from his book-seller £500. These historical compilations possess all the ease, grace, and simplicity peculiar to the general style of their author, and are admirably well calculated to attract young readers by[4] the graces[4] of composition.[4] The success they met[5] with at their first appearance has not yet abated, and they are still considered as the best historical works for the use of youth.

His next work was the poem of *The Deserted Village*. Previous[6] to[6] its publication, the book-seller, who had bargained for the manuscript, gave him a note for one hundred guineas. Having mentioned this soon after to some of his friends, one of them remarked that it was a very great sum for so short a performance.[7] "In truth," said Goldsmith, "I think so too; it is much more than the honest man can afford, or the piece is worth: I have not been easy[8] since I received it; I will, therefore, go back and return him his note." This he actually did, and left it entirely to the book-seller to pay him according to the profits[9] produced by the sale of the piece; which, however, turned out[10] very considerable.

### 137.
### Continuation.

Not discouraged by the cold reception his first play had met with, he resolved to try a second; and notwithstanding the predictions of a total failure, his drama, *She Stoops to Conquer; or, the Mistakes of a Night*, met with universal applause, and still keeps possession of the stage. It was with the greatest difficulty that Colman, the manager of Covent-Garden Theatre, could be got[1] to consent to put[2] the piece in rehearsal,[2] so confident was he that it would not be successful. On the first night of the performance, Goldsmith did not come to the house till towards the close of the representation, having rambled in St. James's park to ruminate on the probable fate of his piece, and even then he was prevailed on with difficulty by a friend, to repair to the theatre.

He had scarcely entered the passage that leads to the stage, when his ears were shocked by a hiss. Such was our poor author's tremor and agitation that, running up to the manager, he exclaimed: "What's that? what's that?" "Pshaw, doctor," replied Colman, in a sarcastic tone, "don't be terrified at squibs, when we have been sitting these two hours upon a barrel³ of gunpowder."³ Goldsmith's pride was so mortified by this remark, that the friendship which had before subsisted⁴ between him and the manager was from that moment dissolved.

He next published *The History of the Earth and Animated Nature*, in the beginning of 1774, on⁵ which he had been engaged about four years. The numerous editions through which it has passed attest that if it is not a profound, it is at least an amusing and useful work. This finally closed the literary labors of Goldsmith. During the progress of this undertaking he is said to have received from the publisher £850 of⁶ copy-money.⁶

## 138.
### Conclusion.

Notwithstanding the great success of his productions, by some of which he cleared¹ £1800 in one year, his circumstances were not in a prosperous situation, partly owing² to the liberality of his disposition, and partly to² a habit of gaming, of the arts of which he knew very little, and thus became the prey of those who took advantage of his simplicity. Before his death he published the prospectus of a Universal Dictionary of Arts and Sciences; and as his literary friends, Sir Joshua Reynolds, Dr. Johnson, Mr. Beauclerk, Mr. Garrick, and others, had undertaken to furnish him [with] articles upon different subjects, he entertained the most sanguine expectations from it. The undertaking, however, did not meet³ with that encouragement from the book-sellers which he had imagined it would receive, and he found himself obliged to abandon the design. It is supposed that he had fondly⁴ promised himself relief from his pecuniary difficulties by this scheme, and consequently his chagrin at the disappointment was the more keenly felt. He frequently lamented the circumstance to his friends, and there is little doubt that it contributed with other vexations to aggravate the disease which ended in his dissolution.

Goldsmith had been for some years afflicted, at different times, with a violent complaint. The attacks of this disease had latterly become more frequent and violent; and these, combined with anxiety of mind on the subject of his accumulating debts, embittered his days, and brought on⁵ almost habitual despondency. In this unhappy condition he was attacked by a nervous fever, which terminated in⁶ his death on the 4th of April, 1774, in the forty-fifth year of his age. For some reasons which have never been explained, his remains were privately⁷ interred in the Temple burying-ground, attended only by a few select friends. A short time afterwards, however, a monument was erected by subscription, in Poet's Corner in Westminster Abbey, between those of Gay and the Duke of Argyle, and the statuary⁹ is admitted⁸ to have produced a good¹⁰ likeness¹⁰ of our author.

# NOTES.

☞ The heavy Arabic numerals on the margin refer to the selections in the text bearing the corresponding numbers. But it has resulted from certain typographical considerations that, when, in the Notes, reference is made to any preceding note, it is designated by the *Roman* numeral with a small Arabic figure annexed. For example, in **4** below, the note marked 4 is: "See II. 4" This means, the note 4 under **2**. Likewise the first note under **5** being: "See III. 2" refers to the note 6 under **3**.

☞ O. followed by numbers, refers to page and paragraph of Otto's German Grammar.

W. followed by numbers, refers to section and paragraph of Whitney's German Grammar.

**1** ¹ O. 251. 2; 389. 2: W. 430. 2; 442. 3. 4c. — ² O. 94. 2: W. 298. — ³ O. 147. 2: W. 153. — ⁴ O. 263. 3; 399. II. 1; W. 386. 1, 4f. — ⁵ O. 394. O. 1: W. 436. 2; 434.

**2** ¹ See I. 4. — ² See I. 1 — ³ O. 328. II; cf. 327. I. 1; W. 325. 1. — ⁴ O. 400. 2: W. 438. 3f. — ⁶ O. 157. V; cf. I. 5; W. 437. 2; 434, 435.— ⁶ O. 344. 7; W. 343. III. 1. — ⁷ an.

**3** ¹ O. 245. 2; 146. 4; 150. 9: W. 155. 3; 286.— ² O. 353. 10; 400. 2. 3. W. 357. a. — ³ O. 383. 'by' 1. — ⁴ O. 394. O 1: W. 444. 2. 3. — ⁶ O. 93. 1; 337. 7; 401. 6: W. 251. 1; 439. 6; 333. — ⁶ O. 297. 12: W. 67.

**4** ¹ O. 296. 5: W. 66. 4c. — ² O. 254 footnote; 391, 10. 13: W. 442. 4c. — ³ See I. 4 — ⁴ See II. 4. — ⁵ O. 149. 8: W. 169. 2. — ⁶ ſtehen, O. 337. 7; W. 333. 1. — ⁷ O. 238. 1: W. 292. 3a. — ⁸ O. 306. 6d. — ⁹ O. 382. 'at' 2.

**5** ¹ See III. 2— ² See I. 1— ³ ʒu.— ⁴ O. 382. 'at' 3.— ⁵ O. 280 'in.'— ⁶ See II. 4— ⁷ ſeßen.— ⁸ O. 319. II. 2; W. 161.— ⁹ See II. 6— ¹⁰ O. 393. 4: W. 443. 1.— ¹¹ erlappen.— ¹² auf.— ¹³ O. 344. 5: W. 345.— ¹⁴ entwiſchen.— ¹⁵ ſchon.— ¹⁶ freilich.

**6** ¹ O. 281. 'to.'— ² O. 346. IV. 10: W. 346. 1.— ³ See III. 2 — ⁴ *Pluperf.*— ⁶ auf or bei.— ⁶ O. 304. 3. Note 2: W. 230. 2.— ⁷ cf. 6; O. 280. 'on'; 384. 'on,' 3.

**7** ¹ See VI. 1 — ². See II. 5 — ³. ask, (= inquire), is rendered by fragen; (= *request*). by bitten.— ⁴ um.— ⁵ O. 78. 5.— ⁶ See I. 3 — ⁷ See VI. 2 — ⁸ darin.— ⁹ hingehen. — ¹⁰ ʒu.— ¹¹ ſich niederbücken.— ¹² W. 188.— ¹³ O. 149. 7: W. 166. 4. 154. 2.— ¹⁴ See III. 2 — ¹⁵ "full of" (voller).— ¹⁶ bei.— ¹⁷ O. 322. 1.

**8** ¹ "makee that you."— ² Da doch.

**9** ¹ O.130. Note 1; W. 325. 1.— ² "when she approached."— ³ O. 368. II. 1: W. 222. 1. 1.— ⁴ O. 305. 4: W. 111. 2.— ⁵ entgegen.— ⁶ bei.— ⁷ O. 350. 4.— ⁸ O. 147. 4: W. 154. 1.— ⁹ See III. 2

**10** ¹ O. 263; 399. II. 1. a.  2: W. 386. 4b; 434, 438.— ² mit Gewalt.— ³ O. 399. II. 1: W. 434; 438. 2.— ⁴ W. 357.— ⁵ für or an.— ⁶ "were sleeping."

**11** ¹ See II. 6 — ² O. 368. II. 1: W. 241. 2b.— ³ O. 379.— ⁴ in.— ⁶ See VI. 2 — ⁶ O. 238. Obs. 2.— ⁷ O. 78. 7: W. 176. 2.— ⁸ Preset. tense.—⁹ iſt.

**12** ¹ See IX. 4 — ² O. 177. 22.— ³ Wollen lieber; O. 343. II. 2: W. 343. I. 1.— ⁴ See IX. 2 — ⁵ O. 296. 7: W. 66. 2.— ⁶ See V. 10.

**13** ¹ See IX. 6 — ² mil.— ⁶ treten.— ⁴ O. 319. II. 1. 2: W. 161.— ⁵ *Past Part.* O. 358. 4 — ⁶ ſo, cf. French que *after* à peine: W. 438. 3. h.

**14** ¹ See XII. 6 — ² See VI. 2 — ³ O. 118. 1; cf. 1: W. 198. 2.— ⁴ "could neither a signal be seen nor etc."— ⁵ See III. 4 — ⁶ "orally."— ⁷ von.— ⁸ O. 304, 3; cf. 194, Reading Lesson: W. 220. 1.— ⁹ O. 114. 8.— ¹⁰ O. 164. Obs. I; 140. 3; W. 185.

**15** ¹ O. 304. 1: W. 216. 2h.— ² See IX. 7 — ³ O. 401. 6.— ⁴ O. 310. 2. 6.— ⁵ O. 382. *'above.'*— ⁶ um.— ⁷ O. 112. 5. Note 2.— ⁸ See III. ² — ⁹ See XIV. 10 — ¹⁰ bringen um.— ¹¹ laſſen übrig.— ¹² O. 254. *' than.'* 3.

**16** ¹ "in his younger years."— ² W. 66. 8.— ³ See V. 13 — ⁴ O. 383. *'from.'* 2. Note.— ⁵ O. 158. 2; 321. 1.— ⁶ O. 78. 1.— ⁷ See XIII. 6 — ⁸ See III. 2; kennen. — ⁹ wiſſen.— ¹⁰ "the answering of."— ¹¹ weiter.— ¹² "to bring to silence."— ¹³ O. 353. 9: W. 436. 3c.— ¹⁴ "I have had you called hither." O. 312. 4; W. 242. 2; 343. 5. 5d.— ¹⁵ O. 72. 5.— ¹⁶ O. 333. I. 1. a; 263: W. 332. 6b; 386. 4e.— ¹⁷ "after which" (wornach).— ¹⁸ See XIII. 1.— ¹⁹ mit.

**17** ¹ W. 357, 358; cf. 147. 3; 148.— ² O. 158. 5; W. 180.— ³ See VI. ⁶ — ⁴ See V 10 — ⁵ nach.— ⁶ bringen.— ⁷ machen.— ⁸ O. 269, Footnote; cf. I. 4 — ⁹ O. 219: W. 299. 1. a.— ¹⁰ das thut Nichts.— ¹¹ See XIII. 1 — ¹² See III. 2.— ¹³ O. 343. II. 3; W. 843. 5. a.— ¹⁴ See IX. 1; O. 394 1: W. 444. 2.

**18** ¹ "When."— ² See XIV. ⁶ — ³ See XIII. ⁹ — ⁴ O. 384. *'on.'* 3.— ⁵ See XIV. 3.— ⁶ O. 306. 6. e: W. 216. 2. d.— ⁷ See VI. 1 — ⁸ anhalten.— ⁹ O. 312. 4; W. 242. 2. — ¹⁰ ſich machen aus dem Staube.— ¹¹ See IV, 8.

**19** ¹ "well-formed."— ² übrigens.— ³ See XVIII. 7 — ⁴ wie.— ⁵ See IV. ⁶ — ⁶ See V. 10 — ⁷ See XV. 3 — ⁸ See 6; O. 338. 10: W. 333. 4.— ⁹ O. 76. II. 2: W. 175.— ¹⁰ See I. ² — ¹¹ O. 240. 6; W. 292. 3.— ¹² O. 118. 2.— ¹³ See V. 4.

**20** ¹ O. 280 *'by.'*— ² O. 108. 6: W. 129. 2.— ³ See XVIII. 4.— ⁴ O. 280. *'at.'*— ⁵ See XVI. 5 — ⁶ See XIX. 10 — ⁷ See IV. 5 — ⁶ O. 56. 16; 305. 5: W. 211. 2.— ⁹ doch.— ¹⁰ See I. ⁸ — ¹¹ O. 346. 10; W. 343. III. 1. a.— ¹² See XVII. 13 — ¹⁶ ſchon recht.— ¹⁴ ſo.

**21** ¹ Patronymic adj. in *'-er.'*— ² See XVII. 14 — ³ See XIV. 8.— ⁴ aus.— ⁵ "very pretentiously."— ⁶ Speiſe.— ⁷ O. 76. I. 2: W. 170. 2.— ⁸ O. 260. Class 1: W. 384.— ⁹ "without (anything) further."— ¹⁰ ausſchütten.— ¹¹ O. 255. *'as.'*— ¹² "eat willingly."— ¹³ reet of = übrig, adj.— ¹⁴ eben ſo — wie.— ¹⁵ See IV. ⁹ — 16. ganz eben ſo.

**22** ¹ See I. 3.— ² nach. See VIII. 13 — ³ an.— ⁴ O. 382. *'at.'* 1.— ⁵ See XIII. 5 — ⁶ O. 240. 7: W. 292. 6.— ⁷ um und um.— ⁸ "There (da) was no clod that remained quiet."— ⁹ See XIV. 10 — ¹⁰ hie und her.— ¹¹ See XIX. 11 — ¹² "then firſt" — ¹³ "ever more."— ¹⁴ *Partitive Gen.*

**23** ¹ O. 264. *'as'*, 4.— ² O. 382. *'at.'* 1; 377.— ³ *Acc.*— ⁴ "that seemed to be about (wollen) to take no end."— ⁵ O. 314. IV. 1.— ⁶ O. 379.— ⁷ O. 306. 6. e: W. 216. 2. d.— ⁸ See XXII. ² — ⁹ ſchweben.— ¹⁰ *sing.*

**24** ¹ ſo ſehr.— ² auf.— ³ O. 166. 2.— ⁴ an.— ⁵ O. 256. 7: W. 363. 3. c.— ⁶ O. 328. 4: W. 324. 3.— ⁷ "was enliſted."— ⁸ "when he saw him."— ⁹ O. 256. 7. Note: W. 365. 1. 6.— ¹⁰ O. 280. *'on.'*— ¹¹ nach dem, wie etc.— ¹² damit ſagen.— ¹³: See V. 5 — ¹⁴ abgeben *Acc.* or werben *Nom.*

**25** ¹ See IX. 7 — ² O. 252. 3; 304. 3: W. 220. 1.— ³ O. 281. *' to', ' with.'*— ⁴ "and left."— ⁵ See XX. 4 — ⁶ O. 385. *'with'*, 1.— ⁷ "From (out of) sympathy with."— ⁸ "stood in communication (Verbindung) with."— ⁹ "let fall."— ¹⁰ "in the chamber."— ¹¹ O. 297. 10; 319. II. 1: W. 161.— ¹² O. 353. 10; 400. 2: W. 325. 1. — ¹³ "of escaping."— ¹⁴ See XXI. 11; cf. O. 297. 10.— ¹⁵ O. 319. II. 2: W. 151.— ¹⁶ geben.— ¹⁷ ſtrecken.— ¹⁸ in.— ¹⁹ als or wie.— ²⁰ O. 271. c: W. 180.— ²¹ nehmen.— ²² ſollen.— ²³ "until the family returned."

**26** ¹ See IX. 7: cf. XVI. ³ — ² "to make a business-journey."— ³ O. 305. 5: W. 211. 5. a.— ⁴ O. 281. *'with'*, *'on.'*— ⁵ bitten.— ⁶ " that it should be restored."— ⁷ ſich ſtellen als ob.— ⁸ cf. XIII. ² — ⁹ bei.— ¹⁰ See XVIII. 7 — ¹¹ See III. ² — ¹² behaupten.— ¹³ einſehen.— ¹⁴ See XIX. 9 — ¹⁵ "if a screechowl carries off."— ¹⁶ ſtattfinden. O. 223. Note 3; W. 312. 2.

**27** ¹ W. 216. 2. f.— ² nach.— ³ auf *acc.*— ⁴ faſſen.— ⁵ See V. 13; O. 351. 5.— ⁶ basmalig.— ⁷ wie.— ⁸ als wie.— ⁹ O. 164. 1: W. 185.— ¹⁰ O. 264. *'than'* 3.— ¹¹ an.

**28** ¹ See XVI. ⁶ — ² See XXVII. ⁸ — ³ See III. 2 — ⁴ no more than = erſt.— ⁵ O. 324. 11.— ⁶ O. 97. Note; 310. 2: W. 254.— ⁷ O. 307. 8.— ⁸ Reit=Uebungen.— ⁹ O. 149. 7: W. 154. 2. 3.— ¹⁰ See III. ² — ¹¹ laſſen bringen.— ¹² O. 353. 9: W. 436. 3. c.— ¹³ ſollte.

**29** ¹ See XVIII. 7 — ² für.— ³ See XVI. 7 — ⁴ "followed."— ⁵ O. 161. 6. 6: W. 179. 4.— ⁶ O. 310. 4.— ⁷ "fitted with."— ⁸ O. 108. 6: W. 129. 1. 2. 3.

**30** ¹ O. 378. *'in'*: cf. XVIII. 7 — ² "in later life."— ³ verbanken.— ⁴ O. 246. Rem.: W. 281.— ⁵ "he was asked." W. 280. 1.— ⁶ an.— ⁷ "while he was seeking." — ⁸ "that if."— ⁹ O. 351. 5; W. 345.— ¹⁰ O. 952. 8.— ¹¹ nur.— ¹² "and I do not be-

NOTES. 125

lieve that."— 13 O. 346. 9: W. 346. 1.— 14 " that my conscience."— 15 O. 353. 9; W. 346. 2.

**31** 1 "As thou to me, so I to thee."— 2 O. 165. 5; W. 186.— 3 See IX. 7 — 4 *supply:* "when."— 5 *Conditional.*— 6 O. 280. '*on*'; 384. '*on.*' 3.— 7 See XIII. 4 — 8 O. 311. 4; W. 255. 2.— 9 möchte.— 10 See XXX. 15 — 11 " who had nothing there against." — 12 trauen.

**32** 1 See XIV. 2 — 2 bei.— 3 " was a friend of."— 4 See XXXI. 5 — 6 See XXX. 9.

**33** 1 stehen in.— 2 von *dat.; or adj.,* "*brazen.*"— 3 See XXIV. 10 — 4 "of which it was believed that it etc."— 5 O. 260.— 6 *Reflexive.*— 7 *Plur.*— 8 See XXVII. 10 — 9 an.— 10 *Plur.*

**34** 1 O. 118. 2; 166. 2; W. 129.— 2 See VI. 2 — 3 O. 240. 7;-142. 8; W. 292. 5; 293.— 4 See XXI. 11 — 5 " forget it."— 6 " while his watch was boiling."— 7 " he was not thinking of."

**35** 1 "in the year."— 2 wie.— 3 *nom.*— 4 See XVI. 6 — 5 "This was nothing easy." O. 109. 8; W. 129. 5.— 6 bei.— 7 einigermaßen.— 8 O. 313. 5.— 9 " when (wenn) they were lighted."— 10 " were wont " pflegen.— 11 O. 343. 3; W. 343. 4.

**36** 1 See XXX. 10 — 2 Die Sankt=Unbreastkirche.— 3 hinauffahren. See III. 2 — 4 See XXX. 13 — 5 auf.— 6 ganz.— 7 See XXX. 9 — 6 durch.— 9 O. 345. 8. Note; W. 343. III. 1. h.

**37** 1 auf.— 2 wegen.— 3 " He said that it was not it."— 4. See XXXIV. 1 — 5 bei. — 6 See XVI. 5 — 7 oben drein.— 8 O. 160. 3; 323. 5; W. 179. 5.— 9 See IV. 9.— 10 O. 261; W. 384. a.— 11 nicht einmal.— 12 wieder geben.

**38** 1 See XXXI. 2 — 2 See XIV. 10 — 3 *Imperf.*— 4 O. 66. Note; W. 66. 4. c.— 5 " while (während) one." See XIV. 3.— 6 einiger. See XVIII. 5 — 7 hinein.— 8 sich auf den Heimweg machen.— 9 " one after the other."

**39** 1 Mensch.— 2 an.— 3 " nowhere." O. 251.— 4 wegen.— 5 See XXVII. 10 — 6 bestehen aus.— 7 sich verantworten.— 8 " was done (happened) as answer to (auf)."— 9 O. 339. Note.

**40** 1 wegen or durch.— 2 wegen.— 3 See XXVII. 10 — 4 wollen (*intentional future*).— 5 O. 315. 4; W. 257. 3.— 6 über.

**41** 1 See VI. 7 — 2 " came by chance."— 3 höher oben.— 4 stromabwärts, *or weiter unten.*— 5 jedoch. W. 385. 4.— 6 See V. 13 — 7 See IX. 8 — 8 See XXXVII. 9 — 9 Sei dem, wie ihm wolle.— 10 See XXVII. 10 — 11 verleumden, *or* schelten über.— 12 See XXVIII 6 — 13 vor mehr als einem Monat. cf. O. 380.— 14 Dann, (at beginning).— 15 O. 265. '*as.*'— 16 " all your breed " (race). cf. O. 322. 2.— 17 " take."

**42** 1 cf. IX. 4 — 2 " neither—nor."— 3 See XXX. 11 — 4 O. 383. '*from.*' 3 von — bis zum.— 5 O. 62. I. 1. Note.— 6 im Krieg.— 7 mit.— 8 " as ransom for."— 9 See XLI. 15 — 12 in Betreff (*Gen.*)— 13 höchst.— 14 See IV. 9 — 15 Savoy=Palast.— 16 " are it."

**43** 1 an.— 2 See XVIII. 9 — 3 " of the."— 4 See XVI. 14 — 6 " repr. his godlessness to him."— 6 sich fassen.— 7 daran.— 8 *Infin.*— 9 " so that he merited." O. 321. 5.— 10 See XXVII. 10

**44** 1 O. 78. 5.— 2 See XLIII. 9 — 3 O. 312. 3; 164. 1; W. 185.— 4 " as that."— 6 " and as if." und als ob.— 6 O. 345. 8. Note.— 7 aus .... heraus, *or unter* .... hervor.— 8 O. 378. '*for.*'— 9 See XIII. 6 — 10 außer Fassung gebracht.— 11 die Flucht ergreifen.— 12 an. O. 307. 8.— 13 engagiren.

**45** 1 " basket full of."— 2 wo, *or* als.— 3 See V. 13 — 4 " the ch. had tasted to her."— 5 See XIX. 9 — 6 Gi.— 7 See VI. 1 — 6 O. 151. Read. Ex. 51. 8. Aufg. 52. 13.— 9 W. 63. 6.— 10 geben lassen.— 11 See VIII. 15 — 12 " that he should " (solle). cf. O. 335. 4.— 13 " Jewish."— 14 " to be obliging to some one in."— 15 " in the opinion, it was done (geschehen, *subj.*) for honor to him."— 16 " with wounded sense-of-honor and with blue-beaten back.".— 17 " was about to go away."

**46** 1 " deserves to be brought."— 2 " for the press."— 3 O. 220. 21.— 4 damit. See XXX. 15 — 5 " after the price."— 6 " with the book."— 7 " I would at-that-time rather have taken only a dollar."— 8 " a by himself occasioned parley."— 9 Nun wohlan.— 10 cf. 7 — 11 an.— 12 O. 167. 4.

**47** 1 " had them thrown."— 2 " where they were obliged to remain."— 3 O. 120. 3; 323. 5; W. 179. 5.— 4 " that they should be." O. 335. 4.— 5 See V. 8 — 6 behalten.— 7 zum Glück für.

**48** ¹ gern zeigen.— ² O. 307. 8; See IV. 9 — ³ See IX. 3 — ⁴ gewiß.— ⁶ "only for the wearing."— ⁶ einbringen, eintragen.— ⁷ liegen lassen.— ⁸ Tand, *sing*.

**49** ¹ vor Gericht führen.— ² "on how he should defend himself", darüber .... wie. See XXX. 15 — ³ "who had been tried (aburtheilen) because he."— ⁴ davon kommen.— ⁵ *supply:* when (wo).— ⁶ vor Gericht.— ⁷ "to be judged."

**50** ¹ "How one catches."— ² O. 352. 7. 8. 9.— ³ See XVI. 14 — ⁴ *Acc. abs.*, W. 230. 3. 6.— ⁵ auf die Börse.— ⁶ "As he went up."— ⁷ "was about to hasten away"— ⁸ See IX. 7 — ⁹ um.— ¹⁰ in (*acc.*) — ¹¹ "afterwards."

**51** ¹ Leute.— ² ein Pfund Sterling.— ³ fest.— ⁴ "arose."— ⁶ in .... herum.— ⁶ "is no m. d. imminent."— ⁷ "extinguished."— ⁸ auf.— ⁹ *dat*.

**52** ¹ O. 281. 'with.'— ² dafür bürgen.— ³ "after his country " (Heimath).— ⁴ durch.— ⁶ auf Gefahr.— ⁶ stoßen.— ⁷ anklagen (daß).— ⁸ nach dem Leben trachten, (*dat*.)

**53** ¹ halten für.— ² mißlingen (*impers.*).— ³ O. 312. 1; 395. 2: W. 439. 2; 348. 2. a.— ⁴ Gnädiger Herr.— ⁶ geruhen.— ⁶ also.— ⁷ bekleiden.

**54** ¹ sich halten für.— ² "and believed."— ³ "in the possession of."— ⁴ an die Regierung.— ⁵ auf, (*acc.*)— ⁶ über.— ⁷ neben jenem.— ⁸ "how great."— ⁹ cf. L. 6 — ¹⁰ "left free course to his anger."

**55** ¹ See XLIII. 9 — ² treffen.— ³ kommen, entstehen.— ⁴ ergreifen.— ⁵ O. 324. 12: W. 198. 3. c.— ⁶ "that he etc.," sich zur Aber lassen.— ⁷ "as it appears."— ⁸ "without doubt."— ⁹ naturgemäß.— ¹⁰ von Geburt.— ¹¹ in dem Maße als.

**56** ¹ *Def. Art.*— ² See XLVIII. 2 — ³ "it was. ᴅ. that they were."— ⁴ See XXVII. 10 — ⁵ See LII. 1

**57** ¹ O. 333. I. 1. b: W. 332. 1. s.— ² See XIV. 3 — ³ "the half of the expenses " (Kosten, *pl.*).— ⁴ See XXX. 9 — ⁵ "they lived."— ⁶ "yet," "however."— ⁷ also.— ⁸ "so also."

**58** ¹ Vermögen, *sing*.— ² vor. cf. O. 380.— ³ See IX. 6 — ⁴ "that we should be able."— ⁵ "how should we."— ⁶ darnach.— ⁷ See XXX. 13 — ⁸ O. 380.— ⁹ "as they had believed them."— ¹⁰ urtheilen über.

**59** ¹ an.— ² "apart."— ³ See VIII. 13 — ⁴ geradewegs führen.— ⁵ durchaus sein. O. 256. 5.— ⁶ O. 362. III. 2: W. 219. 2.— ⁷ O. 311. 5: W. 255. 2.— ⁸ O. 157. 1: W. 183.— ⁹ "left over."— ¹⁰ Was die Ladung .... betrifft.

**60** ¹ See XXV. 3 — ² See XIV. 10 — ³ See XX. 1 — ⁴ See XIV. 8 — ⁵ O. 78. 2.— ⁶ O. 322. 2.— ⁷ durch, or in .... herum.— ⁸ daran erinnern.— ⁹ O. 310. 5.— ¹⁰ O. 98. 4.— ¹¹ See XXV. 6 — ¹² "useful." O. 362. II: W. 229. 2.— ¹³ O. 109. 8: W. 129. 5. — ¹⁴ O. 385. 'with.' 2.— ¹⁵ "who was fond of."

**61** ¹ "every comfort of life."— ² See XXVII. 5; O. 109. 7.— ³ "only in order to."— ⁴ See IX. 7.— ⁵ "sensual (sinnlich) enjoyments."— ⁶ cf. O. 246. 4: W. 290.— ⁷ mit.— ⁸ " a wicked rude husband."— ⁹ O. 352. 7; 353. 9.

**62** ¹ "into a conversation."— ² " all possible inquiries."

**63** ¹ O. 335. 5.— ² "and who took gr. int."— ³ See XXIII. 5.— ⁴ See LII. 1 — ⁵ See XIII. 6 — ⁶ " to meet with."— ⁷ eben erst.

**64** ¹ See XXV. 3 — ² "to buy soap."— ³ "lay."— ⁴ " as."— ⁵ "whereat."— ⁶ " Well, what then, if it be it."— ⁷ zerreißen.— ⁶ verbrauchen.— ⁹ " with still increasing (steigend) warmth."— ¹⁰ jo.— ¹¹ ich bitte.— ¹² bitte.

**65** ¹ noch einmal.— ² um.— ³ kein.— ⁴ " that the boy was greatly concerned."— ⁵ bei.— ⁶ bei.— ⁷ bekommen.— ⁸ "inclined in favor (zu Gunsten) of" (*Gen.*).

**66** ¹ O. 368. 4.— ² See IX. 4 — ³ " which border." cf. VIII. 13 — ⁴ einnehmen.— ⁶ "with."— ⁶ "after."— ⁷ "reign."— ⁸ " are ever."— ⁹ Landrecht.— ¹⁰ nach und nach.— ¹¹ "become similar to one another."

**67** ¹ jagen.— ² "zeal in supporting." O. 351. 6.— ³ " it lies."— ⁴ " to suffer."— ⁵ O. 164. 1; cf. 140. 3.— ⁶ " to bind him."— ⁷ gleichsam, (scheinbar).— ⁸ " have me executed." O. 312. 4.— ⁹ O. 266. ' as.'— ¹⁰ O. 311. 6.

**68** ¹ See III. 2 — ² "how you must deport yourself."— ³ "and begs you to accept."— ⁴ Ei wirklich.— ⁵ "Say," "bring."— ⁶ *sing*.— ⁷ "brought". "compelled."

**69** ¹ bis dahin.— ² "hungry", "in great perplexity."— ³ "distributed."— ⁴ (Title of the French king's eldest brother.)— ⁵ Vorkehrung.— ⁶ "aev", "behold."— 7 "conveniences", "comforts."— 8 erkennen. O. 346. 12; cf. LXVII. 9 — 9 See LXVII. 5

**70** 1 "arising" (entspringen); with its modifications forming an attributive to "happiness." W. 358.— 2 aus. — 3 von.— 4 "country-life."— 5 liegen.— 6 sich emporschwingen.— 7 zu.— 8 machen lassen.— 9 ziehen.— 10 arbeiten.— 11 Gen.

**71** 1 O. 69. 11; W. III. 2.— 2 "though he was."— 3 bei.— 4 ungesehen (superl.).— 5 sich enthalten.— 6 fragen nach.— 7 voraussehen.— 8 darüber, daß.— 9 halten.— 10 fürwahr.— 11 so etwas Großes.— 12 erwidern: O. 264. 3.— 13 andeuten.— 14 See XLVII. 8 — 15 sich erfüllen.— 16 aus dem, was.— 17 "is related."— 18 sich erweisen.— 19 das, was.— 20 vorhersehen.— 21 O. 346. 12. (Cond.).

**72** 1 vormalig.— 2 anfragen.— 3 See XVII. 8 — 4 Sobald.— 5 können.— 6 auftragen.— 7 da.— 8 aus.— 9 vorsichtig sein.— 10 "when they ate."— 11 bei.— 12 dergestalt. 13 "that."— 14 sich setzen.— 15 an den.— 16 hierauf.— 17 welche.— 18 erledigen.— 19 See XXXVI. 9 — 20 künftig.— 21 gießen.— 22 zutrinken (Dat.).

**73** 1 von Profession.— 2 etwas.— 3 machen.— 4 verfallen auf.— 5 "when this was done (geschehen).— 6 führen.— 7 sich rühmen (Gen.).— 8 indem etc. (halten für).— 9 laufen davon.— 10 umsonst.— 11 soviel Glück haben.— 12 Jedoch vor.— 13 erstatten.

**74** 1 nach.— 2 See XXVII. 9 — 3 "which."— 4 durch.— 5 "to make comprehensible (begreiflich) to the tame stork."— 6 etwas.— 7 "thinking of (suspecting) nothing evil."— 8 "as it had."— 9 "and as it thus (so) was."— 10 "presence."— 11 ihm zu Hilfe kommen.— 12 "the enemy was observed."— 13 "of which they might have believed that etc."

**75** 1 liefern.— 2 versetzen.— 3 See LXXIV. 11 — 4 dessen ungeachtet.— 5 mit ihnen fertig.— 6 sich verlieben in.— 7 O. 385. 'with', 2.— 8 Ueberall wohin.— 9 wäre beinahe getödtet worden.— 10 sich entscheiden.— 11 um.— 12 erklären rundweg.— 13 für.— 14 entstehen daraus.

**76** 1 bei.— 2 Wimpel.— 3 Schaar.— 4 durch ganz.— 5 drei Monate lang.— 6 O. 280—1. 'at', 'to.'— 7 dahingleiten.— 8 Unterhaltung.— 9 Lauf.— 10 "love sled-travelling (Schlittenfahren) very much."— 11 gegen.— 12 zur Schau stellen.— 13 im Galopp.

**77** 1 auf.— 2 "more." O. 324. 13.— 3 voraussichtlich.— 4 abgeben.— 5 ausstellen.— 6 zu.— 7 als.— 8 See III. 5 — 9 made remonstrances."— 10 "that his request might (möge) be granted him." O. 335. 5.— 11 drein geben.— 12 trinken lassen.— 13 an.— 14 "if you had not."— 15 O. 320. 4.— 16 "master."— 17 "if I do this."— 18 "fiery coals."

**78** 1 "had."— 2 "for its meaning."— 3 in.— 4 sing.— 5 Reißig.— 6 Feuerung, (Brennmaterial).— 7 "in order to."— 8 Branntwein.— 9 zu.— 10 stellen.— 11 daß.

**79** 1 "they answered: no."— 2 "whose heart beat."— 3 mögen lieber.— 4 schenken.— 5 "barehaaded and barefooted."— 6 über (Acc.).— 7 haben lieber.— 8 Alles Andere.— 9 sich annehmen.— 10 wie (was) er bald that.

**80** 1 beim Einbruch.— 2 bei.— 3 heran.— 4 überhäufen.— 5 sing.— 6 erweisen.— 7 gemeinschaftlich einnehmen.— 8 entschädigen.— 9 schätzen.— 10 "to have saved."— 11 wegen.

**81** 1 "removed from happiness."— 2 "had abundance."— 3 an.— 4 "never a monarch."— 5 Lust haben.— 6 welches.— 7 "hereupon."— 8 hinstellen.— 9 Gesäßen (pl.)— 10 Befehl erhalten.— 11 aufwarten, (bedienen).— 12 fehlen.— 13 See LXXI. 2 — 14 "that they (man) let down."— 15 "which hung."— 16 machen.— 17 kein — mehr.— 18 verlassen.

**82** 1 "which an Eng. a. made."— 2 "where a forest served him as a hidingplace."— 3 aus.— 4 begierig.— 5 verhören.— 6 O. 98. 4. Note.— 7 wünschen, (verlangen).— 8 in.

**83** 1 lassen.— 2 Jedem, der.— 3 See III. 5 — 4 unter.— 5 See III. 5 — 6 herausgeben.— 7 sich beklagen.— 8 bei.— 9 "the pretence."— 10 ausfordern.— 11 "had come." See 5 — 12 von.— 13 O. 350. 4.— 14 nach Umlauf.— 15 darauf.

**84** 1 Unter.— 2 Körper.— 3 von.— 4 O. 370. 2.— 5 erfahren.— 6 Subj.— 7 zu fließen beginnen.— 8 freien Lauf lassen.— 9 mit.— 10 zum Gefangenen machen.— 11 auf.— 12 O. 142. 8; W. 280. 2. 3.

**85** 1 O. 358. 4; W. 357.— 2 O. 158. 3. Nota; 318. 1.— 3 fassen.— 4 aus.— 5 im Gefühl, (Bewußtsein).— 6 "with the words."

**86** ¹ Wohnhaus in der Stadt.— ² O. 315. 4.— ³ entstehen.— ⁴ auf den Spaziergang schicken.— ⁵ "lose him from the eyes."— ⁶ "alone."— ⁷ beim Trinken.— ⁸ bis zum Abend.— ⁹ "as one can easily think to himself."— ¹⁰ O. 91. Note 2.— ¹¹ "sent out."— ¹² Jedem, der.— ¹³ aus.

**87** ¹ "this."— ² *Passive*.— ³ O. 164. 1.— ⁴ an.— ⁵ als. O. 353. 10.— ⁶ weit fort.— ⁷ O. 337. 7.— ⁸ so oft.— ⁹ man kann.— ¹⁰ "adorned with."— ¹¹ Putz.— ¹² vor.

**88** ¹ "is said to have arrived." O. 315. 4.— ² fehlen.— ³ O. 323. 5.— ⁴ Leistung.— ⁵ stellen lassen.— ⁶ "to give attention particularly to that which."— ⁷ die ganze Zeit während.— ⁸ als (für).— ⁹ sich aneignen.— ¹⁰ "could be only very displeased at (über [*Acc.*])."— ¹¹ O. 164. 1.

**89** ¹ Bei.— ² zu Ehren.— ³ O. 312. 4.— ⁴ fangen.— ⁵ stehen.— ⁶ sich zurückziehen.— ⁷ wegen.— ⁸ "as victims."— ⁹ *Gen.*— ¹⁰ an.— ¹¹ also.— ¹² "innocent of it (daran)."

**90** ¹ "wished."— ² *Plur.*— ³ "as partner."— ⁴ bei.— ⁵ sich steigern bis zu.— ⁶ "that I do."— ⁷ zu.— ⁸ "I will lend them to you."— ⁹ Mangel haben an.— ¹⁰ nur schwer, (mit Mühe).— ¹¹ wie.— ¹² an.— ¹³ "how one rewards."

## LETTERS.

**91** ¹ "On (bei) the return of."— ² in Verlegenheit bringen.— ³ Einem frei stehen (*impers.*).— ⁴ jeder.— ⁵ empfehlen.

**92** ¹ fleißig in.— ² auf.— ³ lenken (richten).— ⁴ *sing.*— ⁵ ist es.— ⁶ "attention."— ⁷ in Ausübung bringen.— ⁸ "imitation-worthy."— ⁹ Ihr Sie liebender.

**93** ¹ sehr wünschen.— ² dadurch, daß.— ³ *sing.*— ⁴ Ich verbleibe.

**94** ¹ O. 320. 4.— ² sich erweisen als.— ³ Zuwachs.— ⁴ zu.— ⁵ "quite strange."— ⁶ sich zeigen.— ⁷ "if you forward."— ⁸ neulich vorkommen.— ⁹ "on his arrival."— ¹⁰ jeder.— ¹¹ "which his acq. will afford (gewähren)."— ¹² dankbar.

**95** ¹ "the universal dulness."— ² von.— ³ "which suits (passen für)."— ⁴ Ansicht über.— ⁵ führen.— ⁶ *plur.*— ⁷ bieten, (leisten).— ⁸ für (gegen) Kost und Wohnung.— ⁹ besorgen.— ¹⁰ einnehmen.— ¹¹ an mich.— ¹² Ihr aufrichtiger.

**96** ¹ Verhältnisse.— ² *infin.*— ³ O. 328. 4.— ⁴ bei.— ⁵ auswärts.— ⁶ daß.— ⁷ Anstoß geben.— ⁸ Principal.— ⁹ Bestes.

**97** ¹ "about the journey to L."— ² "kinds."— ³ "I shall be thankful to you."— ⁴ ob.— ⁵ lieber.— ⁶ bald gefällige.— ⁷ Nachschrift.— ⁸ besorgen.

**98** ¹ "to serve you."— ² sodann.— ³ machen.— ⁴ "upon which you will go (fahren) 60 m. upward."— ⁵ in Beziehung auf.— ⁶ sich die Mühe geben, (sich bemühen).— ⁷ "to add" (beifügen).— ⁸ wohl daran thun, daß.— ⁹ auf.— ¹⁰ "distinguished."

**99** ¹ in.— ² sich verschlimmern.— ³ "that he is."— ⁴ "Do not take it ill."— ⁵ "I permit myself."— ⁶ "yield to you" (einräumen).— ⁷ "as it pleases you."

**100** ¹ zuletzt.— ² "wh. pleases me."— ³ in der Stadt herum.— ⁴ alles Sehenswürdige.— ⁵ "if it pleases me further in M."— ⁶ höchst wahrscheinlich.— ⁷ ausrichten.— ⁸ "my friendly greetings."

**101** ¹ "mention-worth."— ² "except that we landed."— ³ vor Anker.— ⁴ "that I swam."— ⁵ "in order to imitate."— ⁶ "than that I must add."— ⁷ darüber.— ⁸ schwimmen über (*Acc.*).

**102** ¹ ankommen.— ² "as the whole region stands under water."— ³ finden. (genießen).— ⁴ Grüße an.— ⁵ Ihr ergebenster.

**103** ¹ Veranlassung.— ² zum.— ³ "brought."— ⁴ veranlassen.— ⁵ über.— ⁶ "prudence."— ⁷ auf.— ⁸ zu Etwas.— ⁹ nur.— ¹⁰ "He dined by chance."— ¹¹ Anlauf, (Versuch).— ¹² Probe.— ¹³ Haltung.— ¹⁴ Benefizvorstellung.— ¹⁵ ziemlich gut ausfallen dürfen.— ¹⁶ anständig.

**104** ¹ mit.— ² "is different."— ³ Rücksicht auf (*Acc.*).— ⁴ "forget not."

**105** ¹ von.— ² angeblich .... sollen.— ³ O. 160. 3.— ⁴ auf's Gerathewohl.— ⁵ Ministerium.— ⁶ "as if."— ⁷ sich eignen.— ⁸ mit.— ⁹ O. 346. 12.— ¹⁰ in Anspruch nehmen.— ¹¹ besser daran thun.

**106** ¹ über den Anlaß.— ² O. 153. 5.— ³ fast nie.— ⁴ Moral, (*Sing.*).— ⁵ Verhältniß. — ⁶ einsehen.— ⁷ "far removed from the wish."— ⁸ "also I am not against" (dagegen, daß). — 9 geeignet. — 10 im Allgemeinen gesprochen. — 11 aus. — 12 "every lightminded (leichtsinnig) man." — 13 hätte ich.

**107** 1 "how very-much (sehr) you need comfort." — 2 O. 158. 5. — 3 *plur.* — 4 einander. — 5 "how great." — 6 Aussicht. — 7 sich grämen um. — 8 Lebenslauf. — 9 auf.

**108** 1 erfahren. — 2 O. 347. 13. — 3 "only." — 4 von. — 5 "of him who etc., one cannot say that etc." — 6 mit. — 7 zur. — 8 für. — 9 annehmen. — 10 ablegen. — 11 Ihr wohlmeinender.

**109** 1 Etwas vorstellen. — 2 sicherlich. — 3 *Gen.* — 4 "surely." — 5 Einem am Herzen liegen. — 6 in Zukunft. — 7 wollen. — 8 durch.

**110** 1 an. — 2 zur leichten Beute. — 3 O. 346. 12. — 4 mit. — 5 "since" (da). — 6 sollen. O. 339. Note. — 7 "at (auf) the." — 8 nach (auf) .... hin. — 9 "grows slowly." — 10 zeitweilig. — 11 glücklicherweise. — 12 dadurch, daß sie. — 13 Richter. — 14 sich einlassen. — 15 in Offensiv- und Defensiv-Streitigkeiten. — 16 "suddenly." — 17 irgend ein. — 18 an. — 19 außer etwa, um .... zu .... — 20 O. 382. 'at', 2; 149. 7. — 21. es kann Jemand .... sein. — 22 Bericht.

## HISTORICAL EXTRACTS.

**111** 1 sein gebildet. — 2 Begriff (von). — 3 verehren. — 4 Leiter. — 5 über (*Acc.*). — 6 Glaube (*sing.*). — 7 treiben. — 8 Glied. — 9 probiren (in). — 10 "of which none pleased him." — 11 sich entschließen (zu). — 12 betrieben. — 13 "strive after." — 14 würdig. — 15 Stil. — 16 *sing.* — 17 uneinig werden. — 18 verbingen. — 19 anstellen. — 20 zum Entwerfen von. — 21 zur — 22 zur Lösung von.

**112** 1 unterhandeln um. — 2 "four years long." — 3 O. 164. 1. — 4 "that he, wearied with." — 5 beendigen. — 6 zuvor. — 7 "which was exacted" (abbringen). — 8 "in case that he should not succeed." — 9 "They (man) even (sogar) gave him to understand." — 10 von. — 11 entgegen kommen. — 12 über. — 13 Theil nehmen an (*Dat.*). — 14 aufgeben. O. 142. 8. — 15 keineswegs. — 16 abgeneigt (*Dat.*).

**113** 1 "There (es) remained (übrig bleiben) only Reg." — 2 "When the turn came to (an) him." — 3 zu. — 4 "all present." — 5 "for (für) the continuance." — 6 *adj.* — 7 Voll. — 8 "quite exhausted by." — 9 bei. — 10 "only." — 11 betheiligt. — 12 in Verlegenheit bringen. — 13 laufen. — 14 "how they should secure" (sicher stellen). — 15 sich entschließen für. — 16 mit. — 17 ein Ende machen. — 18 "that they (man) might permit her." — 19 aufgesucht. — 20 auszufinnen. — 21 "that was stuck (beschlagen) with." — 22 "whose points stood inwards" (nach innen).

**114** 1 über. — 2 "which depend on (von)." — 3 im Verhältniß zu. — 4 O. 164. 1. — 5 "that it explain (erklären)." — 6 sich bewegen. — 7 von derselben. — 8 bleiben herrschend bis auf. — 9 Theorie. — 10 in Beziehung auf. — 11 Behauptung aufstellen. — 12 sich drehen. — 13 dadurch, daß man annimmt, daß. — 14 O. 345. Note.

**115** 1 "had inherited nothing from her parents but (als)." — 2 "need to" (pflegen). — 3 dabei. — 4 "in a prayer-book." — 5 *impf.* — 6 vor, (bei). — 7 Gedankengang. — 8 Heiraths-Anerbieten. — 9 O. 346. 11. — 10 bei. — 11 als. — 12 *Gen.* — 13 O. 312. 4. — 14 zurückwerfen. — 15 früher. — 16 hö-hst. — 17 "in the possession of." — 18 antreten (*Acc.*). — 19 O. 380. 'zu.' — 20 müssen. — 21 "as (je nachdem) the ones or the others by chance (zufällig) became master." — 22 nach Belieben.

**116** 1 "on (an) the way", ("which stood on the way.") — 2 treiben bis zu. — 3 Unteroffizier. — 4 bei. — 5 um. — 6 hergeben. — 7 "do without" (entbehren). — 8 "needed only." — 9 erst. — 10 "so great." — 11 für angemessen halten. — 12 entschlossen (*adj.*). — 13 wenn er gleich. — 14 vorbeugen (*Dat.*). — 15 im Dienst. — 16 O. 88, Note 2: 314. 1. — 17 "began to besiege" (belagern an).

**117** 1 mit Sturm. — 2 über die Klinge springen müssen. — 3 ziemlich vorüber. — 4 müssen. — 5 sich schlagen. — 6 von. — 7 verlangen nach. — 8 "put several questions to (an) her." — 9 sich erkundigen nach. — 10 "followed." — 11 fehlen an, (*impers.*) (*Dat.*). — 12 an. — 13 ihrerseits. — 14 bekleiden (einnehmen). — 15 Lebensstellungen als.

**118** 1 zu. — 2 in jeder Beziehung. — 3 O. 344. 5. — 4 scheltend über. — 5 verhindern. — 6 durch. — 7 "pleased." — 8 aufnehmen. — 9 von denen Jeder. — 10 ausfechten. — 11 "it was resolved to commit (entrust) to them."

**119** 1 O. 350. 4. — 2 vorüber. — 3 an. — 4 niederlegen. — 5 erinnern (an). — 6 "began the contest." — 7 bei. — 8 O. 343. 3. — 9 verdrießlich sein (über).

**120** 1 O. 265. 'as '; 353. 10. wenden (gegen). — 2 zu Hilfe kommen (*Dat.*). — 3 Kampfunfähig in Folge. — 4 "without resistance." — 5 ohne Flecken. — 6 "for (zu) the salvation."— 7 "swimming."— 8 "more than he could bear."— 9 ihm.— 10 O. 142. 8.— 11 indem.

**121** 1 "from (aus) Y."— 2 verbingen als .... an.— 3 "followed."— 4 indem.— 5 "raised to (zu) mate."— 6 sich machen bemerklich.— 7 sollen.— 8 "In order to."— 9 "who was not."— 10 im Seedienst.— 11 Befähigung (*sing*.).— 12 mit.— 13 sich entscheiden für.— 14 O. 368. 3.— 15 kurz schildern.

**122** 1 "came."— 2 durch.— 3 gesuchte Gegenstände.— 4 "for a nail they purchased", (erhandeln).— 5 landen.— 6 ziehen.— 7 fortrubern.— 8 mit.— 9 "for (nach) the Indian Sea."— 10 wegen.— 11 an.— 12 "are rich."

**123** 1 das heftige Stoßen.— 2 umher.— 3 "let in."— 4 daraufnähen.— 5 handvollweise.— 6 "besmeared."— 7 ziehen.— 8 hineinpressen.— 9 nieder.— 10 und zwar an der A.— 11 dadurch, daß.— 12 "on which."— 13 "in order to try."— 14 sich auf den Weg machen.

**124** 1 aller Anschein von.— 2 "that danger was impending", (vorhanden).— 3 vor.— 4 "on the point of doing the same." O. 311. 6.— 5 auf (*Acc*.) (nach).— 6 "did the like."— 7 mit der H. winken.— 8 weiter vom Ufer weg.— 9 tödten.— 10 zuschieben (*impf. pass*.).— 11 Verdienst.— 12 darin.— 13 auf eine Weise.

**125** 1 "westward from."— 2 O. 333. 1. a.— 3 angeben.— 4 "much farther than."— 5 halten für.— 6 auf.— 7 über.— 8 indem etc.— 9 auf Solche. cf. O. 321. 4.— 10 beschuldigen.— 11 O. 321. 6.— 12 auf's Spiel setzen.— 13 O. 353. 9. 3rd Ex.— 14 O. 351. 5.

**126** 1 O. 344. 5. Loswerben (*Gen*.).— 2 "and that it would be etc."— 3 nicht genau.— 4 erkennen.— 5 zu erwecken.— 6 bei.— 7 vermögen (bewegen).— 8 noch eine Zeit lang.

**127** 1 O. 299. 5.— 2 "flight."— 3 "became ever stronger."— 4 übereinstimmen.— 5 umlegen.— 6 unnütz.— 7 ebenso.— 8 aus .... Gründen.— 9 O. 271. 2. als daß ihm konnte gesteuert werden.

**128** 1 O. 271. 6.— 2 auch .... nicht.— 3 indem.— 4 "that land was not far."— 5 "fished up."— 6 O. 313. 5.— 7 und genau Acht zu geben.— 8 "remained."

**129** 1 vorauSsegeln (*Dat*.).— 2 auf.— 3 O. 164. 1.— 4 "in which those .... joined" (einstimmen).— 5 Diesem Gottesdienst folgte ein Act.— 6 für einen Mann.— 7 übermenschlich.— 8 O. 368. 1.

**130** 1 "set his foot."— 2 bloß.— 3 sobann.— 4 O. 353. 4. dafür, daß.— 5 wovon.— 6 "infused (einflößen) such a terror into (*Dat*.) them."— 7 "that now lay before them."— 8 *sing*.— 9 "just as they had them" (wie sie sie gerade hatten).— 10 bei.— 11 machen.— 12 bevorstehen (*Dat*.).

**131** 1 "peculiar feelings."— 2 können. O. 98. 4; 395. 2.— 3 "which is due" (gebühren).— 4 weniger bekümmert um.— 5 von.— 6 für.— 7 sich legen in's Mittel.— 8 "that it was." O. 346. 12.

**132** 1 O. 260.— 2 aufnehmen.— 3 zu der Magisterwürde.— 4 Lebensberuf, (*sing*.).— 5 O. 164. 1.— 6 halten für.— 7 durch.— 8 auf die Klage.— 9 Herr (*before the name*).— 10 auf.

**133** 1 Reiselust.— 2 als Baccalaureus der Medizin.— 3 zeitweise.— 4 gegen Einbruch der N.— 5 Spiel (*sing*.).— 6 "while he was."— 7 von.— 8 in der weiten W.— 9 O. 315. 4.— 10 sein Doktor=Examen machen.— 11 zu.— 12 "cleverness in disputing."— 13 leulen.— 14 "of the peasants."

**134** 1 Kassen=Vorrath.— 2 dahinbringen (es).— 3 an.— 4 *Dat*.— 5 zuwider.— 6 Assistent bei.— 7 "as practical physician."— 8 ziehen.— 9 sich (*Dat*.) helfen durch's Leben, (sich bringen durch).— 10 O. 305. 4.— 11 redigiren.— 12 O. 334. 3.— 13 in Hinsicht auf.

**135** 1 O. 98. 4.— 2 in Verhaft.— 3 ausbezahlen.— 4 Ansehen.— 5 neue Ausgabe.— 6 "which has claim to" (auf *Acc*.).— 7 "which still maintains (behaupten) its rank."— 8 nehmen.

**136** 1 sich verbinden.— 2 "held (einnehmen) a certain rank."— 3 "literary world."— 4 durch die Anmuth des Stils.— 5 "found."— 6 vor.— 7 Arbeit.— 8 ruhig.— 9 Gewinn (*sing*.).— 10 ausfallen.

**137** 1 dazu bringen.— 2 einstubiren lassen.— 3 Pulversatz.— 4 bestehen.— 5 mit.— 6 an Honorar.

**138** 1 einnehmen.— 2 wegen.— 3 finden.— 4 thörichterweise.— 5 herbeiführen.— 6 entbigen mit.— 7 heimlich.— 8 O. 164. 1. annehmen daß.— 9 Bildhauer.— 10 große Aehnlichkeit.

# VOCABULARY.

## A.

Abandon, *v. a.* aufgeben.
Abate, *v. a.* vermindern; (wind) sich legen; (success), nachlassen.
Abbey, *s.* Abtei, *f.*
Abhor, *v. a.* verabscheuen.
Ability, *s.* Fähigkeit, *f.*
Able, to be, *v. n.* können.
Abode, *s.* Wohnung, *f.*
Abolish, *v. a.* vernichten.
Abominable, *a.* abscheulich.
Abound, *v. n.* Ueberfluß haben (an), reich sein (an).
About, *pr.* um, bei; *ad.* herum; ungefähr. to be —, im Begriffe sein.
Above, *ad.* oben.
Abridge, *v. a.* abkürzen.
Abrupt, -ly, *ad.* plötzlich.
Absence, *s.* Abwesenheit, *f.*
Absence of mind, *s.* Geistesabwesenheit, *f.*
Absent, *a.* abwesend.
Absolute, *a.* unbedingt.
Abstraction, *s.* Zerstreutheit, *f.*
Abundance, *s.* Ueberfluß, *m.*
Abundant, *a.* überflüssig, reichlich.
Abuse, *v. a.* mißhandeln. *s.* Mißbrauch, *m.*; Beschimpfung, *f.*
Academy, *s.* Akademie, *f.*
Accept, *v. a.* annehmen.
Acceptable, *a.* annehmbar; angenehm.
Accident, *s.* Zufall, *m.* Unfall, *m.*
Accidental, -ly, *ad.* zufällig.
Acclamation, *s.* Zuruf, *m.*
Accommodate, *v. a.* versorgen.
Accommodation, *s.* Bequemlichkeit, *f.*
Accompany, *v. a.* begleiten.
Accomplice, *s.* Mitschuldige(r), *m.*
Accomplished, *a.* fein gebildet.
Accomplishment, *s.* Ausführung, *f.* -s. *pl.* Eigenschaften, *f. pl.*
According to, nachdem, — als, wie.
Accordingly, *c.* also, darnach, folglich.
Accost, *v. a.* anreden.
Account, *s.* Rechnung, *f.*; Bericht, (of, von, über), *m.*, Grund, *m.*; on — of, halber, wegen, um .... willen. on that —, deßwegen, on what —, weßwegen. to turn to good —, gut ausfallen.
Account for, *v. a.* erklären.
Accounted, to be, *v. n.* gelten (für).
Accumulate, *v. a. & n.* aufhäufen, sammeln.
Accurate, *a.* genau, pünktlich.
Accusation, *s.* Anklage, *f.*
Accuse, *v. a.* anklagen.
Accuser, *s.* Ankläger, *m.*
Accustom, *v. a.* gewöhnen. to be wont, accustomed, pflegen.

Achieve, *v. a.* vollenden, ausführen.
Achievement, *s.* That, *f.*
Acknowledge, *v. a.* anerkennen, gestehen.
Acknowledgment, *s.* Bescheinigung, *f.*
Acquaintance, *s.* Bekannte(r), *m.* (*f.*); Bekanntschaft, *f.*
Acquire, *v. a.* erwerben, erlangen.
Acquisition, *s.* Zuwachs, *m.*
Acquit, *v. a.* freisprechen.
Across, to take, übersetzen.
Act, *v. n.* arbeiten.
Act. *s.* Akt, *m.*
Action, *s.* Handlung, That, *f.*
Active, *a.* thätig, lebhaft.
Activity, *s.* Behendigkeit, *f.*, Lebhaftigkeit, *f.*
Actor, *s.* Schauspieler, *m.*
Actual, -ly, *ad.* wirklich.
Actuate, *v. a.* antreiben.
Add, *v. a.* hinzufügen, hinzusetzen, beifügen, hinzuthun.
Addition, *s.* Hinzuzählung, *f.*
Additional, *a.* noch...., weiter, hinzugefügt.
Address, *s.* Bittschrift, *f.*
Address, *v. a.* sich wenden, anreden; überschreiben (an).
Adduce, *v. a.* beibringen.
Adhere, *v. n.* anhangen.
Adieu, *ad.* lebe wohl!
Adjacent, *a.* angrenzend.
Admeasurement, *s.* Maß, *n.*
Administer, *v. a.* reichen.
Admiral, *s.* Admiral, *m.*
Admiralty, *s.* Admiralität, *f.*
Admiration, *s.* Bewunderung, *f.*
Admire, *v. a.* bewundern.
Admission, (Admittance), to gain, *v. n.* eingelassen sein.
Admit, *v. a.* einlassen, zulassen, annehmen.
Admittance, *s.* Einlaß, *m.*
Admonish, *v. a.* ermahnen.
Ado, *s.* Lärm, *m.* without more ado, ohne Weiteres.
Adopt, *v. a.* annehmen.
Adore, *v. a.* verehren.
Adulation, *s.* Schmeichelei, *f.*
Advance, *v. n.* anrücken, vorrücken; vorschießen. advance to assist, zu Hilfe kommen. advanced age, hohes Alter.
Advantage, *s.* Vortheil, *m.*, Nutzen, *m.* take advantage, Nutzen ziehen.
Advantageous, *a.* vortheilhaft.
Adventure, *s.* Geschichte, *f.*, Abenteuer, *n.*
Adventurer, *s.* Abenteurer, *m.*
Advertisement, *s.* Anzeige, *f.*
Advice, *s.* Rath, *m.*
Advisable, *a.* rathsam.

131

**Advise,** v. a. rathen.
**Affair,** s. Geschäft, n., Angelegenheit, f., Sache, f.
**Affect,** v. a. rühren, v. n. sich stellen.
**Affected,** p. a. bekümmert (um).
**Affection,** s. Liebe, f.
**Affectionate,** a. liebend.
**Affirm,** v. a. behaupten.
**Afflict,** v. a. betrüben (at, über).
**Affliction,** s. Kummer, m., Trübsal, f., Mißgeschick, n.
**Afflicting, Afflictive,** a. betrübend.
**Afford,** v. a. gewähren, geben.
**Affright,** v. a. erschrecken.
**Afraid,** to be, fürchten.
**African,** s. Afrikaner, m.
**After,** pr. nach; ad. nachher.
**Afterlife,** s. späteres Leben.
**Afterward,** ad. nachher, darauf.
**Again,** ad. wieder.
**Against,** pr. gegen, wider. to be —, (opposed to), gegen sein.
**Age,** s. Alter; Zeitalter, n.
**Aged,** a. bejahrt.
**Agent,** s. Agent, m.
**Aggravate,** v. a. verschlimmern.
**Aggression,** s. Anfall, m.
**Agitate,** v. a. aufregen.
**Agitated,** a. bewegt, unruhig.
**Agitation,** s. Bewegung, Erschütterung, f.
**Ago,** ad. a year ago, vor einem Jahre.
**Agree,** v. a. & n. einwilligen.
**Agreed,** a. ausgemacht.
**Agreeable,** a. angenehm.
**Aha,** int., aha.
**Ahead,** keep, vorausgehen.
**Aid,** s. Hülfe, f.
**Aid-de-camp,** s. Adjutant, m.
**Aim,** v. a. aim at, streben nach
**Aim,** s. Plan, m.
**Air,** s. Lied, n.
**Alacrity,** s. Fröhlichkeit, f.
**Alarm,** v. a. to be alarmed, erschrecken, to feel alarmed, unruhig werden, beunruhigen.
**Alarm,** s. Angst, f. v. a. beunruhigen.
**Alarmed,** to be, v. n. erschrecken. to feel —, unruhig werden.
**Alas,** int. ach! leider!
**Alban,** s. Albaner, m.; a. albanisch
**Alchymist,** s. Goldmacher, m.
**Alehouse,** s. Wirthshaus, n.
**Alight,** v. n. sich niederlassen.
**All,** a. aller, alle, alles; ganz; at —, durchaus; not at —, ganz und gar nicht.
**Allege,** v. a. anführen, bemerken.
**Alliance,** s. Bündniß, n.
**Allow,** v. a. erlauben, zugeben, lassen, billigen.
**Allowance,** s. Kostgeld, n.
**Alloy,** s. Flecken, m.
**Almighty,** a. allmächtig.
**Almost,** ad. beinahe, fast.
**Alone,** a. & ad. allein.
**Along,** pr. längs.
**Alphabet,** s. Alphabet, n. Buchstabe, m.

**Already,** ad. schon.
**Also,** ad. auch, ebenfalls. but also, sondern auch.
**Alteration,** s. Veränderung, f.
**Although,** c. obgleich.
**Altogether,** ad. gänzlich, ganz und gar.
**Always,** ad. immer.
**Amazed,** a. erstaunt, betroffen.
**Ambassador,** s. Gesandte(r), m.
**Ambition,** s. Ehrgeiz, m.; Ehrsucht, f.
**Amends,** to make, to. v. a. entschädigen, erstatten, vergelten.
**Amiable,** a. liebenswürdig.
**Amicable,** a. freundschaftlich.
**Amid,** pr. unter, mit.
**Ammunition,** s. Schießbedarf, m.
**Among,** pr. unter.
**Ample,** a. groß, unbegränzt, reichlich.
**Amuse,** v. a. belustigen. [tung, f.
**Amusement,** s. Belustigung, f., Unterhaltung
**Ancestor,** s. Vorfahr, m.
**Anchor,** s. Anker, m.; at anchor, vor Anker.
**Anchor,** v. n. vor Anker liegen.
**Ancient,** a. alt.
**And,** c. und. both — and, sowohl — als.
**Andrew,** Andreas.
**Anecdote,** s. die Anekdote, (von).
**Angry,** a. zornig, böse, aufgebracht.
**Anguish,** s. Angst f.
**Animal,** s. Thier, n.
**Animated,** a. beseelt, lebendig.
**Animosity,** s. Feindseligkeit f.
**Announce,** v. a. ankündigen.
**Anonymous,** a. ungenannt.
**Another,** a. noch ein.
**Answer,** s. Antwort, f. to be in answer, als Antwort geschehen.
**Answer,** v. a. & n. antworten, beantworten; sich verantworten. to answer for, bürgen.
**Answering,** s. Beantwortung, f.
**Ant,** s. Ameise, f.
**Antagonist,** s. Gegner, m.
**Antidote,** s. Gegengift, n.
**Antiquarian,** s. Antiquar, m.
**Antiquity,** s. Alterthum, n.
**Anxiety,** s. Angst, f.
**Anxious, (eager, curious),** a. begierig. to be — to, wünschen, verlangen.
**Any,** a. jeder, jede, jedes; welcher; jemand. not any, kein. anybody, anyone, Jemand. anywhere, irgendwo. anything else, Alles Andere. not anywhere, nirgends.
**Apartment,** s. Zimmer, n.
**Apology,** s. Vertheidigung, f.
**Apparent,** a. -ly. ad. sichtbar, scheinbar.
**Appeal,** v. n. appelliren. make appeal to, appelliren an.
**Appear,** v. n. erscheinen; vor Gericht erscheinen; scheinen, deutlich sein.
**Appearance,** s. Erscheinung, f.; Wahrscheinlichkeit, f. make one's appearance, auftreten.
**Appearing,** s. Erscheinung, f.

# VOCABULARY. 133

Appease, v. a. besänftigen.
Appetite, s. Eßlust, f.; Appetit, m.
Applause, s. Beifall, m.
Apple, s. Apfel, m.
Apply, v. a. anwenden. v. n. sich wenden (an).
Appoint, v. a. anstellen, bestimmen.
Appointment, s. Ernennung, f.
Appreciate, v. a. würdigen, schätzen.
Apprehend, v. a. festnehmen.
Apprehension, s. Besorgniß, f.
Apprentice, s. Lehrling, m.
Apprise, v. a. belehren. [nähern.
Approach, v. a. bevorstehen, nahen, sich
Approach, s. (of night), Einbruch, m.
Approbation, s. Beifall, m.
Appropriate, v. a. widmen.
Approve, v. a. billigen.
Aragon, Arragonien.
Archbishop, s. Erzbischof, m.
Ardor, s. Eifer, m.
Argument, s. Grund, m.; Streitfrage, f.
Arise, v. n. aufsteigen; entstehen; sich erheben, aufstehen.
Arm, s. Arm, m. arm's length, Armslänge, f.
Arms, s. pl. Waffen, f. pl.; Wappen, n.
take up arms, die Waffen ergreifen.
Arm, v. a. bewaffnen.
Armorer, s. Waffenschmied, m.
Army, s. Armee, f.; Kriegsheer, Heer, n.
Around, pr. um (.... herum).
Arrangement, s. Anordnung, f.
Array, s. Schlachtordnung, f.
Arrest, s. Verhaft, m.
Arrest, v. a. verhaften.
Arrival, s. Ankunft, f.
Arrive, v. n. ankommen.
Arrogance, s. Anmaßung, f.
Art, s. Kunst, f.
Artful, a. listig.
Article, s. Artikel, m.; Stück, n.
Article, v. a. verdingen.
Artifice, s. List, f.
Artificial, a. künstlich.
As, c. (similarity), wie; (simultaneity), wie, indem: (proportion, degree), als; (since, (logical reason)), da. (= according as), je nachdem, was, indem, wie; as if, als wie; as well — as —, sowohl.. als (auch); as soon as, so bald als ; as to, in Betreff, (gen.) was betrifft. as it were, gleichsam; scheinbar.
Ascend, v. a. besteigen, steigen auf; aufwärts fahren auf ....
Ashes, s. pl. Asche, f.
Ashamed, a. beschämt.
Ashore, ad. am Ufer; an's Ufer.
Asia, Asien.
Ask, v. a. fragen, bitten; anfragen. ask (questions) of, stellen an. ask a question of one, e'ne Frage an einen richten (stellen). ask for, verlangen.
Asleep, to fall, v. n. einschlafen. to be.— v. n. schlafen.
Aspect, s. Anblick, m.; Aussehen, n.

Aspire, v. n. wollen, streben.
Ass, s. Esel, m.
Assail, v. a. aufallen.
Assailant, s. Angreifer, m.
Assault, s. Sturm, m.
Assemble, v. a. & n. sich versammeln.
Assembly, s. Versammlung, f.
Assiduous, a. emsig.
Assign, v. a. anweisen.
Assimilate, v. n. (einander) ähnlich werden.
Assist, v. a. beistehen, unterstützen, helfen.
Assistance, s. Hülfe, f.; Beistand, m.
Assistant, s. Gehülfe, m.; Hülfslehrer, m.; Assistent, m. [binden.
Associate, s. Kamerad, m. v. n. sich verAssociation, s. Gesellschaft, f. Bible-association, s. Bibel-Gesellschaft, f.
Assume, v. a. annehmen.
Assure, v. a. versichern.
Astonish, v. a. erstaunen; in Erstaunen setzen. to be astonished, staunen.
Astonishing, a. erstaunlich.
Astonishment, s. Erstaunen, n.
Astronomer, s. Astronom, m.
Astronomical, a. astronomisch.
Astronomy, s. Astronomie, f.
Asunder, ad. abgesondert.
At, pr. zu, bei, in.
Atheist, s. Atheist, m.
Athletic, a. athletisch.
Attach, v. a. fesseln. attached to, anhänglich an.
Attack, v. a. angreifen.
Attainment, s. Erlangung, f.
Attempt, s. Versuch. attempt at escape, s. Fluchtversuch, m.
Attempt, v. a. versuchen.
Attend, v. a. begleiten; aufwarten.
Attendant, s. Begleiter, m.; Aufwärter, m.
Attention, s. Acht, f.; Aufmerksamkeit, f.
pay attention to, Acht geben (auf).
Attentive, a. fleißig (in), aufmerksam.
Attest, v. a. bezeugen.
Attitude, s. Haltung, f.; Körperstellung, f.
Attorney, s. Anwalt, m.
Attract, v. a. anziehen.
Attractive, a. anziehend.
Attribute, v. a. beilegen.
Audacious, a. kühn.
Audacity, s. Frechheit, f.
Audience, s. Audienz, f.; Gehör, n.
Auditor, s. Zuhörer, m.
Augment, v. a. vermehren.
Aunt, s. Tante, f.
Auspices, s. Regierung, f.
Author, s. Urheber, Verfasser, m.; Schriftsteller, m.; Verfertiger, m.
Authority, s. Autorität, f. authorities, pl. Behörden, f. pl.
Autobiography, s. Selbstbiographie, f.
Autumn, s. Herbst, m.
Auxiliaries, s. pl. Hülfstruppen, f. pl.
Avail, of no, unnütz.
Avarice, s. Geiz, m.
Avaricious, a. geizig.
Avoid, v. a. vermeiden.

Await, v. a. erwarten.
Awake, v. a. aufwecken. a. wach.
Aware, a. wohl wissend. to be aware, wohl wissen.
Away, ad. weg, fort.
Awful, a. furchtbar.

# B.

Bachelor, s. Baccalaureus (der Medizin), m.
Back, s. Rücken, m.; Rückseite, f. back of the head, Hinterkopf, m.
Back, ad. zurück.
Backwindow, s. Hinterfenster, n.
Bad, ad. schlecht.
Bagpiper, s. Sackpfeifer, m.
Bailiff, s. Amtmann, m.
Ball, s. Ball, m.
Banish, v. a. verbannen.
Bank, s. Ufer, n.
Banker, s. Banquier, Wechsler, m.
Banknote, s. Banknote, f., Bankzettel, m.
Banquet, s. Festmahl, n.; Gastmahl, n.
Bar, s. Schranke, f.
Barbarity, s. Unmenschlichkeit, f.
Barbarous, a. barbarisch.
Bard, s. Sänger, m.
Bare, a. bloß; bar.
Bare, v. a. entblößen.
Barefoot(ed), a. barfüßig.
Bareheaded, a. barhäuptig, bloßköpfig.
Bargain, s. Handel, m. into the bargain, oben drein. give into the bargain, drein geben.
Bargain, v. n. handeln.
Bark, s. Baumrinde, f.
Bark, v. n. bellen.
Barrel, s. Faß, n. barrel of gunpowder, Pulverfaß, n.
Barren, a. & ad. unfruchtbar.
Baseness, s. Niedrigkeit, f.
Basket, s. Korb, m., Körbchen, n.
Bathe, v. a. baden. bathed (in tears), (in Thränen) schwimmend.
Battalion, s. Bataillon, n.
Battle, s. Schlacht, f.
Bawbles, s. Spielwerk, n. Tand, m.
Bay, s. Bucht, f.
Be, v. n. sein. to be to, sollen, müssen. there is, es gibt, es ist, es steht; (consist of (in), bestehen aus, stehen. to be really, vorhanden sein:
Bead, s. Glasperle, f.
Bear, v. a. tragen.
Beard, s. Bart, m.
Bearer, s. Ueberbringer, m.
Beast, s. Thier, n.
Beat, v. n. klopfen (heart), schlagen.
Beautiful, a. schön.
Beauty, s. Schönheit, f.
Because, c. weil. [den aus.
Become, v. n. werden. become of, werBed, s. Bett, n. bed of death, Todbett, n. go to bed, zu Bette gehen.
Bed-chamber, s. Schlafzimmer, n.
Beeves, pl. Rindvieh, n.

Beer, s. Bier, n.
Before, c. bevor, ehe; ad. vorher; pr. vor.
Beg, v. a. bitten (for) um, sich erlauben.
Begin, v. a. & n. anfangen, beginnen.
Behave, v. n. sich benehmen, sich betragen.
Behavior, s. Betragen, n.
Behead, v. a. enthaupten.
Behind, pr. hinter.
Behold, v. a. sehen.
Being, s. Wesen, n.
Belief, s. Glaube, m. slow of belief, schwergläubig.
Believe, v. a. glauben, vertrauen. believe me, ich verbleibe.
Bell, s. Glocke, f.
Bellows, s. pl. Blasebalg, m.
Belly, s. Bauch, m.
Belong, v. n. gehören (zu).
Below, ad. unten.
Bemoan, v. a. beklagen. refl. sich beklagen.
Bench, s. Bank, f.
Beneath, pr. unter.
Benefactor, s. Wohlthäter, m
Benefit, s. Vortheil, m.; Benefizvorstellung, f.
Benevolence, s. Wohlwollen, n.
Benevolent, a. wohlwollend.
Bequeath, v. a. vermachen.
Berry, s. Beere, f.
Beseech, v. a. anflehen.
Beside, Besides, pr. neben. ad. außerdem, überdieß.
Besiege, v. a. belagern.
Bestow, v. a. schenken, anwenden.
Betray, v. a. verrathen.
Betroth, v. a. verloben.
Better, a. besser, lieber. love better, mehr lieben. like better, lieber haben. to have better, lieber sollen.
Between, Betwixt, pr. zwischen.
Beware, v. n. sich hüten.
Beyond, pr. über.
Bible, s. Bibel, f.
Bible-association, s. Bibel-Gesellschaft, f.
Bid, v. a. befehlen.
Bill, s. Zettel, m.; Rechnung, f., Wechsel, m.
Billow, s. Welle, f.
Bind, v. a. binden, verpflichten. bind (apprentice) to, verdingen an.
Binding, s. Einband, m.
Bird, s. Vogel, m.
Bird-trap, s. Vogelschlag, m.
Birth, s. Geburt, f.
Birthday, s. Geburtstag, m.
Bishop, s. Bischof, m.
Bite, v. a. beißen, anbeißen.
Bite, s. Biß, m.
Black, a. schwarz.
Blacksmith, s. Schmied, m.
Blame, s. Schuld, f.
Bleed, v. a. zur Ader lassen.
Blind, a. blind.
Blockhead, s. Dummkopf, m.
Blood, s. Blut, n.
Bloody-minded, a. blutgierig, grausam.
Blow, s. Schlag, m.

## VOCABULARY. 135

Blow, *v. n.* wehen; *v. a.* (bellows) ziehen.
Blue, *a.* blau.
Blush, *v. n.* erröthen.
Board, *s.* Tafel, Kost, *f.* on board, auf Kost und Wohnung.
Board, *v. n.* in der Kost sein.
Boarding-school, *s.* Kostschule, *f.*
Boat, *s.* Boot, *n.*
Boatman, *s.* Schiffer, *m.*
Body, *s.* Leib, Körper, *m.*
Boil, *v. a. & n.* kochen.
Bold, *a.* kühn.
Bond, *s.* Fessel, *f.*
Bondage, *s.* Knechtschaft, Verbindlichkeit, *f.*
Bone, *s.* Knochen, *m.*, Bein, *n.*
Book, *s.* Buch, *n.* Book of devotion, Gebetbuch, *n.*
Bookseller, *s.* Buchhändler, *m.*
Bookstand, *s.* Bücherbrett, *n.*
Boot, *s.* Stiefel, *m.*
Booth, *s.* Bude, *f.*
Booty, *s.* Beute, *f.*
Border, *s.* Grenze (Gränze), *f.*
Born, *p. & a.* geboren.
Borrow, *v. a.* borgen.
Both, *a.* beide. both — and, *c.* sowohl als.
Bottom, *s.* Grund, *m.*, Kiel, *m.*, Ende, *n.*
Bounds, *s.* Grenzen, *f.*
Bow, *v. n.* sich verneigen, sich verbeugen. *s.* Verbeugung, *f.*
Bowl, *s.* Schüssel, *f.*
Boy, *s.* Knabe, *m.*, Bursche, *m.*
Bracelet, *s.* Armband, *n.*
Brains, *s.* Gehirn, *n.*
Bran, *s.* Kleie, *f.*
Branch, *s.* Zweig, Ast, *m.*
Brandish, *v. a.* schwingen.
Brave, *a.* tapfer.
Bravo, *int.* brava!
Bread-fruit, *s.* die Frucht des Brodbaums.
Break, *v. a.* brechen, vernichten. break out, ausbrechen. break open, aufbrechen. break off, abbrechen.
Breakfast, *v. n.* frühstücken; *s.* Frühstück, *n.* breakfast-time, Frühstückszeit, *f.*
Breast, *s.* Brust, *f.*, Busen, *m.*
Breed, *s.* Brut, *f.*, Geschlecht, *n.*
Brevity, *s.* Kürze, *f.*
Brickdust, *s.* Ziegelmehl, *n.*
Bride, *s.* Braut, *f.*
Bright, *a.* hell.
Brilliant, *a.* glänzend.
Bring, *v. a.* bringen; (produce), einbringen, eintragen; bring out, ausbringen, herausbringen; bring down (fell), strecken. bring up, erziehen, heraufbringen, aufziehen. bring under, unterwerfen. bring on, anführen, anleiten, herbeiführen.
British, *a.* britisch.
Broad, *a.* -ly. *ad.* breit.
Bronze, *s.* Erz, *n.*; *a.* ehern.
Brook, *s.* Bach, *m.*
Brother, *s.* Bruder, *m.*
Bubble, *s.* Spielball, *m.*

Build, *v. a.* bauen.
Building, *s.* Gebäude, *n.*
Bumping, *s.* heftiges Stoßen, *n.*
Bundle, *s.* Bündel, *n.*
Burden, *s.* Ladung, *f.*
Burial-place, *s.* Begräbnißplatz, *m.*
Barn, *v. a.* brennen, verbrennen.
Burst, *v. n.* ausbrechen.
Bury, *v. a.* begraben, vergraben.
Buryingground, *s.* Begräbnißplatz, *m.*
Business, *s.* Geschäft, *n.*; Handel, *m.* to travel on business, eine Geschäftsreise machen.
Bustle, *s.* Handel, *m.*; Getümmel, *n.*
Busy, *a.* geschäftig; beschäftigt.
But, *c.* aber, sondern, nur, als. (after doubt), daß. yet but, erst.
Butcher, *s.* Fleischer, *m.*
Button, *s.* Knopf, *m.*
Buy, *v. a.* kaufen.
By, *pr.* von, neben. *ad.* dabei. by-and-by, nachher. by the side of, neben. by this time, um diese Zeit.

## C.

Cabal, *s.* Kabale, *f.*
Cabbage, *s.* Krautkopf, *m.*
Cabin, *s.* Kajüte, *f.*
Cabinet, *s.* Kabinet, *n.*
Cady, *s.* Cadi, *m.*; Richter, *m.*
Cake, *s.* Kuchen, *m.* cake of wax, ein Boden Wachs.
Calamity, *s.* Unglück, *n.*
Calculate, *v. a.* berechnen. *v. n.* rechnen.
Calculator, *s.* Rechner, *m.*
Calendar, *s.* Kalender, *m.*
Caliph, *s.* Khalife, *m.*
Call, *v. a.* rufen, nennen, heißen. call on, (visit), besuchen. call on (invoke), anrufen. call off, abrufen. to call for, nachfragen, fordern; verlangen nach.
Calm, *a.* ruhig.
Calmness, *s.* Ruhe, *f.*
Camel, *s.* Kameel, *n.*
Campaign, *s.* Feldzug, *m.*
Can, *v. n.* können.
Canal, *s.* Kanal, *m.*
Canary Islands, *s.* Kanarieninseln, *f. pl.*
Candid, *a.* -ly. *ad.* aufrichtig.
Candle, *s.* Licht, *n.*
Candy, *v. a.* überzuckern.
Cane, *s.* Rohr, *n.*
Canoe, *s.* Baumkahn, *m.*
Cap, *s.* Mütze, *f.*
Capable, *a.* fähig, (von).
Capacious, *a.* geräumig.
Cape, *s.* Vorgebirge, *n.* C. of Good Hope, das Vorgebirge der guten Hoffnung.
Captain, *s.* Hauptmann, *m.*
Captivity, *s.* Gefangenschaft, *f.*
Caravansary, *s.* Karawanen-Herberge, *f.*, Karawanserei, *f.*
Cardinal, *s.* Kardinal, *m.*

Care, *s.* Sorge, Vorsicht, *f.* take care,
Acht geben; Sorge tragen, sich bemühen.
Career, *s.* Laufbahn, *f.*
Careful, *a.* sorgfältig.
Careless, *a.* -ly. *ad.* unachtsamer Weise.
Carelessness, *s.* Sorglosigkeit, *f.*
Cargo, *s.* Ladung, *f.*
Carange, *s.* Schlachten, *n.*
Carpet, *s.* Teppich, *m.*
Carriage, *s.* Wagen, *m.*
Carry, *v. a.* führen, bringen, tragen. carry on, *v. a.* führen. carry off, wegtragen, wegraffen. carry to, treiben bis zu.
Cart, *s.* Karren, *m.* [leute.
Carter, *s.* Fuhrmann, *m.* Carters, Fuhr=
Carthage, *s.* Karthago, *f.* [ger. *m.*
Carthaginian, *a.* karthagisch. *s.* Karthas
Carve, *v. a.* aushauen.
Case, *s.* Fall, *m.* in case of necessity, im Nothfall. in case (of, daß) im Falle.
Cash, *s.* Kasse, *f.* stock of cash, Kassen= Vorrath, *m.*
Cask, *s.* Faß, *n.*
Cast, *v. a.* gießen.
Catastrophe, *s.* Entwickelung, *f.*
Catch, *v. a.* fangen, ertappen.
Catherina, Katharine.
Cattle, *s.* Vieh, Rindvieh, *n.*
Cause, *s.* Ursache, *f.*; Sache, *f. v. a.* lassen.
Caution, *s.* Vorsicht; Warnung, *f.*
Cautious, -ly. *ad.* vorsichtig.
Cavalcade, *s.* Reiterschaar, *f.*
Cavalier, *s.* Reiter, *m.*
Cease, *v. n.* aufhören.
Celebrate, *v. a.* preisen, feierlich begehen.
Celebrated, *a.* berühmt.
Celtic, *a.* keltisch.
Cement, *s.* Band, *n.*
Cement, *v. a.* zusammenhängen.
Central, *a.* central.
Centre, *s.* Mittelpunkt, *m.*
Century, *s.* Jahrhundert, *n.*
Ceremony, *s.* Gepränge, *n.*; Ceremonie, *f.*; Umstand, *m.*, Feierlichkeit, *f.*, Hof= etiquette, *f.*
Certain, *a.* gewiß.
Chagrin, *s.* Verdruß, Aerger, *m.*
Chain, *s.* Kette, *f.*
Chair, *s.* Stuhl, *m.* Easy-chair, Lehn= stuhl, *m.*
Chamber, *s.* Zimmer, *n.*
Chamber-maid, *s.* Kammermädchen, *n.*
Champion, *s.* Kämpfer, Held, *m.*
Chance, *s.* Gelegenheit, *f.*, Zufall, *m.* by chance, zufällig.
Change, *v. a.* ändern, wechseln, verändern. *v. n.* sich ändern. change horses, die Pferde wechseln (umspannen).
Change, *s.* Veränderung, *f.*; Aenderung, *f.*; Börse, *f.*
Chaplain, *s.* Kapellan, (Kaplan), *m.*
Chaplet, *s.* Kranz, *m.*
Character, *s.* Charakter, *m.*; Ansehen, *n.*; Handschrift, *f.*; Schrift, *f.* act, maintain a character, vorstellen. (of a play), Per= son, *f.*

Characteristic(al), *a.* charakteristisch.
Charge, *v. a.* beladen; anklagen; verpflich= ten, fordern, verlangen.
Charge, *s.* Anklage, *f.*; Angriff, *m.*, La= bung, *f.*; to have charge of (purse), tra= gen.
Charles, Karl.
Charm, *v. a.* entzücken. *s.* Zauber, *m.*
Chat, *s.* Geschwätz, *n.*
Chattering, *s.* Gezwitscher, *n.*
Cheap, *a.* -ly. *ad.* wohlfeil, billig.
Check, *v. a.* (a torrent), steuern.
Cheek, *s.* Wange, *f.*
Cheerful, *a.* fröhlich.
Chemist, *s.* Chemiker, *m.*
Chemistry, *s.* Chemie, *f.*
Cherry, *s.* Kirsche, *f.*
Chest, *s.* Kiste, *f.*
Chide, *v. a.* schelten.
Chief, *a.* angeseh(e)nst; hauptsächlich.
Child, *s.* Kind, *n.*
Childhood, *s.* Kindheit, *f.*
Chimerical, *a.* chimärisch.
Chimney, *s.* Kamin, *n.*, Schornstein, *m.*
Chimney-sweeper, *s.* Schornsteinfeger, *m.*
Chinese, *a.* chinesisch.
Chisel, *s.* Meißel, *m.*
Choice, *s.* Wahl, *f.*
Choose, *v. a.* wählen, vorziehen, wollen. Choose rather, wollen lieber.
Chopper, *s.* Hackmesser, *n.*
Christ, *s.* Christus.
Christendom, *s.* Christenheit, *f.*
Christian, *a.* christlich. *s.* Christ, *m.*
Chuckle, *s.* to a —, bis auf das Kichern.
Church, *s.* Kirche, *f.* Established church, herrschende Kirche, anglicanische Kirche. St. Andrew's church, Sankt=Andreaskirche. church-establishment, Kirchen=Einrich= tung, *f.*, Kirchenverfassung, *f.*
Churchyard, *s.* Kirchhof, *m.*
Circle, *s.* Kreis, *m.*
Circuit, *s.* Kreislauf, *m.*
Circulation, *s.* Kreislauf, *m.*
Circumnavigator, *s.* Weltumsegler, *m.*
Circumstance, *s.* Umstand, *m.*, Verhält= niß, *n.*
Citizen, *s.* Bürger, *m.* [stadt, *f.*
City, *s.* Stadt, *f.* native city, Mutter=
Civility, *s.* Artigkeit, *f.*, Freundlichkeit, *f.*
Claim, *s.* Anspruch, *m.* have a claim on, Anspruch haben auf.
Class, *s.* Klasse, *f.*
Classic, *s.* Klassiker, *m.*
Classical, *a.* klassisch.
Clean, *a.* rein.
Clear, *a.* -ly. *ad.* klar, rein; deutlich; un= schuldig.
Clear up, *v. a.* aufklären; (profits) einneh= men; (of weather), sich aufklären.
Clemency, *s.* Gnade, Milde, *f.*
Clergy-man, *s.* Geistliche(r), *m.*
Clerk, *s.* Gehülfe, *m.*, Schreiber, *m.*
Climate, *s.* Himmelsstrich, *m.*, Klima, *n.*
Clip, *v. a.* beschneiden.
Cloak, *s.* Mantel, *m.*

## VOCABULARY. 137

Clock, s. Uhr, f.
Clod, s. Kloß, m.
Close, v. a. verschließen.
Close, a. (to = an) dicht.
Closed, a. geschlossen.
Cloth, s. Tuch, n. oiled cloth, Wachstuch, n.
Clothes, s. pl. Kleider, n.
Cloud, s. Wolke, f.
Club, s. Keule, f.; Gesellschaft, f.; Klubb, m.
Clustering, a. klebrig.
Clutch, s. Klaue, f.
Coal, s. Kohle, f. coals of fire, feurige Kohlen.
Coalvessel, s. Kohlenschiff, n.
Coast, s. Küste, f.
Coat, s. Rock, m. coat of arms, s. Wappenschild, m.
Cocoa, s. Kakaobaum, m.; Cocasbaum, m.
Cocoanut, s. Cocosnuß, f.
Cold, a. kalt; gefühllos. s. Kälte, f. to be cold, frieren. to take (catch) cold, sich erkälten.
Collect, v. a. sammeln.
College, s. Collegium, n.
Colony, s. Kolonie, f.
Color, s. Farbe, f. —s, s. pl. Fahnen, (pl.), Fahne, f.
Combat, s. Kampf, m.
Combatant, s. Kämpfer, m.
Combination, s. Verbindung, f.
Combine, v. a. verbinden.
Come, v. n. kommen. come in to one's assistance, zu — Hülfe kommen. come down, abkommen. come to pass, sich erfüllen, geschehen. come up, heran-, heraufkommen. come off, davon kommen. come after, folgen. to come, a. künftig.
Come, int. wohlan! Nun wohlan.
Comfort, s. Trost, m.; Bequemlichkeit, f.
Comfortable, a. bequem.
Command, v. n. befehlen. s. Befehl, m.; Herrschaft, f.
Commence, v. a. anfangen; beginnen.
Commission, s. Auftrag, m.; Offizierspatent, n.; Ernennung, f.
Commit, v. a. anvertrauen; begehen
Commodity, s. Waare, f.
Common, a. gemein, gewöhnlich.
Common-sense, s. gesunder (Menschen)verstand, m.
Communicate, v. a. mittheilen, in Verbindung stehen.
Communication, s. Umgang, m.
Communion, s. Abendmahl, n.
Companion, s. Genoß, m.; Gefährte(r) m.
Company, s. Compagnie, f.; Gesellschaft, f.
Compassion, s. Mitgefühl (mit), n.
Compel, v. a. zwingen, bewegen.
Compilation, s. Sammlung, f.
Complain, v. n. sich beklagen (über = of) (bei = to).
Complaint, s. Klage, f.; Krankheit, f.
Complaisant, a. gefällig, höflich.
Complete, a. vollendet. v. a. vollständig machen, vollenden, zu Stande bringen.

Complexion, s. Gesichtsfarbe, f.
Complicated, a. verwickelt.
Compliment, s. Compliment, n. v. a. beloben (wegen).
Comply, v. n. willfahren, nachgeben.
Compose, v. a. bestehen (aus).
Composition, s. Zusammensetzung, f.; Stil, m. taste in composition, Stil, m.
Composure, s. Fassung, f.
Comprehend, v. a. zusammenfassen; begreifen, verstehen.
Comptroller, s. Oberaufseher, m.
Conceal, v. a. verhehlen, verstecken, verbergen.
Concealment, s. Versteck, n.
Conceivable, a. erdenklich.
Conceive, v. a. fassen, begreifen.
Concern, s. Theilnahme, f.; Sorge, f.
Concerned, p. & a. betrübt; betheiligt.
Concerning, pr. betreffend, über.
Concert, v. a. überdenken.
Conclude, v. a. schließen, sich entschließen.
Concur, v. n. —in opinion, übereinstimmen.
Condemn, v. a. verdammen, verurtheilen.
Condemnation, s. Verdammung, f.
Condescend, v. n. sich herablassen; geruhen.
Condition, s. Zustand, m.; Lebensverhältniß, n.; Bedingung, f.
Condacive, a. behülflich.
Conduct, s. Betragen, n.
Conduct, v. a. verwalten; geleiten, begleiten, führen. conduct about, herum führen, rebigiren.
Conductor, s. Anführer, m.
Confederacy, s. Bündniß, n.
Confer, v. a. erweisen.
Conference, s. Unterredung, f.
Confess, v. a. bekennen, gestehen.
Confession, s. Geständniß; Bekenntniß, n.
Confide, v. a. anvertrauen.
Confidence, s. Vertrauen, n.
Confidential, a. vertraulich.
Confine, v. a. beschränken.
Confinement, s. Verhaftung, f.
Confirm, v. a. bestätigen, bewähren.
Confiscate, v. a. confisciren.
Conform, v. n. sich schicken in.
Comformable, a. angemessen. conformably to the laws of nature, naturgemäß.
Confounded, a. beschämt.
Confuse, v. a. verwirren.
Confusion, s. Verwirrung, f.
Congeal, v. n. gefrieren.
Congratulate, v. a. beglückwünschen.
Congratulation, s. Glückwunsch, m.
Congress, s. Kongreß, m.
Conjecture, s. Muthmaßung, f.
Conjugal, a. ehelich.
Connect, v. a. verbinden.
Connections, s. Verwandten, pl.
Connexion, s Verbindung, f.
Conquer, v. a. besiegen.
Conqueror, s. Sieger, m.
Conscience, s. Gewissen, n.
Conscientious, a. -ly. ad. gewissenhaft.

Consecrate, v. a. weihen.
Consent, s. Einwilligung, f.; v. n. einwilligen.
Consequence, s. Folge, f. in consequence of, in, zu Folge.
Consequent, a. -ly. ad. folglich.
Consider, v. a. betrachten, halten für, schätzen; — one's self, sich halten.
Considerable, a. ansehnlich.
Consideration, s. Rücksicht, f.; in consideration of, für, gegen.
Consist, (of) = (aus), v. n. bestehen.
Consistent, a. übereinstimmend.
Console, v. a. trösten.
Conspiracy, s. Verschwörung, f.
Constant, a. -ly. ad. beständig, beharrlich.
Constitute, v. a. ausmachen.
Construct, v. a. errichten, bauen, erbauen.
Construction, s. Bau, m.
Consular, a. consularisch.
Consult, v. a. um Rath fragen, befragen.
Consultation, s. Berathschlagung, f.
Consume, v. a. verzehren.
Consumption, s. Verbrennung, f.; Auszehrung, f. (disease).
Contagion, s. Seuche, f.
Contain, v. a. in sich fassen, enthalten. contain one's self (refrain), sich enthalten.
Contempt, s. Verachtung, f.
Contend, v. n. streiten; behaupten.
Content, s. Inhalt, m. content one's self, v. n. sich begnügen.
Contention, s. Streit, m.
Contiguous, a. benachbart.
Continent, s. Festland, n.
Continual, -ly. ad. fortwährend, beständig.
Continuance, s. Fortsetzung, Fortdauer, f.; Aufenthalt, m.
Continuation, s. Fortsetzung, f.
Continue, v. a. fortsetzen; v. n. bauern, fortdauern, immer sein, bleiben. — (to do,) ferner (thun).
Continuing, s. Fortsetzung, f.
Contract, v. a. (a debt), machen, schließen.
Contrary, pr. entgegengesetzt, zuwider, gegen; im Widerspruch mit. s. Gegentheil, n. on the contrary, im Gegentheil, hingegen.
Contrast, v. a. kontrastiren, entgegensetzen.
Contribute, v. a. mitwirken.
Contrive, v. n. es dahinbringen.
Convenient, a. bequem, gelegen.
Conversation, s. Gespräch, n.; Unterredung, f.
Converse, v. n. sich unterhalten.
Conveyance, s. Fuhrwerk, n.
Convict, v. a. überführen.
Convince, v. a. überzeugen.
Cook, s. Koch, m.; Köchin, f. v. a. zubereiten.
Copper, s. (coin), Kupfermünze, f.
Copper-color, s. Kupferfarbe, f.
Coppercolored, a. kupferfarben.
Copy-money, s. Honorar, n.
Coquetry, s. Koketterie, f.

Coral-reef, s. Korallenriff, n.
Corn, s. Getreide, n.
Corner, s. Winkel, m.; Ecke, f.
Corporal, a. körperlich.
Corporeal, a. körperlich; sinnlich.
Correct, v. a. verbessern; tadeln.
Correspondence(cy), s. Korrespondenz, f.
Correspondent, s. Korrespondent, m.
Cost, v. n. kosten.
Cottage, s. Hütte, f.
Cotton, s. Baumwolle, f.
Couch, s. Lager, n.
Council, s. Rath, m.; Kirchenversammlung, f. privy council, geheimer Rath, m.
Count, s. Graf, m.
Count, v. a. zählen.
Countenance, s. Angesicht, n.
Counter, s. Ladentisch, m.
Country, s. Gegend, f.; Land, n.; Heimath, f.
Country-house, s. Landhaus, n.
Countryman, s. (compatriot) Landsmann, m.; (rustic) Landmann, m.
Country-people, s. Landleute, pl.
Country-seat, s. Landsitz, m.
County, s. Provinz, f.
Courage, s. Muth, m.; Tapferkeit, f.
Conrageons, a. muthig.
Course, s. Lauf, Gang, m.; Richtung, f.; of course, folglich; natürlich.
Court, s. Hof; Gerichtshof, m.; Gericht, n. court-of-justice, Gericht, n.
Courtier, s. Höfling, m. Courtiers, Hofleute.
Court-yard, s. Vorplatz, m.
Cousin, s. Vetter, m.; Muhme, f.
Cover, v. a. decken, bedecken; bemänteln.
Covered, (with paper) (of a book), mit Papier überzogen.
Coward, a. -ly. feig.
Cowardice, s. Feigheit, f.
Cradle, s. Wiege, f.
Crawl, v. a. kriechen. crawl out, herauskriechen.
Crazy, a. gebrechlich.
Creature, s. Geschöpf, n.
Credit, v. a. glauben. letter of credit, s. Creditbrief, m.; Creditiv, n.
Credulity, s. Leichtgläubigkeit, f.
Credulous, a. leichtgläubig.
Crew, s. Schiffsvolk, n.; Mannschaft, f.
Crier, s. Ausrufer, m.
Crime, s. Verbrechen, n.
Critic, s. Kritiker, m.
Critical, a. kritisch.
Crop, v. a. abweiden, abfressen.
Cross, s. Kreuz, n.
Cross, v. a. hinübersetzen, überschreiten, schwimmen über.
Crowd, s. Gedränge, n. — v. a. drängen, crowd round, umringen.
Crown, s. Krone, f.
Crucifix, s. Krucifix, n.
Cruel, a. grausam.
Cruelty, s. Grausamkeit, f.
Cruiser, s. Kreuzer, m.

# VOCABULARY. 139

**Crusade,** *s.* Kreuzzug, *m.*
**Cry,** *v. n.* (scream) schreien; (weep) weinen. — out, ausrufen. *v. a.* (for sale or advertisement) ausrufen, ausschellen.
**Cries,** *s.* Geschrei, *n.*
**Culpable,** *a.* schuldig.
**Crying,** *s.* Geschrei, *n.*, Weinen, *n.*
**Cultivate,** *v. a.* ausbilden.
**Cultivation (land),** *s.* Ausbildung, *f.*, Bau, Anbau, *m.*
**Cunning,** *a.* schlau.
**Cup,** *s.* Becher, *m.*, Tasse, *f.*
**Curate,** *s.* Pfarrer, *m.*
**Curiosity,** *s.* Sehenswürdigkeit, *f.*, Neugier, Neugierde, *f.*; with no curiosity, nicht genau. inquisitive curiosity, Majestätheit.
**Curious,** *a.* merkwürdig, sonderbar.
**Current,** *s.* Strom, *m.*; down the current, strom-abwärts, weiter unten.
**Curse,** *v. n.* fluchen.
**Curtain,** *s.* Vorhang, *m.*
**Custody,** *s.* Haft, *f.*
**Custom,** *s.* Gebrauch, *m.*, Gewohnheit, *f.*, Sitte, *f.*
**Custom-house,** *s.* Zollhaus, *n.* Custom-house-officer, Zollbeamtete(r), *m.*
**Cut,** *v. a..* schneiden, aufschneiden. cut off, abschneiden, abhauen.
**Cat,** *s.* Schnitt, Hieb, *m.*
**Caller,** *s.* Messerschmied, *m.*
**Cutter,** *s.* Putter, *m.*
**Catting,** *s.* (— off), Lösung (von),

## D.

**Dagger,** *s.* Dolch, *m.*
**Daily,** *a.* täglich.
**Dalmatia,** Dalmatien.
**Damage,** *v. a.* beschädigen.
**Damsel,** *s.* Mädchen, *n.*
**Dance,** *v. n.* tanzen.
**Dancing,** *s.* Tanzen, *n.*
**Danger,** *s.* Gefahr, *f.*
**Dangerous,** *a.* gefährlich.
**Danube,** Donau, *f.*
**Daring,** *a.* kühn. I dare say, gewiß.
**Dark,** *a.* dunkel.
**Dastard,** -ly, *ad.* feig.
**Daughter,** *s.* Tochter, *f.*; daughter-in-law, Schwiegertochter, *f.*
**Dauphin,** (French king's eldest son), *s.* Dauphin, *m.*
**Dawn,** *v. a.* dämmern, tagen.
**Day,** *s.* Tag, *m.* day by day, mit jedem Tage.
**Dead,** *a.* todt.
**Deadly,** *a.* tödtlich.
**Deal,** *s.* Theil, *m.* a good deal, a great deal, viel, sehr. *v. a.* deal (a blow), versetzen. *v. n.* handeln.
**Dealing,** *s.* Benehmen, *n.*
**Dean,** *s.* Dekan, *m.*
**Dear,** *a.* theuer; *s.* Geliebte(r), lieb, *m. & f.*

**Death,** *s.* Tod, *m.* bed of death, Todbett, *n.*
**Debate,** *s.* Wortwechsel, *m.*
**Debauchery** *s.* Ausschweifung, *f.*
**Debt,** *s.* Schuld, *f.*
**Decapitation,** *s.* Enthauptung, Hinrichtung, *f.*
**Decease,** *v. n.* sterben.
**Deceit,** *s.* Betrug, *m.*
**Deceive,** *v. a.* betrügen, täuschen, anführen.
**Deception,** *s.* Betrug, *m.*
**Decide,** *v a.* entscheiden.
**Decipherer,** *s.* Entzifferer, *m.*
**Decision,** *s.* Entscheidung, *f.*
**Decisive,** *a.* entscheidend.
**Deck,** *s.* Verdeck, *n.*
**Declaration,** *s.* Erklärung, *f.*
**Declare,** *v. a.* erklären. declare for, sich entscheiden; declare off, erklären, rundweg sich lossagen.
**Decline,** *v. a.* ablehnen.
**Decorate,** *v. a.* verzieren
**Decrepit,** *a.* abgelebt.
**Dedicate,** *v. a.* widmen.
**Deem,** *v. a.* halten für.
**Deep,** *a.* -ly, *ad.* tief.
**Defeat,** *v. a.* vereiteln. *s.* Niederlage, *f.*
**Defect,** *s.* Fehler, *m.*
**Defence,** *s.* Vertheidigung, *f.*
**Defenceless,** *a.* schutzlos, vertheidigungslos.
**Defend,** *v. a.* schützen (gegen), vertheidigen.
**Defendant,** *s.* Beklagte(r), *m.*
**Defensive,** *a.* defensiv.
**Defray,** *v. a.* bestreiten.
**Degree,** *s.* Grad, *m.*, Rang, *m.* in some degree, einigermaßen. (academic), Würde, *f.* — of M.A. Magisterwürde. medical degree, Doctor-Examen, *n.*
**Deign,** *v. n.* geruhen.
**Delay,** *v. a.* aufschieben. *s.* Verzug, *m.*
**Delegate,** *s.* Abgeordnete(r), *m.*
**Deliberate,** *a.* bedachtsam.
**Delicacy,** *s.* Delikatesse, *f.*, Leckerbissen, *m.*, Zartgefühl, *n.*
**Delicious,** *a.* köstlich.
**Delight,** *s.* Freude, *f. v. a.* freuen, entzücken.
**Delighted,** *a.* erfreut.
**Deliver,** *v. a.* ausliefern; (message) ausrichten, überlief. rn.
**Deliverance,** *s.* Ueberlieferung, *f*
**Deliverer,** *s.* Erretter, *m.*
**Delude,** *v. a.* betrügen, täuschen.
**Demand,** *v. a.* fordern, fragen, verlangen, anhalten um.
**Demise,** *s.* Tod, *m.*
**Demolish,** *v. a.* vernichten
**Denmark,** Dänemark, *n.*
**Denote,** *v. a.* anzeigen.
**Denounce,** *v. a.* anzeigen.
**Deny,** *v. a.* verneinen, sagen daß .... nicht....
**Depart,** *v. n.* weggehen.
**Departure,** *s.* Abreise, *f.*
**Depend,** *v. n.* abhangen, sich verlassen.
**Dependency,** *s.* Besitzung, *f.*, Abhängigkeit, *f.*

Deposit, v. a. niederlegen, in Verwahrung geben, ablegen. s. Verwahrgut, n.
Depot, s Wartesaal, m., Depot, n.
Deprive, v. a. bringen um, berauben
Deputation, s. Deputation, f.
Derange, v. a. stören.
Derive, v. a. ableiten, ziehen. to be derived, entspringen, gewähren.
Dervise, s. Derwisch, m.
Descend, v. n. absteigen.
Describe, v. a. beschreiben.
Description, s. Beschreibung, f.
Desert, s. Wüste, f.
Desert, v. a. verlassen.
Deserve, v. a. verdienen.
Design, s. Vorhaben, n., Absicht, f., Plan, m.
Designedly, ad. absichtlich.
Desire, s. Verlangen, n. v. a. wünschen, verlangen, bitten, erwünschen.
Desirous, a. wünschend. become desirous, wünschen.
Desist, v. n. abstehen.
Desk, s. Pult, n.
Desolation, s. Verwüstung, Oede,
Despair, s. Verzweiflung, f.
Despatch, see dispatch.
Desperate, a. verwegen.
Despise, v. a. verachten.
Despondence (cy), s. Verzweiflung, f.
Destroy, v. a. zerstören.
Destruction, s. Untergang, m., Zerstörung, f.
Destructive, a. zerstörend.
Detain, v. a. zurückhalten.
Determination, s. Entscheidung,
Determine, v. n. (sich) entschließen
Determined, a. entschlossen.
Detest, v. a. verabscheuen.
Device, s. Entwurf, m.
Devil, s. Teufel, m.
Devise, v. a. ersinnen.
Devote, v. a. ergeben.
Devotion, s. Hingebung, f. Book of devotion, Gebetbuch, n.
Devour, v. a. verschlingen, fressen, auffressen.
Dexterity, s. Gewandtheit, Fertigkeit, f.
Diabolic, a. teuflisch.
Diamond, s. Diamant, m. a. diamanten.
Dictate, v. a. vorsagen.
Dictionary, s. Wörterbuch, n.
Die, v. n. sterben.
Differ, v. n. verschieden sein.
Difference, s. Unterschied, m., Streitigkeit, f.
Different, a. verschieden.
Difficult, a. schwierig.
Difficulty, s. Schwierigkeit, f.
Diffuse, v. a. verbreiten.
Diffused, a. verbreitet.
Dig, v. a. graben (for = nach).
Dig up, v. a. aufgraben.
Dignity, s. Würde, f.
Dilemma, s. Verlegenheit, f.
Din, s. Lärm, m., Getümmel, n.
Dine, v. n. (zu Mittag) speisen.
Dining-room, s. Speisezimmer, n.

Dinner, s. Mittagsmahl, n., Mittagsessen, n.
Dionysius, Dionys.
Direct, a. gerade. -ly, ad. gerade, unmittelbar. v. a. richten lassen, anordnen, aufgeben.
Direction, s. Richtung, Leitung, f.
Director, s. Leiter, m.
Dirty, a. schmutzig.
Disabled, a. kampfunfähig.
Disadvantageous, a. nachtheilig (für).
Disaffection, s. Mißvergnügen, n.
Disagree, v. n. uneinig werden.
Disagreement, s. Mißhelligkeit, f.
Disappoint, v. a. vereiteln, täuschen.
Disappointment, s. Vereitelung, f.
Disapprove of, v. a. mißbilligen.
Discern, v. a. wahrnehmen.
Discharge, v. a. entlassen.
Disconcerted, a. verlegen, außer Fassung gebracht.
Disconcert, v. a. (einen) mißmuthig machen.
Discontinue, v. a. beendigen.
Discourage, v. a. entmuthigen.
Discourse, s. Gespräch, n. v. a. sprechen.
Discover, v. a. verspüren, entdecken, offenbaren.
Discovery, s. Entdeckung, f.
Discretion, s. Belieben, n.
Discussion, s. Gespräch, n.
Disease, s. Krankheit, f.
Disengage, v. a. herausbringen.
Disfigure, v. a. entstellen.
Disgrace, s. Schande, f.
Disguise, v. a. verstellen.
Dish, s. Speise, f.
Dishonesty, s. Unredlichkeit, f.
Disinclined, a. abgeneigt.
Dismal, a. gräßlich.
Dismount, v. n. absteigen.
Dispatch, v. a. tödten; (execute at once), hinrichten lassen.
Dispel, v. a. vertreiben.
Disperse, v. a. zerstreuen.
Dispersion, s. Zerstreuung, f.
Display, v. a. entfalten, zur Schau stellen.
Displease, v. n. mißfallen.
Displeased, a. unzufrieden, aufgebracht. to be displeased, es übel nehmen.
Displeasure, s. Unwillen. m., Verdruß, m.
Dispose, v. a. (distribute), vertheilen.
Disposed, p. & a. geneigt.
Disposition, s. Neigung, f., Anlage, f., Gemüthsart, f., Gesinnung, f., Gutmüthigkeit, f.
Disputation, s. Disputiren, n.
Dispute, v. n. streiten, disputiren. s. Streit, m.
Disquiet, s. Unruhe, f.
Dissatisfied, a. unzufrieden.
Dissenter, s. Andersgläubiger, m.
Dissolution, s. Auflösung, f.
Dissolve, v. a. auflösen.
Dissuade, v. a. abrathen.
Distance, s. Entfernung, Weite, f. at no great distance, nicht ferne.

## VOCABULARY. 141

Distant, a. entfernt.
Distasteful, a. (to), zuwiber.
Distemper, s. Krankheit, f.
Distiller, s. Branntweinbrenner, m.
Distinct, -ly. ad. unterschieden; deutlich.
Distinction, of, a. angesehen.
Distinguish, v. a. unterscheiden. distinguish one's self, sich auszeichnen.
Distruct, v. a. abziehen.
Distress, s. Verkümmerung, f., Noth, f.
Distressing, a. schmerzlich, peinlich.
District, s. Bezirk, m.
Disturb, v. a. stören, trüben, beunruhigen, in Verlegenheit bringen.
Dive, v. n. untertauchen.
Divert, v. a. belustigen.
Divide, v. a. theilen, abtheilen.
Divine, a. göttlich. s. Geistliche(r), m.
Division, s. Abtheilung, f.
Divulge, v. a. ausbreiten.
Do, v. a. thun, machen; ausführen; do (honor), erweisen; imperative (for urgent request), bitte.
Doctor, s. Arzt, Doktor, m.
Doctrine, s. Lehre, f.
Document, s. Urkunde, f.
Dog, s. Hund, m.
Dollar, s. Thaler, m.
Dolphin, s. Delphin, m.
Domestic, a. häuslich. domestic establishment, Haushalt, m.
Donkey, s. Esel, m.
Door, s. Thür, f.
Dormant, a. schlafend, geheim.
Doubt, v. a. & n. zweifeln, bezweifeln. s. Zweifel, m.; no doubt, schon.
Doubtful, a. zweifelhaft.
Down, pr. nieder.
Downward(s), ad. niederwärts, hinab.
Doze, s. Schlummer, m.
Dozen, s. Dutzend, n.
Dr., Dr., Doct.
Drag, v. a. ziehen.
Drama, s. Drama, n., Schauspiel, n.
Drapery, s. Mantel, m.
Draw, v. a. ziehen; bringen, nöthigen (into, zu); (attention), lenken, richten; (of a ship) (water), einlassen; — out (in array) aufstellen; — out, herausziehen; — on (one's self), zuziehen.
Drawer, s. Schublade, f.
Drawing, s. Zeichnung, f. drawing up, s. Entwerfen, n.
Drawing-room, s. Gesellschaftszimmer, n.
Dread. v. a. erschrecken.
Dreadful, a. schrecklich.
Dress, s. Anzug, m. v. a. ankleiden, putzen. dress in, schmücken mit.
Drink, v. a. & n. trinken, saufen. give drink, lassen trinken.
Drive, v. a. treiben, wegtreiben; jagen. v. n. fahren. drive on, zufahren, fortfahren. drive out, austreiben. drive to despair, in Verzweiflung bringen.
Droll, s. Possenreißer, m.
Drop, v. n. fallen; v. a. fallen lassen.

Drown, v. n. ertrinken.
Drowning, s. Ertrinken, n.
Drowsy, a. schläfrig.
Drunk, a. betrunken.
Drunkenness, s. Trunkenheit f.
Dry, a. trocken. v. a. trocknen. dry up, abtrocknen.
Duck, s. Ente, f.
Due, a. verfallen, fällig, birett. to be due, gebühren.
Duel, s. Duell, n.
Duke, s. Herzog, m.
Dull, a. einfältig, dumm.
Dulness, s. (of business) Flauheit, f.
Dumb, a. stumm.
Duration, s. Dauer, f.
During, pr. während.
Dusk, s. Einbruch der Nacht, m.
Dusky, a. dunkel.
Dusty, a. staubig.
Dutch, a. holländisch.
Dutiful, a. ehrerbietig.
Duty, s. Pflicht, f. on —, im Dienst.
Dwarf, s. Zwerg, m.

## E.

Each, pn. jeder, jede, jedes, der Eine oder der Andere. each other, einander.
Ear, s. Ohr, n.
Early, a. ad. früh. early part of life, jüngere Jahre.
Earn, v. a. erwerben.
Earnest, a. ernstlich.
Earth, s. Erde, f. on earth, auf Erben.
Ease, s. Leichtigkeit, f.
East, s. Osten, m.
Eastern, a. östlich, orientalisch.
Easy, a. -ily, ad. leicht, ruhig, frei.
Eat, v. a. & n. essen; fressen.
Ebb, s. Ebbe, f.; Verfall, m.
Ecclesiastic(al), a. geistlich.
Economie(al), a. sparsam.
Economizer, s. Sparer, m. economizer of time, Zeitsparer, m.
Economy, s. Sparsamkeit, f.
Edge, s. Schärfe, f.; Rand, m.
Edifice, s. Gebäude, n.
Edition, s. Auflage, f.
Education, s. Erziehung, f.
Edward, Eduard.
Eel, s. Aal, m.
Effect, s. Wirkung, f.; Erfolg, m. v. a. bewirken.
Effort, s. Anstrengung, f.
Egg, s. Ei, n.
Eighty, a. achtzig.
Elder, a. älter.
Elect, v. a. erwählen.
Elegance, s. Zierlichkeit, f.
Elegant, a. wohlgebildet, zierlich, geschmackvoll.
Element, s. Element, n.; Bestandtheil, m.; Anfangsgründe, m. pl.

Elevate, v. a. erhöhen, erheben.
Eloquence, s. Beredsamkeit, f.
Else, anything else, Alles Andere.
Elude, v. a. entwischen.
Embark, v. n. sich einschiffen.
Embarrass, v. a. verwirren.
Embarrassed, a. in Verlegenheit.
Embarrassment, s. Verlegenheit, f.
Embitter, v. a. verbittern.
Embrace, v. a. umarmen; (a proposal), aufnehmen. s. Umarmung, f.
Embroidery, s. Stickerei, f.
Emerald, s. Smaragd, m.
Eminence, s. Talent, n.
Eminent, a. hoch, ausgezeichnet.
Emotion, s. Rührung, f.
Emperor, s. Kaiser, m.
Emphasis, s. Nachdruck, m.
Empire, s. Reich, n.
Employ, v. a. anstellen; anwenden; beschäftigen. employ one's self (meddle), sich mischen.
Employer, s. Principal, m.
Empress, s. Kaiserin, f.
Empty, a. leer.
Enable, v. a. in Stand setzen; fähig machen.
Encamp, v. a. & n. (sich) lagern.
Enclose, v. a. einschließen.
Encourage, v. a. hetzen, anfeuern.
Encouragement, s. Ermuthigung, f.
End, s. Ende, n.; Spitze, f.; Tod, m.; at an end, am Ende. v. a. beendigen. v. n. aufhören.
Endear, v. a. theuer machen.
Endeavour, s. Bestreben, n., Bestrebung, f. v. n. suchen, sich bemühen, versuchen.
Endow, v. a. begaben.
Endure, v. a. erdulden, ertragen.
Enemy, s. Feind, m.
Energy, s. Thatkraft, f.; Wärme, f.
Engage, v. a. anstellen; engagiren; (to be engaged, occupied in), beschäftigt mit. v. n. sich einlassen; sich verbindlich machen; den Kampf beginnen.
Engaged, a. (involved), verwickelt.
Engagement, s. Verpfändung; Einladung, f.
English, a. englisch. Englishman, Engländer, m.
Enjoy, v. a. erfreuen, genießen.
Enjoyment, s. Genuß, m.
Enlightened, a. aufgeklärt.
Enlist, v. a. anwerben.
Enmity, s. Feindschaft, f.
Enough, ad. genug.
Enraged, a. wüthend, zornig.
Entangle, v. a. verwickeln.
Enter, v. a. hineingehen, eintreten.
Enterprise, s. Unternehmung, f.
Entertain, v. a. unterhalten; bewirthen. entertain a design, Absicht fassen.
Enthusiast, s. Schwärmer, m.
Enthusiastic(al), a. schwärmerisch.
Entice, v. a. reizen.
Entire, -ly. ad. ganz, gänzlich.
Entitled, to be, v. n. Anspruch haben auf.

Entreat, v. a. bitten.
Environs, s. pl. Umgebung, f.
Envy, s. Neid, m.
Epitaph, s. Grabschrift, f.
Epoch, s. Zeit, f.
Equal, a. -ly. ad. gleichmäßig. v. a. gleich sein.
Equality, s. Gleichheit, f.
Equipage, s. Ausrüstung; Equipage, f.
Erect, v. a. errichten. a. aufrecht.
Errand, s. Auftrag, m. (send) on errands, um Aufträge zu besorgen.
Error, s. Irrthum, m.
Escape, v. n. entrinnen, entkommen, entgehen. s. Entkommen, n.
Especial, -ly. ad. besonders.
Esquire, s. (— Esq.), Herr —.
Essay, s. Aufsatz, m.
Establish, v. a. errichten.
Establishment, s. Behörde, f.; church—, s. Kirchen-Einrichtung, f.; domestic—, s. Haushalt, m.; religious —, s. Kloster, n.
Estate, s. Vermögen, n.; Sitz, m.; Landsitz, m.
Esteem, s. Hochschätzung, f.; Achtung, f.
Estimate, s. Schätzung, f.
Etiquette, s. Etikette, f.
Europe, s. Europa.
European, s. Europäer, m. a. europäisch.
Even, ad. eben. not even, nicht einmal. even though, wenn gleich.
Evening, s. Abend m.
Event, s. Ereigniß, n.; Begebenheit, f.
Ever, ad. je, jemals, immer. forever, immerfort, immer und ewig.
Everlasting, a. immerwährend.
Every, a. jeder. every one, Jedermann. everywhere, überall. everything, Alles.
Evidence, s. Zeugniß, n.; Beweis, m.
Exact, a. -ly, ad. genau. v. a. fordern; befehlen.
Exalt, v. a. erhöhen.
Examination, s. Prüfung; Untersuchung, f.
Examine, v. a. untersuchen, prüfen.
Example, s. Beispiel, Muster, n.
Exceed, v. a. übertreffen.
Excel, v. n. sich auszeichnen.
Excellence, s. Verdienst, m.
Excellency, s. Excellenz, f.
Excellent, a. vortrefflich.
Except, pr. ausgenommen.
Excess, s. Uebermaß, n.
Excessive, a. -ly. ad. übermäßig; übertrieben; äußerst.
Exchange, v. a. wechseln, tauschen. s. Tausch, m.
Excite, v. a. erregen.
Exclaim, v. n. ausrufen.
Exclamation, s. Ausruf, m.
Exclusion, s. Ausschließung, f.
Exclusive, of, a. abgerechnet.
Excuse, v. a. entschuldigen. excuse one's self (from), sich entschuldigen (wegen). s. Ausrede, f.; Entschuldigung, Verzeihung, f.
Execute, v. a. besorgen, vollziehen.

**Execution,** s. Ausführung; Hinrichtung, f.
**Executioner,** s. Henker, m.
**Exercise,** s. Uebung. (riding) exercise, Reitübung, f.
**Exert,** v. a. anstrengen.
**Exertion,** s. Bemühung. f.
**Exhaust,** v. a. erschöpfen.
**Exhibit,** v. a. ausüben, ausstellen.
**Exhort,** v. a. ermahnen.
**Existence(cy),** s. Dasein, n.; Leben, n.
**Ex-king,** s. vormaliger König.
**Expand,** v. a. ausspannen.
**Expect,** v. a. erwarten.
**Expectation,** s. Erwartung, f.
**Expedience(cy),** s. Räthlichkeit, f.
**Expedient,** s. Mittel, Nothmittel, n.
**Expedition,** s. Feldzug, m.; Untersuchungsreise, f.; Expedition, f.
**Expeditious,** a. hurtig.
**Expel,** v. a. wegtreiben.
**Expense,** s. (-s pl.) Kosten, f. pl.
**Expensive,** a. theuer, kostspielig.
**Experience,** s. Erfahrung, f. v. a. erfahren, leiden.
**Experiment,** s. Versuch, m.; Experiment, n.
**Expiration,** s. Umlauf, m.; Ablauf, m.
**Explain,** v. a. erklären.
**Explanation,** s. Erklärung, f.
**Explore,** v. a. ausforschen.
**Expose,** v. a. aussetzen, ausstellen.
**Expostulate,** v. n. streiten.
**Express,** v. a. ausdrücken.
**Expression,** s. Ausbruck, m.
**Exquisite,** a. auserlesen.
**Extend,** v. a. ausstrecken; v. n. sich ausdehnen.
**Extensive,** a. ausgedehnt.
**Extinguish,** v. a. auslöschen, vertilgen.
**Extract,** s. Auszug, m.
**Extraordinary,** a. außerordentlich.
**Extravagance,** s. Verschwendung, f.
**Extreme, -ly.** ad. äußerst, höchst.
**Extricate,** v. a. herauswickeln.
**Exult,** v. n. frohlocken.
**Eye,** s. Auge, n.

## F.

**Face,** s. Gesicht, n.
**Facility,** s. Leichtigkeit, f.
**Fagot,** s. Welle, f.
**Fail,** v. n. verfehlen, mißlingen, ermangeln, mangeln.
**Failure,** s. Fehlschlagen, n.
**Faint,** a. schwach.
**Fair,** a. hübsch; rein; schön. s. Jahrmarkt, m.
**Faith,** s. Glaube, m., Treue, f. want of faith, Wortbruch, m., Wortbrüchigkeit, f.
**Faithful,** a. treu, treulich.
**Full,** v. n. fallen; — asleep, einschlafen; — in love with, sich verlieben in; fall upon, v. a. überfallen.
**Fallacious,** a. betrüglich.

**False,** a. falsch.
**Falsehood,** s. Falschheit, f.
**Fame,** s. Ruhm, Ruf, m.
**Familiar,** a. bekannt, leutselig.
**Family,** s. Familie, f.
**Famous,** a. -ly, ad. berühmt.
**Fancy,** v. a. glauben.
**Fantastic(al),** a. sonderbar.
**Far,** ad. weit, fern. to be far from, weit entfernt sein von. by far, bei weitem.
**Fare,** s. Kost, f.
**Farewell,** int. lebe wohl.
**Farm,** s. Pachtgut, n.
**Farther,** ad. weiter.
**Farthing,** s. Farthing, m.
**Fast,** v. n. fasten.
**Fast,** ad. fest.
**Fasting,** s. Fasten, n.
**Fatal,** a. traurig, verhängnißvoll.
**Fate,** s. Schicksal, n.
**Father,** s. Vater, m. to father, v. a. sich aneignen.
**Fatigue,** s. Anstrengung, f., Müdigkeit, f. v. a. ermüden.
**Fault,** s. Fehler, m.
**Faulty,** a. fehlerhaft.
**Favor,** s. Gunst, f. in favour of, zu Gunsten. —s, pl. Gunstbezeigungen.
**Favourable,** a. günstig.
**Favourite,** a. geliebt. s. Günstling, m.
**Fear,** s. Furcht, f. v. n. sich fürchten.
**Fearful,** a. fürchterlich.
**Feast,** s. Fest, n.
**Feather,** s. Feder, f. v. a. befiedern, bereichern.
**Feature,** s. Gesichtszug, Zug, m.
**Feeble,** a. schwach.
**Feed,** v. a. unterhalten.
**Feel,** v. n. fühlen, sich fühlen.
**Feeling,** s. Gefühl, n.
**Feign,** v. n. sich stellen.
**Felicitation,** s. Glückwünschung, f., Glückwunsch, m.
**Fell,** v. a. fällen.
**Fellow,** s. Kerl, m. fellow-citizen, s. Mitbürger, m. fellow-prisoner, s. Mitgefangene(r), m. fellow-slave, s. Mitsklave, m. fellow-student, s. Mitstudent, m.
**Female,** a. weiblich.
**Ferry,** s. Fähre, f.
**Festival,** s. Festtag, m.
**Fetch,** v. a. holen, hervorbringen. fetch up, heraufholen.
**Fever,** s. Fieber, n.
**Few,** a. wenig; a few, wenige.
**Fidelity,** s. Treue, f.
**Field,** s. Feld; Schlachtfeld, n.
**Fieldfare,** s. Krametsvogel, m.
**Fierce,** a. grimmig.
**Fifty,** a. fünfzig.
**Fight,** v. n. ausfechten, kämpfen, fechten. fight (a battle), liefern.
**Figure,** s. Gestalt, f.
**Filial,** a. kindlich. [bekleiben.
**Fill,** v. a. füllen; (an office), einnehmen,

Fin, s. Floßfeder, f. (Hand, f.)
Final, a. -ly. ad. endlich.
Find, v. a. finden, antreffen; bemerken; erfinden. to be found, sich finden. find out, ausfindig machen.
Fine, a. -ly. ad. schön; kostbar.
Finery, s. Schmuck, m., Putz, m.
Finger, s. Finger, m.
Finish, v. a. fertig machen, endigen, vollenden. to be finished, fertig sein.
Fire, s. Feuer, n. coals of fire, feurige Kohlen.
Fire, v. n. schießen. set fire to, in Brand stecken.
Fireplace, s. Kamin, n., Herd, m.
Fire-side, s. Kamin, n., Ofen, m.
Firing, s. Feuerung, f.
Firm, -ly. ad. fest.
First, a. erste; ad. erstens, zuerst.
Fish, s. Fisch, m.
Fisherman, s. Fischer, m.
Fishing-vessel, s. Fischerboot, n.
Fishing-tackle, s. Fischzeug, n.
Fishhook, s. Fischangel, f.
Fit, a. (adapted to), geeignet; to be —, sich eignen (zu).
Five, a. fünf.
Fix, v. a. festsetzen, richten; (abode) nehmen; v. n. fest werden.
Flag, s. Flagge, f.
Flail, s. Dreschflegel, m.
Flambeau, s. Fackel, f.
Flanders, s. Flandern.
Flap, s. Rockschoß, m.
Flat, a. platt.
Flatter, v. a. schmeicheln.
Flatterer, s. Schmeichler, m.
Floe, v. n. fliehen.
Flesh, s. Fleisch, n. human flesh, Menschenfleisch.
Flight, s. Flucht, f., Anlauf, Versuch, m.
Fling, v. a. werfen.
Float, v. n. schweben. float about, umherschwimmen.
Flock, s. Schaar, f.
Flood, s. Fluth, f.
Floor, s. Fußboden, m.
Florin, s. Gulden, m.
Flour, s. Mehl, n.
Flourish, v. n. blühen.
Flower, s. Blume, f.
Flute, s. Flöte, f.
Fly, v. n. fliehen. fly to arms, zu den Waffen eilen.
Fly, s. Fliege, f.
Fold, s. Falte, f.
Follow, v. a. folgen, nachahmen. worthy to be followed, nachahmungswerth.
Following, a. folgend.
Folly, s. Thorheit; Ausschweifung, f.
Fond, a. vernarrt, thörichterweise. to be — of doing, gern thun; to be — of, ein Freund von (Einem) sein; sehr lieben; trachten nach, gern haben.
Fool, s. Thor, Narr, m.
Foot, s. Fuß, m. set foot (on), Fuß setzen. from head to foot, vom Scheitel bis zur Sohle, über und über. on foot, zu Fuß.
Footman, s. Läufer, m.
Footstep, s. Fußstapfe, f.
For, pr. (purpose), um; für, zu. c. denn; (= as) als.
Force, s. Gewalt, f. -s, pl. Truppen, m. pl. by force, mit Gewalt. v. a. — inwards, hineinpressen.
Ford, s. Furt, f.
Forecastle, s. Vorderkastell, n.
Foreign, a. ausländisch; fremd.
Foreigner s. Ausländer, m.
Foremost, a. vorderste.
Foresee, v. a. voraussehen, vorhersehen.
Foresight, s. Vorsicht, f.
Forest, s. Forst, m.
Forever, ad. immerfort, zeitlebens.
Forfeit, v. a. verscherzen.
Forge, s. Schmiede, f.
Forget, v. a. vergessen.
Fork, s. Gabel, f.
Form, s. Form, Gestalt, f. v. a. bilden, machen, fassen, gestalten. form a project, einen Plan fassen.
Formality, s. Förmlichkeit, f.
Former, a. -ly. ad. vorig; vormalig, früher; jener; der, die, das Erstere.
Forsake, v. a. verlassen.
Forthwith, ad. geradewegs.
Fortitude, s. Tapferkeit, f.; Geistesstärke, f.
Fortnight, s. vierzehn Tage.
Fortunate a. -ly. ad. glücklich.
Fortune, s. Glück; Vermögen, n. to make a fortune, sich ein Vermögen machen.
Forty, a. vierzig.
Forward, v. a. befördern.
Forwards, ad. vorwärts.
Four, a. vier.
Fourteen, a. vierzehn.
Fourteenth, a. vierzehnte.
Fourtimes, ad. viermal.
Fowl, s. Huhn, n.
Frail, a. gebrechlich.
Franc, s. Franken, m.
France, Frankreich.
Frank, -ly. ad. frei.
Frankness, s. Freimüthigkeit, f.
Fray, s. Streit, f.
Frederick, Friedrich.
Free, v. a. befreien.
Freeze, v. n. frieren.
French, s. Franzose, m. a. französisch in French, auf französisch.
Frequent, -ly. ad. oft.
Frequent, v. a. oft besuchen.
Fresh, a. frisch.
Friend, s. Freund(in), m. & f.
Friendly, a. freundlich.
Friendship, s. Freundschaft, f.
Frigate, s. Fregatte, f.
Frighten, v. a. erschrecken.
Frosty, a. frostig.
Frugal, a. sparsam.
Frugality, s. Sparsamkeit, f.

Fruit, s. Frucht, f.
Fruitful, a. fruchtbar.
Frustrate, v. a. vereiteln.
Fuel, s. Brennmaterial, n.; Feuerung, f.
Fugitive, a. flüchtig.
Fulfilment, s. Erfüllung, f.
Full, a. voll; gefüllt. at full speed, im Galopp.
Fumble, v. n. tänbeln, spielen.
Funeral, s. Leichenbegängniß, n.
Fur, s. Pelz, m.
Furious, a. wüthend, rasend.
Furl, (die Segel) einziehen.
Furnish, v. a. versehen, leihen, ausmöbliren.
Furniture, s. Möbel, (pl.) f.
Further, a. weiter.
Fury, s. Wuth, f. in a fury, wüthend.
Future, a. künftig. s. Zukunft, f. in future, künftig, in Zukunft.

## G.

Gaily, ad. lustig.
Gain, s. Gewinn, m. v. a. erreichen, gewinnen.
Gallery, s. Gallerie, f.
Galley, s. Galeere, f.
Gaming, s. Spielen, n.
Gamekeeper, s. Förster, m.; Wildhüter, m.
Gang, s. Bande, f.; Trupp, m. gang of robbers, Räuberbande, f.
Garden, s. Garten, m.
Garrison, s. Besatzung, f.
Gascony, Gasconien.
Gate, s. Thor, n.
Gather, v. a. sammeln, pflücken.
Gay, a. lustig.
Gaze, v. n. anstarren. s. Blick, m.
General, s. General, m., Feldherr, m. a. allgemein, gewöhnlich. generally speaking, im Allgemeinen gesprochen.
Generation, s. Generation, f.
Generosity, s. Freigebigkeit, f.; Großmuth, f.
Generous, a. edelmüthig, großmüthig.
Geneva, s. Genf.
Genius, s. Genius, Geist, m.
Genteel, a. fein.
Gentle, a. sanft.
Gentleman, s. Herr, m. like a gentleman, anständig.
Gently, ad. sanft.
George, Georg.
German, s. Deutsche(r), m.; a. deutsch.
Germany, Deutschland.
Get, v. a. erhalten, bekommen, kommen. get off (away), sich machen aus dem Staube. get up, aufstehen. get a living, Brod verdienen. get here, antommen. get rid of, ablegen, loswerden. get (one to do), dazu bringen.
Giant, s. Riese, m.
Gift, s. Geschenk, n.
Gigantic, a. riesengroß.
Gild, v. a. vergolden.
Gin, s. Branntwein, m.
Gipsy, s. Zigeuner(in), m. (& f.).
Girl, s. Mädchen, n.
Give, v. a. geben; bieten, leisten; (afford), machen; (bestow, confer), schenken; — (trouble), machen; — out, angeben; — pleasure, Vergnügen machen;—up, übergeben, herausgeben; — into the bargain, dreingeben.
Glad, a. froh. to be glad, sich erfreuen.
Gladly, ad. gern, mit Freuden.
Glaring, a. blendend.
Glass, s. Glas, n. magnifying glass, Vergrößerungsglas, n. glassbead, Glaskoralle, f.
Glide, v. n. gleiten. glide away, dahingleiten.
Glitter, v. n. glänzen, schimmern.
Gloom, s. Trübsinn, m.
Gloomy, a. düster, traurig.
Glorious, a. rühmlich.
Glory, s. Ruhm, m.
Glove, s. Handschuh, m.
Glow, v. n. glühen.
Gnash, v. n. & v. a. fletschen.
Go, v. n. gehen; to be going to do, im Begriff sein zu thun, thun wollen. go on (= under way), fortfahren. go along on, hingehen an.
God, s. Gott, m.
Going, s. Reise, f.
Gold, s. Gold, m.
Golden, a. golden.
Gone, ad. weg, fort.
Good, a. gut; s. Beste, n.
Goods, s. Vermögen, n.
Goodnatured, a. gutmüthig.
Goose, s. Gans, f.
Gosling, s. Gänschen, n.
Gossip, v. n. plaudern.
Govern, v. a. regieren.
Governess, s. Gouvernante, f., Erzieherin, f.
Government, s. Regierung, f.
Governor, s. Verwalter, m.
Grace, s. Gnade, Anmuth, f.
Gracious, -ly, ad. gnädig.
Gradual, -ly, ad. nach und nach.
Grand, a. groß.
Grandeur, s. Größe, f.
Grateful, a. dankbar.
Gratify, v. a. gönnen.
Grating, s. Kratzen, n.
Gratitude, s. Dankbarkeit, f. office of gratitude to Heaven, Gottesdienst, m.
Gratuitous, a. unbezahlt.
Grave, s. Grab, n.
Graze, v. n. grasen.
Great, a. groß.
Great Britain, Großbritannien.
Greatly, ad. sehr.
Grecian, s. Grieche, m. a. griechisch.
Greedy, -ily, ad. begierig.
Greek, a. griechisch.

Grenadier, s. Grenadier, m.
Grief, s. Kummer, m.
Grieve, v. a. dauern, sich grämen (um).
Grievous, -ly, ad. schmerzlich.
Grocer, s. Krämer, m.
Ground, s. Grund, Boden, m. v. n. laufen auf den Grund.
Grow, v. n. wachsen; werden. grow up, wachsen, aufwachsen. grow to (into), sich steigern bis zu.
Guard, s. Wache, f., Garde, f. (= guard house), Hauptwache, f. regiment of the guard, Garderegiment, n. to be on one's guard, vorsichtig sein.
Guess, v. n. & a. errathen.
Guest, s. Gast, m.
Guide, v. a. leiten.
Guilty, a. schuldig, schuldbewußt.
Guinea, s. Guinee, f.
Gun, s. Geschütz, n., Flinte, f.
Gunpowder, s. Pulver, n.
Gush, v. n. strömen, fließen, beginnen.

# H.

Habit, s. Beschaffenheit, f., Gewohnheit, f. be in the habit, pflegen.
Habitation, s. Wohnung, f.
Habitual, a. angewöhnt.
Hair, s. Haar, n.
Half, a. halb; s. Hälfte, f.
Half-pay, s. halber Sold, m.
Half-way, adv. auf halbem Wege.
Hall, s. Saal, m.
Halt, v. n. Halt machen.
Hammer, s. Hammer, m.
Hand, s. Hand, Handschrift, f. at (on) hand, vorhanden. on the one hand, auf (von) der einen Seite; einerseits. on the other hand, auf (von) der andern Seite; andererseits.
Handbill, s. Billet, n.
Handful, s. Handvoll, f. by handfuls, handvollweise.
Handkerchief, s. Schnupftuch, n.
Handle, s. Stiel, m.
Handsome, -ly, ad. anständig, reichlich, hübsch.
Hang, v. n. hangen.
Happen, v. n. sich ereignen, begegnen, geschehen. to happen to do, thun zufällig. (= occur, take place), stattfinden.
Happiness, s. Glückseligkeit, f., Glück, n.
Happy, -ily, ad. zum Glück, glücklich.
Harass, v. a. —out, ganz erschöpfen.
Hardly, ad. kaum. hardly ever, fast nie.
Harm, s. Böses, n., Schade, m.
Harmless, a. unschädlich.
Harmony, s. Eintracht, f., Einigkeit, f.
Haste, s. Eile, f. make haste, schnell machen.
Hasten, v. n. eilen.
Hasty, a. eilig, hastig.
Hatchet, s. Axt, f.

Hate, v. a. hassen.
Hatred, s. Haß, m.
Haughty, a. stolz, übermüthig.
Haul, v. a. ziehen.
Have, v. a. haben. let (one) —, geben; — to, brauchen; — any thing done, etwas thun (machen) lassen; — at heart, (Einem) am Herzen liegen; —on, anhaben.
Hawk-bell, s. Falkenglocke, f.
Hay, s. Heu, n.
Hazard, v. a. aufs Spiel setzen, riskiren.
Head, s. Haupt, n., Kopf, m. head to foot, vom Scheitel bis zur Sohle, über und über. back of the head, Hinterkopf, m. take into one's head, sich in den Kopf setzen.
Healed, a. heil.
Health, s. Gesundheit, f.
Heap, v. a. sammeln.
Hear, v. a. hören, erfahren.
Heart, s. Herz, n. to have at heart, (einem) am Herzen liegen.
Hearty, -ily, ad. herzlich.
Heathen, s. Heide, m., Heidin, f.
Heaven, s. Himmel, m.
Heavenly, a. himmlisch.
Heavy, -ily, ad. hoch, schwer.
Heel, s. Ferse, f. to take to one's heels, die Flucht ergreifen.
Heir, s. Erbe, m.
Heiress, s. Erbin, f.
Hellfire, s. Höllenfeuer, höllisches Feuer, n.
Help, v. n. helfen; (restrain one's self (from)), sich enthalten; v. a. — to, (= aid in obtaining), verhelfen.
Hence, ad. daher.
Henry, Heinrich.
Herb, s. Kraut, n.
Herbage, s. Gras, n.
Here, ad. hier (=hither), hierher.
Hereupon, hierauf.
Hermit, s. Einsiedler, m.
Hero, s. Held, m.
Heroic, -ally, ad. heldenmüthig.
Heroism, s. Heldenmuth, m.
Hesitation, s. Zögern, n.
Hibernian, s. Irländer, m.
Hide, v. a. verbergen; verstecken.
Hideous, a. traurig.
Hiding-place, s. Versteck, m.
High, a. hoch; ad. hoch, höchst.
Highness, s. Hoheit, f.
Highway, s. Straße, f.
Highwayman, s. Wegelagerer, m.
Hill, s. Hügel, m.
Hire, v. a. miethen.
His, pn. sein.
Hiss, s. Gezisch, n.
Hist, still! st!
Historian, s. Geschichtschreiber, m.
Historic(al), a. geschichtlich.
History, s. Geschichte, f.
Hit, v. n. hit (upon), kommen, verfallen (auf).
Hither, ad. hierher. hitherto, bis hierher.
Hoe, s. Karst, m.
Hold, v. a. halten, haben, (rank) einnehmen.

# VOCABULARY. 147

Hole, s. Loch, n.
Holiday, s. Feiertag, m.
Hollanda, s. Branntwein, m.
Hollow, s. Höhle, f.
Holy, a. heilig.
Home, ad. heim; nach, zu Hause. set off towards home, sich machen auf den Heimweg.
Honesty, s. Ehrlichkeit, f.
Honey, s. Honig, m.
Honor, s. Ehre, f.; in — of, zu Ehren; do —, Ehre erweisen, (erzeigen). v. a. ehren, beehren; (pay honor), ehren.
Honorable, a. ehrbar, würdig; ehrenvoll.
Hook, s. Hafen, m. v. a. einhafen.
Hope, s. Hoffnung f. in hopes, in der Hoffnung. v. n. hoffen.
Hopeful, a. hoffnungsvoll.
Hopeless, a. hoffnungslos.
Horn, s. Horn, n.
Horrid, a. schrecklich.
Horse, s. Pferd, n. on horseback, zu Pferde.
Hospitable, a. gastfrei.
Hospitality, s. Gastfreundlichkeit, f.
Host, s. Wirth, m.
Hostage, s. Geißel, m.
Hostler, s. Stallknecht, m.
Hot, a. heiß.
Hotel, s. Gasthof, m.; Hotel, n.
Hound, s. Jagdhund, m.
Hour, s. Stunde, f.
House, s. Haus, n.
Housekeeper, s. Haushälterin, f.
Housewife, s. Hausfrau, f.
How, ad. wie.
However, ad. jedoch, doch, indessen, dennoch.
Howl, v. n. heulen.
Human, a. menschlich. more than human, übermenschlich.
Humanity, s. Menschlichkeit, f.
Humble, a. -bly. ad. niedrig; demüthig; nieder.
Humility, s. Demuth, f.
Humour, s. Scherzhaftigkeit, f.
Hundred, a. hundert. s. Hundert, n.
Hundred-weight, s. Zentner, n.
Hunger, s. Hunger, m.; v. n. hungern.
Hungry, a. hungrig.
Hunter, s. Jäger, m.
Hurricane, s. Orkan, m.
Harry, s. Eile, f. v. a. führen.
Husband, s. Gatte, m.; Ehemann, m. brute of a husband, ein roher Ehemann.
Hush ! i. stille.
Hymn of thanksgiving, s. Loblied, n.
Hypocrisy, s. Heuchelei, f.

## I.

Ice, s. Eis, n.
Idea, s. Gedanken, m.; Einbildung, f.; Ansicht, f.; Begriff, m.; Idee, f.
Idle, a. müßig.

Idolater, s. Götzendiener, m.
If, c. wenn. (whether), ob.
Ignorance, s. Unwissenheit, f.
Ignorant, a. unwissend.
Ill, a. krank, unwohl; schlecht. ad. schwer; mit Mühe.
Ill-natured, a. böse.
Illness, s. Krankheit, f.
Illusive, a. täuschend, trüglich.
Illustrate, v. a. erzeigen, zeichnen, schildern.
Illustrious a. berühmt.
Imaginable, a. denkbar.
Imagine, v. a. sich einbilden; denken, glauben; nicht recht wissen, annehmen.
Imbrue, v. a. beflecken.
Imitate, v. a. nachahmen.
Imitation, s. Nachahmung, f. in imitation of, um nachzuahmen.
Immediate, a. unmittelbar. -ly. ad. sogleich, augenblicklich.
Immense, a. unermeßlich.
Imminent, a. vorhanden.
Immutable, a. unveränderlich.
Impatience, s. Ungeduld, f.
Impatient, impatient of, unwillig über.
Impetuous, a. ungestüm, heftig.
Impiety, s. Gottlosigkeit, f.
Impious, a. gottlos.
Implement, s. Werkzeug, n.
Importance, s. Wichtigkeit, f.
important, a. wichtig, bedeutend.
Impossible, a. -bly, ad. unmöglich.
Impotent, a. unmächtig.
Impression, s. Eindruck, m.
Imprisonment, s. Gefangenschaft, f.
Improbable, a. unwahrscheinlich.
Improper, a. unpassend.
Improve, v. a. verbessern. v. n. sich ausbilden, besser werden.
Improvement, s. Verbesserung, f.; Ausbildung, f.
Improvidence, s. Unvorsichtigkeit, f.
Imprudence, s. Unklugheit, f.
Imprudent, a. unklug.
Impudence, s. Frechheit, f.
Impute, v. a. zurechnen, zuschieben.
In, pr. in. ad. hinein, herein.
Inactivity, s. Unthätigkeit, f.
Inattention, s. Gleichgültigkeit, f.
Incapable, a. unfähig, untauglich.
Incessant, a. unaufhörlich.
Inch, s. Zoll, m.
Incitement, s. Antrieb, m.
Inclination, s. Neigung, f.
Inconsiderate, a. unbedachtsam.
Inconvenience, s. Unbequemlichkeit, f.; Verlegenheit, f.
Increase, v. a. vergrößern, vermehren. v. n. (of a fever), sich verschlimmern.
Increasing, a. steigend.
Incredible, a. unglaublich.
Incredulity, s. Unglaube, m.
Incredulous, a. ungläubig.
Incur, v. a. sich zuziehen; laufen.
Indecency, s. Unanständigkeit, f.
Indeed, ad. in der That, freilich, ja.

Indefatigable, a. unermüdlich.
Independence, s. Unabhängigkeit, f.
Independent, a. unabhängig.
Indian, a. indisch.
Indicate, v. a. anzeigen.
Indication, s. Anzeige, f.
Indies, s. pl. Indien, n.
Indifferent, a. gleichgültig.
Indigence, s. Dürftigkeit, f.
Indignation, s. Unwille(n), m.
Indirect, -ly. ad. mittelbar.
Indiscreet, a. unbescheiden.
Indiscretion, s. Unbescheidenheit, f.
Indisposed, a. unpäßlich.
Induce, v. a. bewegen.
Indulge, v. a. befriedigen, folgen.
Indulgence, s. Nachsicht, f.
Industry, s. Fleißigkeit, f.
Ineffectual, a. unwirksam.
Inevitable, a. unvermeidlich.
Inexorable, a. unerbittlich.
Infallible, a. unfehlbar.
Infant, s. Kind, n.
Infant, a. kindisch.
Infested, a. unsicher gemacht.
Infidel, s. Ungläubige(r), m.
Infirm, a. schwach.
Inflame, v. a. entflammen.
Inflexible, a. unbiegsam.
Influence, s. Einfluß, m.
Inform, v. a. benachrichtigen, unterrichten.
Information, s. Auskunft, f.; Bildung, f.
Ingenious, a. sinnreich, geistreich.
Ingenuity, s. Erfindungsgeist, m.
Ingraft, v. a. einprägen.
Ingratitude, s. Undankbarkeit, f.
Inhabit, v. a. bewohnen.
Inhabitant, s. Einwohner, m.
Inherit, v. a. erben.
Inheritance, s. Erbschaft, f.; Besitz, m.
Injure, v. a. verletzen, beleidigen.
Injury, s. Schade(n), m.; Beleidigung, f.
Injustice, s. Ungerechtigkeit, f.
Inn, s. Wirthshaus, n.
Inn-keeper, s. Wirth, m.
Innocence, s. Unschuld, f.
Innocent, a. unschädlich, arglos, unschuldig.
Innumerable, a. unzählig.
Inquire, v. n. nachfragen, sich erkundigen; inquire into, untersuchen, fragen.
Inquiry, s. Untersuchung; Nachfrage, f. make inquiries, Nachforschungen or Nachfragen anstellen.
Inquisitive, a. neugierig. inquisitive curiosity, s. Naseweisheit, f.
Inscribe, v. a. einschreiben.
Inscription, s. Aufschrift, f.
Insensible, a. besinnungslos.
Insignificant, a. bedeutungslos.
Insinuation, s. Einschmeichelung, f.
Insist, v. n. bestehen, behaupten.
Insolence, s. Frechheit, f.
Inspiration, s. göttliche Eingebung, f.
Inspire, v. a. begeistern.
Instance, s. Probe, f.
Instant, s. Augenblick, m.

Instantly, ad. augenblicklich.
Instead, pr. anstatt.
Instigate, v. a. veranlassen.
Institute, v. a. stiften.
Institution, s. Verordnung, f.
Instruction, s. Unterricht, m.
Instructor, s. Lehrer, m.
Instrument, s. Werkzeug, n.
Insult, s. Beschimpfung, f.
Insurrection, s. Empörung, f.
Integrity, s. Rechtschaffenheit, f.
Intellect, s. Verstand, m.
Intelligence, s. Verstand, m., Nachricht, f. give —, Nachricht geben; benachrichtigen.
Intelligent, a. verständig.
Intend, v. a. beabsichtigen.
Intense, a. gespannt, stark, lebhaft.
Intent, a. gespannt.
Intention, s. Absicht, f. to have — against, trachten nach.
Inter, v. a. begraben.
Intercede, v. n. Fürbitte einlegen.
Interest, s. Interesse, n., Vortheil, Nutzen, m.; Zinsen (pl.) f.
Interest, v. a. unterhalten.
Interested, a. to be interested (in), Antheil nehmen (an).
Interesting, a. interessant.
Interior, s. Innere, n.
Interpose, v. n. sich legen ins Mittel.
Interrogate, v. a. befragen, ausfragen, verhören.
Interrogation, s. Prüfung, f.
Interrupt, v. a. unterbrechen.
Interview, s. Zusammenkunft, f.
Intimacy, s. Vertraulichkeit, f.
Intimate, a. vertraut.
Intimidate, v. a. einschüchtern.
Intrinsic(al), a. inner; wesentlich.
Introduce, v. a. einführen, vorstellen, bekannt machen.
Invention, s. Erfindung, f.
Investigation, s. Erforschung, f.
Invitation, s. Einladung, f.
Invite, v. a. einladen.
Invocation, s. Anrufung, f.
Involve, v. a. einwickeln.
Inward, s. ad. -ly. nach innen, inwendig; innig.
Ireland, s. Irland, n.
Irishman, s. Irländer, m.
Iron, a. eisern.
Irritate, v. a. erzürnen.
Island, s. Insel, f.
Islander, s. Insulaner, m.
Issue, s. Ausgang; Erfolg, m.
Italian, s. Italiener, m. a. italienisch.

## J.

Jamaica, s. Jamaika, n.
James, s. Jakob, m.
Jealous, a. eifersüchtig (of, über).
Jest, s. Scherz, m.

## VOCABULARY. 149

**Jesus,** s. Jesus, m.
**Jew,** s. Jude, m.
**Jewel,** s. Juwele, f.
**Jeweller,** s. Juwelier, m.
**Jewish,** a. jüdisch.
**John,** s. Johann, m.
**Join,** v. a. stoßen (zu); zugesellen. v. n. sich verbinden, einstimmen.
**Jokingly,** ad. scherzhaft.
**Journey,** s. Reise, f. v. n. reisen.
**Joy,** s. Freude, f.
**Joyful,** a. freudig, freude(n)voll.
**Judge,** s. Richter, m.; v. n. entscheiden, urtheilen (über).
**Judgment,** s. Urtheil, n.
**Judicial,** a. richterlich.
**Judicious,** a. klug.
**Juniper,** s. Wachholder, m. **Juniperberry,** s. Wachholderbeere, f.
**Jury,** s. die Geschworenen, pl.
**Just,** a. gerecht, recht, richtig. ad. eben, gerade. but just, eben erst. just as, eben als.
**Justice,** s. Gerechtigkeit, f., Richtigkeit, f. to bring to justice, vor Gericht führen.
**Justification,** s. Rechtfertigung, f.
**Justify,** v. a. rechtfertigen.

## K.

**Keel,** s. Kiel, m.
**Keen,** a. scharf.
**Keep,** v. a. halten, erhalten, bewahren. — (books), führen; — watch, Acht geben. v. n. sich halten, bleiben. — ahead, vorauseilen; — from, abhalten.
**Key,** s. Schlüssel, m.
**Kill,** v. a. tödten.
**Kind,** s. Art, f. a. gütig, freundlich.
**Kindness,** a. Güte, Freundlichkeit, f.
**Kindred,** s. Verwandtschaft, f.
**King,** s. König, m.
**Kingdom,** s. Königreich, n., Reich, n.
**Kinsman,** s. Verwandte(r), m.
**Kiss,** v. a. küssen.
**Kitchen,** s. Küche, f.
**Knave,** s. Schurke, m.
**Knee,** s. Knie, n. knee-deep, a. bis an die Knie tief.
**Kneel,** v. n. knieen.
**Knife,** s. Messer, n.
**Knighthood,** s. Ritterschaft, f.
**Knock,** v. a. schlagen, stoßen. s. Klopfen, n.
**Know,** v. a. wissen, kennen, erfahren; (recognise as), erkennen. let —, wissen lassen, zu wissen thun.
**Knowledge,** s. Wissen, n., Kenntniß, f., Erkenntniß, f.
**Known,** a. bekannt.

## L.

**Laborious,** a. fleißig, arbeitsam.
**Labour,** s. Arbeit, f. v. n. arbeiten, (for, an.)
**Lace,** s. Schnur, Spitze, f.

**Lacerate,** v. a. zerreißen.
**Ladder,** s. Leiter, f.
**Lady,** s. Frau, Dame, f. young lady, Fräulein, n.
**Lamb,** s. Lamm, n.
**Lame,** a. lahm.
**Lament,** v. n. klagen, jammern.
**Lamentable,** -bly. ad. kläglich.
**Lamentation,** s. Wehklage, f.
**Land,** s. Land, n. v. n. landen.
**Landbird,** s. Landvogel, m.
**Landlady,** s. Wirthin, f.
**Landlord,** s. Wirth, m.
**Lane,** s. Gäßchen, n.
**Language,** s. Sprache, f.
**Lapse,** s. Verfluß, m.
**Large,** a. -ly, ad. groß.
**Lash,** s. Streich, m.
**Last,** a. letzte, vorig. ad. zuletzt, endlich. at last, zuletzt.
**Last,** v. n. dauern.
**Late,** a. & ad. spät, neulich, selig, verstorben. of late, neulich.
**Lately,** ad. neulich.
**Latter,** a. dieser, der letztere.
**Laudable,** a. lobenswerth.
**Laugh,** v. n. lachen. s. Lachen, n.
**Laughable,** a. lächerlich.
**Law,** s. Gesetz, n. Common law, s. Landrecht, n.
**Lawsuit,** s. Rechtshandel, m., Prozeß, m.
**Lay,** v. a. legen, stellen. lay (blame), zuschieben. lay down, niederlegen. to be laid, stehen. lay siege to, anfangen zu belagern.
**Lead,** v. a. führen, leiten. lead forth, ausführen.
**Leaf,** s. Blatt, n.
**League,** s. Seemeile, f.
**Leak,** s. Leck, m.
**Lean,** v. n. sich lehnen.
**Learn,** v. a. lernen, erfahren. learn wiedom, klug werden.
**Learning,** s. Gelehrsamkeit, f.
**Leave,** s. Erlaubniß, f., Abschied, m. v. a. lassen, verlassen, hinterlassen, übrig lassen, zurücklassen, überlassen. leave on record, erzählen. leave behind one, hinterlassen.
**Lecture,** s. Vorlesung, f.
**Ledge,** s. Rand, m.
**Ledger,** s. Hauptbuch, n.
**Left,** a. links. left (over), übrig.
**Leg,** s. Bein, n.
**Legacy,** s. Vermächtniß, n.
**Legislative,** a. gesetzgebend.
**Legislature,** s. Gesetzgebung, f.
**Leisure,** s. Muße, f.
**Leisure,** a. müßig.
**Lend,** v. a. leihen.
**Length,** s. Länge, Dauer, f. at length, zuletzt.
**Less,** ad. weniger. no less, ebenso.
**Lesson,** s. Unterricht, m.; Stunde, f.; gute Lehre, Warnung, Lehre, f.
**Lest,** c. damit nicht.

Let, v. a. laſſen. let have, geben. let in, einlaſſen. let down, herablaſſen.
Lethargy, s. Schlafsucht, f. drunken lethargy, todtenähnlicher Zustand der Betrunkenheit.
Letter, s. Brief. m. letter of credit, s. Creditbrief, m. letter of advice, s. Avisbrief, m. world of letters, literariſche Welt, f.
Level, v. a. eben machen; (gun), anlegen.
Levity, s. Leichtsinn, m.
Liable, a. unterworfen, ausgesetzt.
Liberal, -ly, ad. freigebig.
Liberality, s. Freigebigkeit, f.
Liberty, s. Freiheit, f. he is at liberty, es steht einem frei. to set at liberty, befreien, in Freiheit ſetzen.
Library, s. Bibliothek, f.
Lickerish, a. naschhaft.
Lie, v. n. liegen. lie to, vor Anker liegen, beiliegen.
Lieutenant, s. Lieutenant, m., (police), Commissär, m.
Life, s. Leben, n.
Lift, v. a. heben, aufheben.
Light, of a light turn, a. leichtsinnig.
Light, s. Licht, n.
Light, v. a. anzünden.
Lighten, v. a. erleichtern.
Lightning, s. Blitz, m.
Like, ad. wie. to have like, beinahe sein. like that, so.
Like, v. a. & n. gefallen, gern essen.
Likely, ad. voraussichtlich.
Likeness, s. Aehnlichkeit, f.
Likewise, ad. gleichfalls.
Line, s. Linie, f.
Lineament, s. Zug, m.
Lion, s. Löwe, m.
Lip, s. Lippe, f.
Listen, v. n. zuhören.
Literary, a. literarisch; wissenschaftlich.
Little, a. & ad. klein, wenig.
Live, v. n. wohnen.
Live, a. lebendig.
Lively, a. lebhaft; leibhaftig.
Living, s. Kost, f., Unterhalt, m. to get a —, Brod verdienen.
Load, s. Ladung, f. v. a. überhäufen, laden.
Lock, s. Schloß, n.
Lodge, v. n. logiren, sich lagern.
Lodging, s. Wohnung, f.; night's lodging, Nachtherberge, Schlafstätte, f.
Logic, s. Denklehre, f.; Logik, f.
Lone, a. -ly, ad. einsam.
Long, a. ad. lang, lange. no longer, nicht mehr.
Long, v. n. sich sehnen.
Look, v. n. sehen. —about, sich umsehen; —at, betrachten, ansehen; —down, hinunterblicken; —for, suchen; (of a room) —into (the street), gehen auf (acc.); —out, hinausschauen, (keep a lookout) beobachten; —out for, sich umsehen nach; —

over (books), durchblättern; —upon (as), halten (für).
Look, s. sieh!
Lord, s. Lord; Herr, m. My lord, gnädiger Herr.
Lose, v. a. verlieren.
Loss, s. Verlust, m.; Schade(n), m. to be at a loss, in Verlegenheit sein; nicht recht wissen.
Lost, to be, verloren werden, verloren gehen.
Loud, a. laut.
Louisd'or, s. Louisd'or, m.
Lounger, s. Bummler, m.; Müſſiggänger, m.
Love, v. a. lieben. love better, mehr lieben. fall in love with, sich verlieben in.
Lover, s. Liebhaber, m.
Low, a. niedrig, wohlfeil.
Lower, a. untere.
Luck, s. Glück, n. by good luck, glücklicherweise.
Lucrative, a. einträglich.
Lull, v. a. beschwichtigen.
Lump, s. Klumpen, m.
Lunch, s. Abendbrod, n.
Lustre, s. Glanz, m.
Lutheran, a. lutherisch.

## M.

Machination, s. Anschlag, m.
Machine, s. Maschine, f.
Mad, a. verrückt.
Madam, s. Madame, f.
Madman, s. Narr, m.
Magazine, s. Monatsschrift, f.
Magistrate, s. Richter, m.; Behörde, f. civil magistrate, Richter, m.
Magnanimity, s. Großmuth, f.
Magnificence, s. Pracht, f.
Magnificent, a. -ly. ad. prächtig, prachtvoll.
Magnifying-glass, s. Vergrößerungsglas, n.
Mahometan, a. mahomedanisch.
Maid, s. Jungfer, f.
Mail, s. Postkutsche, f.; Briefpost, f.
Maintain, v. a. behaupten. maintain a character, (act a part), vorstellen.
Maintenance, s. Unterhalt, m.
Majesty, s. Majestät, f.
Major-domo, s. Ceremonienmeister, m.
Make, v. a., machen; (cause, induce) veranlassen; (of a bargain), schließen; (he. become), abgeben, werden; — appearance, auftreten; — amends, entschädigen; —(convert) into verarbeiten zu; —off. davonlaufen: — a present, zum Geschenk machen; — shift to live, sich durchbringen, sich (dat.) durch's Leben helfen.
Male, a. männlich.
Malevolence, s. Bosheit, f.
Malice, s. Bosheit, f.
Mamma, s. Mamma, f.

Man, s. Mensch; Mann; Soldat, m. v. a. bemannen.
Management, s. Verwaltung, f. Leitung, f.
Manager, s. Director, m.
Manhood, s. Mannbarkeit, f.
Manifest, v. a. entdecken.
Manifesto, s. Manifest, n.
Mankind, s. Menschheit, f.; Menschengeschlecht, n.
Manner, s. Haltung, f.; Art; Lebensart, f. Sitte, f. -s, pl. Sitten, f. pl. in such a manner, auf solche Weise, so.
Mansion, s. Wohnung, f.
Manufactory, s. Fabrikation, f.
Manufacture, v. a. verfertigen. to be manufactured, werden.
Manuscript, s. Handschrift, f.
Many, a. viele, mancher.
March, s. Marsch, m. v. n. marschiren.
Margaret, s. Margarethe, f.
Marine, s. Seesoldat, m.
Mark, s. Zeichen, n., Beweis, m., Maal, n.; Mark, f., Thaler, m.; v. a. bezeichnen, bemerken.
Market, s. Markt; Marktplatz, m.
Marriage, s. Heirath, (to) (mit).
Marry, v. a. (take to wife or husband) heirathen; (give in marriage), verheirathen; (join in marriage) trauen.
Marshal, s. Marschall, m.
Martial, a. militärisch.
Martyr, s. Märtyrer, m.
Mast, s. Mastbaum, m.
Master, s. Meister; Herr, m. master of arts, s. Magister, m.
Master-chimmy-sweeper, s. Kaminfegermeister, m.
Mat, s. Matte, f.
Mate, s. Schiffs-Cadet, m.
Material, -ly. ad. wichtig.
Mathematician, s. Mathematiker, m.
Matrimony, s. Ehestand, m.
Matter, s. Sache, f.; Gegenstand, m. no matter for that, das thut Nichts.
Mattock, s. Hacke, f.
Maxim, s. Lehre, f.
Mayor, s. Bürgermeister, m.
Meal, s. Mahl, n.; Mittagsmahl, n.; Mahlzeit, f.
Mean, -s, pl. Mittel, n. pl.; Vermögen, n.
Mean, v. a. meinen; sagen wollen.
Meantime, (in the mean time, while, space), adv. in der Zwischenzeit, inzwischen, einstweilen, indessen.
Meaning, s. Meinung, f.; Bedeutung, f.
Meanness, s. Niedrigkeit, f.
Measure, s. Maßregel, f.
Medical, a. medizinisch. Medical practitioner, praktischer Arzt, m.
Medicine, s. Medizin, f.
Meditate, v. a. nachdenken.
Meet, v. a. zusammentreffen (mit). go to meet, entgegengehen. come to meet, entgegenkommen. meet with (= obtain), erfahren, finden, genießen.

Melancholy, s. Schwermuth, f. a. schwermüthig.
Melt, v. a. schmelzen.
Member, s. Glied, n.
Memorial, s. Denkmal, n.; Bittschrift, f.
Memory, s. Gedächtniß; Andenken, n. in memory of, zum Andenken an.
Menace, s. Drohung, f.
Mend, v. n. sich bessern.
Mention, v. a. erwähnen. worth mentioning, erwähnenswerth.
Merchant, s. Kaufmann, m.
Merchant-ship, s. Handelsschiff, n.
Mercury, Merkur.
Mercy, s. Barmherzigkeit, Gnade, f. to have mercy on, Erbarmen haben mit.
Merit, s. Werth, m.; Verdienst, n. v. a. verdienen.
Merry, a. lustig, fröhlich.
Message, s. Botschaft, f.
Messenger, s. Bote, m.
Metal, s. Metall, n.
Method, s. Methode, f.; Mittel, n.
Metropolis, s. Hauptstadt, f.
Mid-day, s. Mittag, m.
Middle, s. Mitte, f.
Middle-aged, a. von mittlerem Alter.
Midnight, Mitternacht, f.
Midshipman, s. Seekadett, m.
Midst, s. Mitte, f. in the midst of, mitten in.
Mighty, a. mächtig.
Migration, s. Wanderung, f.
Mild, a. sanft, mild.
Milk, s. Milch, f.
Mill, s. Mühle, f.
Miller, s. Müller, m.
Million, s. Million, f.
Mind, s. Gemüth, n.; Geist, m. have a mind (to), Lust haben. v. a. never mind, laß es gut sein.
Mingle, v. a. mischen.
Minister, s. Pfarrer, m.
Minute, s. Minute, f.
Mischief, s. Unglück, n.
Miser, s. Geizhals, m.
Miserable, a. elend.
Misery, s. Elend, n.
Misfortune, s. Unglück, n.; Unglücksfall, m.
Miss, v. a. vermissen; verfehlen; nicht treffen; v. n. fehlen.
Mistake, v. a. verkennen. v. n. sich irren. s. Irrthum, m., Versehen, n. by —, aus Irrthum.
Mistaken, a. betrogen, verführt.
Mister, s. Herr, m.
Mistress, s. Frau, Herrin, f.
Mix, v. a. mischen, vermischen.
Mode, s. Art, f. mode of escape, Mittel zu entkommen.
Model, s. Muster, n.
Moderate, a. mäßig.
Modern, a. neu.
Modesty, s. Bescheidenheit, f.
Moment, s. Augenblick, m.

Monarch, s. Alleinherrscher, m.; Herrscher, Monarch, m.
Monday, s. Montag, m.
Money, s. Geld, n.
Monk, s. Mönch, m.
Monsieur, (title of the French king's eldest brother), s. Monsieur, m.
Month, s. Monat, m.
Monthly, a. monatlich.
Monument, s. Denkmal, n.
Moon, s. Mond, m.
Moonlight, s. Mondenlicht, n.
Moral, s. -s. pl. Moral, f.
Morality, s. Sittlichkeit, f.
More, a. pr. (= others), weitere. no more than, erst. so much the more, um so viel mehr.
Morning, s. Morgen, m.
Mortal, a. sterblich.
Mortify, v. a. bemüthigen.
Mosque, s. Moschee, f.
Most, ad. ganz.
Mother-country, s. Mutterland, n.
Motion, s. Bewegung, f.; Flug, m.
Motive, s. Beweggrund, m.
Motto, s. Motto, n.; Sinnspruch, m.
Mount, v. n. aufsteigen.
Mountain, s. Berg, m.
Mountainous, a. gebirgig.
Mouth, s. Mund, m.; Maul, n. by word of mouth, mündlich.
Move, v. n. gehen, ziehen.
Movement, s. Bewegung, f.
Much, a. & ad. viel. as much — as, so viel — als. so much, so sehr.
Muddy, a. schmutzig. mud-walled, mit Lehm gemauert.
Multitude, s. Menge, f.; Schaar, f.
Murder, v. a. ermorden.
Murmur, s. Gemurmel, n. v. n. murmeln.
Muse, s. Muse, f.
Music, s. Musik, f.
Musician, s. Tonkünstler, m.
Musket, s. Flinte, f.
Mutiny, s. Meuterei, f.
Mutual, a. gegenseitig; wechselweise.
Mysterious, a. geheimnißvoll.
Mystery, s. Geheimniß, n.

# N.

Nail, s. Nagel, m.
Naked, a. nackt, bloß.
Name, s. Name, m. Christian name, Taufname. by name, Namens. v. a. nennen.
Named, a. Namens, genannt.
Narrow, a. enge.
Nation, Volk, n.; Nation, f.
Native, a. gebürtig (aus). native of, (sein) aus. s. Eingeborner, m.
Natural, a. -ly. ad. natürlich.
Nature, s. Natur, f.
Nautical, a. nautisch.
Naval, a. nautisch.

Navigation, s. Schifffahrt, f.
Navigator, s. Seefahrer, m.
Near, a. nahe; pr. neben.
Nearly, ad. beinahe.
Necessary, a. nothwendig.
Necessity, s. Nothwendigkeit, Noth, f.; Dürftigkeit, f.
Neck, s. Hals, m.
Necklace, s. Halsband, n.
Need, v. n. nöthig haben, bedürfen.
Negative, a. in the negative, nein.
Neglect, v. a. vernachlässigen. s. Vernachlässigung, f.
Negotiate, v. n. unterhandeln.
Negro, s. Neger, m.
Negro-dealer, s. Negerhändler, m.
Neighbor. s. Nachbar, m.
Neighborhood, s. Nachbarschaft, f.
Neighboring, a. in der Nähe.
Neither, c. weder. neither — nor, weder — noch.
Nephew, s. Neffe, m.
Nervous, a. nervig.
Nest, s. Nest, n.
Never, ad. nie, niemals.
Nevertheless, ad. dessenungeachtet.
New, a. neu.
Newly, ad. neulich. [keit, f.
News, s. Nachricht, f.; das Neue, n.; Neuigkeit
Newspaper, s. Zeitung, f.
Next, a. nächst, folgend. ad. sodann.
Night, s. Nacht, f.
Nightfall, s. Einbruch der Nacht, m.
Ninety, a. neunzig.
No, a. kein.
Nobility, s. Adel, m.
Noble, a. edel. s. Adelige(r), m.; pl. Edelleute.
Nobleman, s. Edelmann, m.
Nod, s. Wink, m.
Noise, s. Lärm, m.; Geräusch, n.
Nominal, a. namentlich.
Nor, c. noch; auch nicht. [wärts.
North, s. Norden, m. to the north, nordNorthern, a. nördlich.
Northward(s), ad. nordwärts.
Norway, s. Norwegen, n.
Not, ad. nicht.
Note, s. Briefchen, n.; Billet, n.; Note, f.
Nothing, ad. nichts. s. Nichts.
Notice, s. Beachtung, f.; Aufmerksamkeit, f.; Bemerkung, f. worthy of notice, sehenswürdig. to raise to notice, bemerklich machen.
Notify, v. a. (einem) kund thun.
Notion, s. Begriff, m.
Notwithstanding, pr. ungeachtet.
Novel, s. Erzählung, f.; Novelle, f.
Novelist, s. Novellenschreiber, m.
Novelty, s. Neuheit, f.
Now, ad. nun, jetzt.
Noway(s), ad. keineswegs.
Nowhere, ad. nirgends.
Number, s. Zahl; Menge, f.; Anzahl, f.
Numerous, a. zahlreich.
Nuptials, s. pl. Hochzeit, f.

## O.

**Oakum,** s. Werg, n.
**Oats,** s. Hafer, m.
**Oath,** s. Eid, m.
**Obedient,** a. gehorsam.
**Obey,** v. a. gehorchen.
**Object,** s. Ziel, n., Ding, n., Gegenstand, m.
**Objection,** s. Entgegensetzung, f., Einwand, m. to have no objection (to it), Nichts (dagegen) haben.
**Oblige,** v. a. nöthigen (= compel); gefällig sein (= accommodate); verpflichten.
**Obliged,** a. dankbar.
**Obscure,** a. wenig bekannt, dunkel.
**Obscurity,** s. Unberühmtheit, f., Dunkelheit, f.
**Observation,** s. Bemerkung, f., Beobachtung, f.
**Observe,** v. a. beobachten, bemerken.
**Obstacle,** s. Hinderniß, n.
**Obstinacy,** s. Hartnäckigkeit, f.
**Obstinate,** a. -ly, ad. hartnäckig.
**Obstruct,** v. a. hindern.
**Obtain,** v. a. erlangen, erreichen.
**Occasion,** s. Gelegenheit, Veranlassung, f., Anlaß, m., Angelegenheit, f. v. a. veranlassen.
**Occasional,** -ly, ad. gelegentlich, gelegenheitlich.
**Occupy,** v. a. beschäftigen (mit), einnehmen, besetzen.
**Occur,** v. n. vorkommen, geschehen.
**Ocean,** s. Weltmeer, n.
**Odious,** a. gehässig.
**Off,** ad. & pr. von, von .... weg. get off (away), sich machen aus dem Staube.
**Offence,** s. Aergerniß, n. give offence, Anstoß geben.
**Offend,** v. a. beleidigen.
**Offensive,** a. offensiv.
**Offer,** v. a. anbieten, ausstellen (zum Verkauf), darbieten, darbringen, antragen. s. Anerbieten, n.
**Office,** s. Dienst, m., Gottesdienst, m.
**Officer,** s. Beamte(r), Offizier, m.
**Oft, Often,** ad. oft.
**Ointment,** s. Salbe, f.
**Old,** a. alt.
**Omen,** s. Omen (Anzeichen), n., Vorbedeutung, f.
**Omnipresent,** a. allgegenwärtig.
**Once,** ad. einmal, einst. at —, auf einmal.
**One,** a. ein. pr. einer. one by one, einer nach dem andern.
**Only,** a. einzig; ad. nur. not only — but also, nicht allein (nur) — sondern auch.
**Onset,** s. Angriff, m.
**Open,** a. offen. v. a. öffnen. v. n. bevorstehen.
**Opening,** s. Gelegenheit, f.
**Openness,** s. Offenherzigkeit, f.
**Operation,** s. Wirkung, f., Operation, f.
**Opinion,** s. Meinung, f.
**Opponent,** s. Gegner, m.
**Opportunity,** s. Gelegenheit, f.
**Oppose,** v. a. sich widersetzen.
**Opposite,** a. entgegengesetzt. pr. gegenüber.
**Oppress,** v. a. drücken, unterdrücken.
**Order,** s. Ordnung, f.; Bestellung, f.; Befehl, m.; Orden, m.; Absicht, f. in — to, in der Absicht, um .... zu. in — that, damit. v. a. befehlen, lassen. to be ordered, Befehl erhalten.
**Ordinary,** a. ordentlich, gemein.
**Organ,** s. Organ, n.
**Origin,** s. Ursprung, Anfang, m.
**Original,** a. ursprünglich, anfänglich.
**Ornament,** s. Verzierung, f., Putz, m.
**Otaheitian,** a. otaheitisch.
**Other,** a. der, die, das andere.
**Otherwise,** ad. anders, sonst.
**Out,** pr. aus. ad. heraus, hinaus. out of town, auswärts.
**Outdo,** v. a. übertreffen.
**Oven,** s. Ofen, m.
**Over,** pr. über. ad. vorüber, vorbei.
**Overcome,** v. a. überwältigen.
**Overjoyed,** a. überglücklich.
**Overtake,** v. a. einholen, betreffen.
**Overthrow,** v. a. umstürzen.
**Overturn,** v. a. umwerfen.
**Owe,** v. a. schuldig sein, verdanken.
**Owing to,** pr. wegen. it is owing to (that), man verdankt es (dat.).
**Own,** a. eigen. v. a. gestehen.
**Owner,** s. Eigenthümer, m.
**Oyster,** s. Auster, f.
**Oyster-bed,** s. Austerlager, n.

## P.

**Pace,** s. Schritt, Gang, m. v. n. hin- und hergehen.
**Pacha,** s. Pascha, m.
**Pack up,** v. a. einpacken, verpacken.
**Paddle,** v. n. rudern. paddle off, fortrudern.
**Paganism,** s. Heidenthum, n.
**Page,** s. Page, Junker, m.
**Pain,** s. Schmerz, m., Qual, f. —s, pl. Mühe, Bemühungen, f.
**Painful.** a. schmerzhaft.
**Paint,** v. a. malen.
**Painter,** s. Maler, m.
**Painting,** s. Malerei, f., Gemälde, n.
**Palace,** s. Palast, m. Palace of the Savoy, Savoy-Palast.
**Palate,** s. Gaumen, m.
**Pale,** a. bleich. v. n. turn pale, erbleichen.
**Paper,** s. Papier, n. waste-paper, s. Makulaturpapier, n., Tütenpapier, n.
**Parcel,** s. Päckchen, n.
**Parchment,** s. Pergament, n.
**Pardon,** v. a. verzeihen, begnadigen.
**Parent,** s. Vater, m. —s, pl. Eltern, pl.

Parity, s. Gleichheit, f.
Park, s. Part, m.
Parley, s. Unterredung, f.
Parliament, s. Parlament, n.
Parole, s. Ehrenwort, n.
Part, s. Theil, m. v. a. theilen, trennen.
— with, sich trennen von, hergeben.
Partake, v. n. Theil nehmen (an). — of, v. a. gemeinschaftlich einnehmen.
Particular, a. besonder, vorzüglich. ad. in particular, besonders. s. Einzelheit, f.
Partly, ad. theils.
Partnership, s. Handlungsgesellschaft, f. take into partnership, als Theilnehmer (Associé) annehmen.
Party, s. Partei, Gesellschaft, f.
Pass, v. n. gehen, passiren, vorübergehen.
— by, vorbeigehen, vorübergehen, vorüberkommen; — up, hinauffahren, hinaufgehen; — away, schwinden. v. a. hinbringen.
Passage, s. Ueberfahrt, f., Durchgang, m. take passage, sich einschiffen.
Passion, s. Leidenschaft, f., Schmerz, m. passion for travel, Reiselust, f.
Patch up, v. a. (a ship), verstopfen.
Path, s. Pfad, m.
Patience, s. Geduld, f. to be out of patience, die Geduld verlieren.
Patient, s. Patient, m.
Patrimony, s. Erbgut, n.
Patriotism, s. Vaterlandsliebe, f.
Patron, s. Gönner, m.
Patronage, s. Theilnahme, f.; Gunst, f.
Patronise, v. a. beschützen.
Pattern, s. Muster, n.
Pause, s. Pause, f.
Pave, v. a. pflastern, bahnen.
Pavement, s. Pflaster, n.
Paw, s. Pfote, f.
Pawnbroker, s. Pfandleiher, m.
Pay, v. a. zahlen, bezahlen; (show) erweisen; pay (attention), zollen; — attention (give heed), Acht geben; — down, ausbezahlen; — honour, ehren; — out, auszahlen; — a visit, Besuch erstatten, (machen). s. Sold, m.
Payment, s. Bezahlung, f.
Peace, s. Friede, m.; Ruhe, f.
Peaceful, a. friedlich, ruhig.
Peacock, s. Pfauhahn, m.
Peasant, s. Bauer, m.
Peasantry, s. Bauern, m. pl.
Pebble, s. Steinchen, n.
Peck, s. Metze, f.
Peculiar, a. eigenthümlich, verschieden.
Peculiarity, s. Eigenthümlichkeit, f.
Pecuniary, a. Geld betreffend.
Pedestal, s. Fußgestell, n.
Pedestrian, s. Fußgänger, m.
Pen, s. (Schreib)feder, f.
Pencil, s. Pinsel; Bleistift, m.
Pendant, s. Wimpel, m.
People, s. Volk, n.; Leute, pl.
Pepper, s. Pfeffer, m.

Pepper-box, s. Pfefferfaß, n.
Perceive, v. a. einsehen; wahrnehmen; merken.
Perfect, a. vollkommen. v. a. vervollkommnen; geschickt machen.
Perfection, s. Vollkommenheit, f.
Perfidious, a. treulos.
Perform, v. a. verrichten, erfüllen, thun.
Performance, s. Arbeit, f. —s, pl. Spiel, m.
Perfume, s. Wohlgeruch, m.
Perhaps, ad. vielleicht.
Perilous, a. gefährlich.
Perish, v. n. umkommen.
Permission, s. Erlaubniß, f.
Permit, v. a. erlauben.
Perpetual, a. fortwährend, beständig.
Persecute, v. a. verfolgen.
Perseverance, s. Beharrlichkeit, f.
Persian, a. persisch.
Persist, v. n. beharren.
Person, s. Person, f.; Mann, m.; Gestalt, f., Körper, m., (somebody), Jemand; —s, pl. Leute, Menschen.
Personal, a. persönlich.
Persuade, v. a. überreden, überzeugen.
Persuasive, a. überzeugend.
Peruse, v. a. durchlesen.
Philanthropic, a. menschenfreundlich.
Philosopher, s. Weltweiser, m.; Philosoph, m.
Philosophical, a. philosophisch.
Philosophy, s. Weltweisheit, f.
Physic, s. Arzeneikunde, f.
Physician, s. Arzt, m.
Pick, v. a. pflücken; (a quarrel), anfangen. pick up, auflesen, sammeln.
Pickpocket, s. Taschendieb, m.
Picture, s. Gemälde, n.; Bildniß, n.
Piece, s. Stück, n. piece of gold, Goldstück, n. piece by piece, Stück für Stück.
Piety, s. Frömmigkeit, f.
Pike, s. Hecht, m.
Pile, s. Haufen, m.
Pilgrimage, s. Wallfahrt, f.
Pillow, s. Kopfkissen, n.
Pilot, s. Lootse, m.
Pinnace, s. Pinasse, f.
Pipe, s. Pfeife, f. v. n. flöten.
Piper, s. Pfeifer, m.
Pistol, s. Pistole, f.
Pit, s. Grube, f.
Pitch upon, v. a. sich entscheiden für.
Pitchfork, s. Mistgabel, f.
Piteous, a. -ly. ad. jämmerlich, erbärmlich.
Pity, s. Mitleid (mit). it is a pity, es ist Schade. what a pity it is, wie schade ist es. v. a. bedauern.
Place, s. Ort, m., Platz, m., Stelle, f.; Rang, m., Amt, n. v. a. stellen, setzen, legen, hinstellen; (in college) aufnehmen; take —, Statt finden.
Plague, s. Pest, f.

Plain, a. -ly, ad., einfach, beutlich. s. Boden, m., Ebene, f.
Planet, s. Wandelstern, m.
Planking. s. Planken, f. pl.
Plant, s. Pflanze, f. v. a. pflanzen.
Plantation, s. Pflanzung, Pflanzschule, f.
Plaster, s. Pflaster, n.
Plate, s. Gefäße (pl.) n.
Play, s. Schauspiel, n. v. a. spielen.
Plead, v. a. vorschützen.
Pleasant, a. angenehm.
Please, v. a. gefallen, befriebigen; gefällig sein; please, imperat., (for urgent request) ich bitte.
Pleased (with), a. erfreut (über).
Pleasure, s. Vergnügen, n. give pleasure, Vergnügen machen. a man of pleasure, ein Vergnugungssüchtiger. pleasure-boat, Lustboot, n.
Pledge, v. a. zutrinken.
Plentiful, a. -ly. überflüssig.
Plenty, s. Fülle, f.
Plight, s. Zustand, m.; Befinden, n.
Plot, s. Plan; Anschlag, m.
Pluck, v. a. pflücken, rupfen.
Plum-pudding, s. Rosinenkloß, m.
Plunder, v. a. plündern.
Plunge, v. a. tauchen.
Pocket, s. Tasche, f.
Pocket-book, s. Taschenbuch, n.
Pocket-money, s. Taschengeld, n.
Poem, s. Gedicht, n.
Poet, s. Dichter, m.
Poetic(al), a. dichterisch.
Point, s. Spitze, f. in — of, in Hinsicht auf; be on the point of, im Begriffe sein. v. a. bezeichnen; — at, bezeichnen; — out, erkennen, anbeuten, beuten (auf); — to, hinbeuten.
Poison, s. Gift, n.
Police, s. Polizei, f. Lieutenant of the police, Polizei-Commissär. m.
Politeness, s. Höflichkeit, Artigkeit, f.
Politics. pl. s. Politik, f.
Political, a. politisch.
Pomp, s. Pracht, f.
Pond, s. Teich, m.
Poniard, s. Dolch, m.
Poodle, s. Pubel, m.
Poodledog, s. Pudelhund, m.
Poor, a. -ly, ad. arm, schwach, armselig.
Pope, s. Papst, m.
Populace, s. Volk, n.
Popularity, s. Popularität, f., Volksgunst, f.
Port, s. Hafen, m.
Portion, s. Theil, m., Mitgift, f.
Portuguese, s. Portugiese, m.
Position, s. Stellung, f.
Possess, v. a. besitzen.
Possession, s. Besitz, m. take possession, einnehmen, in den Besitz treten.
Possessed of, a. im Besitz von.
Possible, a. möglich.
Possibly, ad. möglich, möglicher Weise.

Posterity, s. Nachkommenschaft, f., Nachwelt, f.
Postilion, s. Postillion, m.
Post-office, s. Post restante, f.
Postscript, s. Nachschrift, f.
Posture, s. Stellung, Lage, f.
Pot, s. Topf, m.
Pounce (upon), v. n. herfallen (über).
Pound, s. Pfund, n.
Poverty, s. Armuth, f.
Powder, s. Pulver, n.
Power, s. Macht, f. powers, Mächte, Leistungen, f. pl. to be in one's power (to do), in seiner Macht liegen.
Powerful, a. gewaltig, mächtig.
Practical, a. praktisch.
Practice, s. Ausübung, Anwendung, Gewohnheit, Practik, f. put in practice, in Ausübung bringen.
Practise, v. a. üben.
Practitioner, medical, s. praktischer Arzt, m.
Praise, s. Lob, n.
Pray, v. n. beten.
Pray, interj. bitte.
Prayer, s. Gebet. n.
Preach, v. a. & n. predigen.
Precaution, s. Vorsicht, Vorsichtsmaßregel, f.
Precept, s. Regel, f., Lehre, f.
Preceptor, s. Lehrer, m.
Precious, a. kostbar, köstlich.
Precious stone, s. Edelstein, m.
Precipitate, a. -ly, ad. voreilig.
Predecessor, s. Vorgänger, m.
Predict, v. a. vorhersagen.
Prediction, s. Weissagung, f.
Preeminence, s. Vorrang, m.
Prefer, v. a. vorziehen.
Prejudice, s. Vorurtheil, n.
Prelate, s. Prälat, m.
Preparation, s. Vorbereitung, f., Anstalt, f.
Prepare, v. a. bereiten, vorbereiten; veranstalten. v. n. sich rüsten.
Presage, s. Vorbedeutung, f.
Prescribe, v. a. vorschreiben.
Presence, s. Gegenwart, f. presence of mind, Geistesgegenwart.
Present, a. anwesend, gegenwärtig. at present, gegenwärtig. s. Geschenk, n. make a present, zum Geschenk machen.
Present, v. a. barstellen, vorstellen; ausrichten, darbieten; überreichen. refl. sich darbieten.
Presently, ad. sogleich, gleich, gerabe, balb nachher.
Preservation, s. Verwahrung, f.
Preserve, v. a. verwahren, aufbewahren, behalten, erhalten.
Preside, v. n. den Vorsitz haben, vorsitzen, präsidiren.
President, s. Präsident, m.
Press, s. Presse, f. v. a. pressen, brängen.
Pressing, u. bringend.

**Pressure,** s. Pressen, n.
**Presumption,** s. Anmaßung, f.
**Pretence,** s. Vorwand, m.
**Pretend,** v. a. vorgeben, vorwenden, sich stellen (als ob), behaupten.
**Pretended,** a. verstellt.
**Pretentious,** a. anmaßend.
**Pretext,** s. Vorwand, m.
**Pretty,** a. nieblich. ad. ziemlich. pretty well over, ad. ziemlich vorüber.
**Prevail,** v. n. herrschen. prevail upon, v. a. bewegen, vermögen.
**Prevalence,** s. Dauer, f., Vorherrschen, n.
**Prevnient,** a. vorherrschend.
**Prevent,** v. a. hindern, vorbeugen.
**Previous,** a. & ad. vorhergehend. previous to, prep. vor.
**Prey,** s. Beute, f.
**Priam,** s. Priamus, m.
**Price,** s. Preis, m.
**Pride,** s. Stolz, m. to pride one's self (on), sich rühmen (Gen.).
**Prince,** s. Fürst, Prinz, m.
**Princess,** s. Prinzessin, Fürstin, f.
**Principal,** a. vorzüglich. s. Kapital, n.
**Printer,** s. Buchdrucker, m.
**Printing-office,** s. Druckerei, f.
**Prior,** s. Prior, m.
**Prison,** s. Gefängniß, n.
**Prisoner,** s. Gefangene(r), m. to take prisoner, zum Gefangenen machen, gefangen nehmen.
**Pristine,** a. früher.
**Private,** a. -ly, ad. geheim, privat, eigen. in private, im Geheim.
**Probability,** s. Wahrscheinlichkeit, f. in all probability, höchst wahrscheinlich.
**Probable,** -bly, ad. wahrscheinlich.
**Problem,** s. Problem, n.
**Procedure,** s. Verfahren, n.
**Proceed,** v. n. fortfahren, sich anschicken, Anstalt machen.
**Procure,** v. a. verwalten, verschaffen, erreichen, erlangen.
**Prodigal,** a. verschwenderisch.
**Prodigious,** a. erstaunlich.
**Prodigy,** s. Wunder, n.
**Produce,** v. a. hervorbringen, vorstellen, aufweisen, erwecken.
**Produce,** s. Erzeugniß, n.
**Production,** s. Erzeugniß, n.
**Productive,** a. fruchtbar.
**Profession,** s. Bekenntniß, n., Beruf, m.
**Professor,** s. Professor, m.
**Profit,** s. Gewinn, m. v. a. profit by, nützen.
**Profitable,** a. einträglich.
**Profound,** a. tief, tiefsinnig.
**Prognostic,** s. Vorbedeutung, f.
**Progress,** s. Fortschritt, m.
**Project,** s. Plan, m. form a project, einen Plan fassen.
**Projector,** s. Planmacher, m., Entwerfer, m.
**Prologue,** s. Vorrede, f.
**Prolong,** v. a. verlängern.

**Promise,** s. Versprechen, n. v. a. versprechen.
**Promising,** a. hoffnungsvoll.
**Promote,** v. a. befördern.
**Promotion,** s. Beförderung, f., Vorrücken, n.
**Prompt,** -ly, ad. lebhaft. v. a. treiben.
**Pronounce,** v. a. erklären.
**Proof,** s. Beweis, m., Probe, f. put to the proof, auf die Probe stellen.
**Propagate,** v. a. verbreiten.
**Proper,** -ly, ad. tauglich, sorgfältig. think proper, für gut befinden.
**Property,** s. Vermögen, n.
**Prophet,** s. Prophet, m.
**Prophetic,** a. prophetisch.
**Proportion,** s. Verhältniß, n. in proportion as; in dem Maße als. in proportion, verhältnißmäßig.
**Proposal,** s. Vorschlag, m.
**Propose,** v. a. vorlegen, vorschlagen.
**Proposition,** s. Vorschlag, Antrag, m.
**Proscribe,** v. a. verbannen.
**Prosecute,** v. a. fortsetzen, verfolgen.
**Prospect,** s. Ansicht, Aussicht, f.
**Prospectus,** s. Prospectus, m.
**Prosperous,** a. gedeihlich.
**Prostrate,** one's self, v. refl. niederfallen.
**Protect,** v. a. schützen, schonen.
**Protector,** s. Protector, m., Beschützer, m.
**Protestation,** s. Verwahrung, f.
**Protract,** v. a. in die Länge ziehen.
**Prove,** v. a. beweisen. v. n. sich erweisen, sich zeigen.
**Provide,** v. a. vorsehen, versehen, schaffen; (for one's self), sich schaffen.
**Provided (that)** c. wenn nur.
**Providence,** s. Vorsehung, f.
**Province,** s. Provinz, f.
**Provision,** s. Vorkehrung, f. -s, pl. Lebensmittel, n. pl.
**Provoke,** v. a. reizen.
**Prudence,** s. Klugheit, f.
**Prudent,** a. klug.
**Prussia,** s. Preußen, n.
**Prussian,** s. Preuße, m. a. preußisch.
**Public,** a. öffentlich. s. Publikum, n.
**Public-house,** s. Wirthshaus, m.
**Publication,** s. Veröffentlichung, f.; Ausgabe, f.
**Publish,** v. a. herausgeben.
**Pull out,** v. a. ausziehen, herausziehen.
**Pump,** s. Pumpe, f.
**Punctilious,** a. spitzfindig.
**Punctual,** a. -ly, ad. pünktlich.
**Punish,** v. a. strafen (wegen), bestrafen.
**Punishment,** s. Strafe, Bestrafung, f.
**Purchase,** s. Kauf, m.; Einkauf, m. v. a. kaufen, erhandeln.
**Purchaser,** s. Käufer, m.
**Pure,** a. rein, ächt, bloß.
**Purpose,** s. Zweck, m.; Absicht, f.; Vorhaben, n. on purpose, in der Absicht.
**Purse,** s. Beutel, m.
**Pursue,** v. a. verfolgen. [beruf, m.
**Pursuit,** s. Verfolgung, f.; -s, pl. Lebens-

**Put**, *v. a.* setzen, stellen, legen; bringen; gießen. — (a question), richten, stellen. — down, niederstellen. — in, einrücken. — to inconvenience, in Verlegenheit bringen. — in mind (remind), (Jemand) daran erinnern. — in practice, in Ausübung bringen. — out (relieve of), ziehen aus, befreien von; (extinguish), auslöschen. — up (at an inn), einkehren. — a stop, ein Ende machen, Einhalt thun. — upon (one), aufheften.

## Q.

**Quadrant**, *s.* Quadrant, *m.*
**Qualification**, *s.* Befähigung, *f.*
**Qualify**, *v. a.* befähigen.
**Quality**, *s.* Eigenschaft, *f.* in quality of, als.
**Quantity**, *s.* Menge, *f.*
**Quarrel**, *s.* Streit, *m.*
**Quarter**, *s.* Viertel, *n.*; Quartier, *n.*; Richtung, *f.*
**Queen**, *s.* Königin, *f.*
**Quell**, *v. a.* unterdrücken.
**Quench**, *v. a.* löschen.
**Question**, *s.* Frage, *f.* cross questions, Querfragen. put questions to one, an einen Fragen stellen, (richten). ask a question, fragen.
**Quick**, *ad.* -ly. *ad.* schnell.
**Quiet**, *a.* ruhig.
**Quit**, *v. a.* niederlegen, verlassen.
**Quite**, *ad.* gänzlich, ganz, sehr, recht.

## R.

**Rabbit**, *s.* Kaninchen, *n.*
**Race**, *s.* Lebenslauf, *m.*
**Rage**, *s.* Wuth, Zorn, *m.* in rage, vor Wuth.
**Ragged**, *a.* zerrissen.
**Railleries**, *s.* Spott, *m.*
**Rain**, *s.* Regen, *m.*
**Raise**, *v. a.* erheben; erregen.
**Rake**, *s.* Harke, *f.*
**Ramble**, *v. n.* herumschweifen.
**Rampart**, *s.* Brustwehre, *f.*
**Rank**, *s.* Rang, *m.*; Stand, *m.*; Classe, *f.*; Stufe, *f.* to be ranked, seinen Rang behaupten.
**Ransom**, *s.* Lösegeld, *n.*
**Rapacious**, *a.* raubgierig.
**Rapid**, *a.* -ly. *ad.* schnell.
**Rare**, *a.* selten.
**Rascal**, *s.* Schurke, *m.*
**Rash**, *a.* unbesonnen.

**Rat**, *s.* Ratte, *f.*
**Rather**, *ad.* ein wenig; lieber.
**Reach**, *v. a.* erreichen. *v. n.* sich erstrecken.
**Read**, *v. n.* lesen, vorlesen.
**Reader**, *s.* Leser, *m.*
**Readiness**, *s.* Gefälligkeit, *f.*
**Ready**, *a.* fertig, bereit, bereitwillig; schnell. get ready, fertig (bereit) machen. ready-money, baar Geld.
**Real**, -ly. *ad.* wirklich, wohl.
**Reality**, *s.* Wirklichkeit, *f.*
**Reap**, *v. a.* (Vortheil) ziehen.
**Reason**, *s.* Beweggrund, *m.* *v. n.* wortwechseln; streiten.
**Reasonable**, *a.* vernünftig; ziemlich.
**Recall**, *v. a.* zurückrufen.
**Receipt**, *s.* Empfangschein, *m.*; Quittung, *f.*
**Receive**, *v. a.* empfangen, erhalten, aufnehmen.
**Reception**, *s.* Annahme, *f.*; Empfang, *m.*
**Recipe**, *s.* Recept, *n.*
**Reciprocal**, *a.* gegenseitig.
**Recital**, *s.* Erzählung, *f.*
**Recite**, *v. a.* hersagen.
**Reckon**, *v. a.* rechnen.
**Reckoning**, *s.* Rechnung, *f.*; Zeche, *f.*
**Recognise**, *v. a.* erkennen. [lassen.
**Recollect**, *v. a.* sich besinnen. *v. n.* sich
**Recollection**, *s.* Gedächtniß, *n.*
**Recommend**, *v. a.* empfehlen.
**Recommendation**, *s.* Empfehlung, *f.* letter of recommendation, Empfehlungsbrief, *m.*; Empfehlungsschreiben, *n.*
**Recompense**, *s.* Belohnung, *f.*
**Reconcile**, *v. a.* versöhnen.
**Record**, leave on record. *v. a.* erzählen.
**Recourse**, *s.* Zuflucht; Rückkehr, *f.* to have recourse, Zuflucht nehmen, sich wenden (an).
**Recover**, *v. a.* wieder gewinnen, wieder bekommen. *v. n.* genesen, sich erholen.
**Recovery**, *s.* Wiedereroberung, *f.*
**Red**, *a.* roth.
**Reduce**, *v. a.* bringen; stürzen; zurückwerfen. reduced (to), gestürzt (in).
**Reelevate**, *v. a.* wieder erheben.
**Reenter**, *v. a.* wieder eintreten.
**Reference**, *s.* Bezug, *m.*
**Reflect**, *v. n.* nachdenken.
**Reflection**, *s.* Nachdenken, *n.*
**Reformation**, *s.* Verbesserung, *f.*
**Refreshment**, *s.* Erfrischung, *f.*
**Refuge**, *s.* Zuflucht, *f.*
**Refusal**, *s.* Weigerung, *f.*
**Refuse**, *v. a.* sich weigern, verweigern.
**Refuse**, *s.* Auswurf, *m.*
**Regain**, *v. a.* wiedergewinnen.
**Regard**, *v. a.* ansehen, achten. with regard to, im Verhältniß zu, in Beziehung auf. as regards, als es betrifft.
**Regards**, *s.* Grüße, *pl. m.*
**Regardless**, *a.* rücksichtslos.
**Regiment**, *s.* Regiment, *n.* regiment of guards, Garderegiment, *n.*

**Region**, s. Gegend, f.
**Regret**, s. Reue, f. v. a. bebauern, bereuen.
**Regular**, a. regelmäßig.
**Regulate**, v. a. ordnen.
**Rehearse**, v. a. einstudiren. put in rehearsal, einstudiren lassen.
**Reign**, v. n. regieren. s. Regierung, f.
**Reimburse** (one's self), v. refl. sich wieder bezahlt machen.
**Rejoice**, v. n. sich freuen.
**Rejoin**, v. n. erwidern, versetzen.
**Rekindle**, v. a. wieder anzünden.
**Relapse**, v. n. zurückfallen.
**Relate**, v. a. erzählen, berichten.
**Relation**, s. Verwandtschaft, f.
**Release**, v. a. befreien.
**Reliance**, s. Vertrauen, n.
**Relief**, s. Erleichterung, f.
**Relieve**, v. a. entsetzen, ein Ende machen.
**Religion**, s. Religion, f.
**Religious**, a. gottesfürchtig.
**Reload**, v. a. wieder aufladen.
**Rely**, v. n. sich verlassen, vertrauen.
**Remain**, v. n. bleiben, verbleiben. let remain, liegen lassen. **Remains**, s. pl. Ueberreste, m.
**Reminder**, s. Rest, m.
**Remark**, v. a. bemerken. s. Anmerkung, f.
**Remarkable**, a. merkwürdig.
**Remedy**, s. Hülfsmittel, n.
**Remember**, v. a. sich erinnern, empfehlen, nicht vergessen. [gen, f.
**Remembrances**, s. Grüße, m., Empfehlungen.
**Remind**, v. a. erinnern.
**Remonstrance**, s. Vorstellung, Gegenvorstellung, f.
**Remove**, v. a. verlassen, entfernen, ziehen.
**Render**, v. a. leisten, machen.
**Renowned**, a. berühmt.
**Rent**, s. Miethzins, m.
**Repair**, v. n. sich wohin begeben.
**Repast**, s. Mahlzeit, f.
**Repeal**, v. a. wiederholen.
**Repentance**, s. Reue, f.
**Repine**, v. n. verdrießlich sein (über).
**Reply**, v. n. erwiedern. s. Antwort, Erwiederung, f. make a reply, Antwort geben.
**Report**, v. a. ausbreiten, annehmen.
**Repose**, v. n. ruhen, schlafen.
**Representation**, s. Vorstellung, f.
**Repress**, v. a. unterdrücken, zurückweisen.
**Reprimand**, v. a. tadeln, verweisen.
**Reproach**, v. a. Vorwürfe machen, vorwerfen. s. Vorwurf. bear reproaches, Vorwürfe leiden.
**Reproof**, s. Vorwurf, m., Zurechtweisung, f.
**Reprove**, v. a. tadeln.
**Republic**, s. Freistaat, m.
**Republication**, s. neue Ausgabe, f.
**Reputation**, s. guter Ruf, m., guter Name, m.
**Request**, s. Bitte, f. v. a. bitten, ersuchen. of request, a. gesucht.

**Require**, v. a. verlangen.
**Research**, s. Untersuchung, f.
**Resemble**, v. a. vergleichen.
**Resentment**, s. Rachegefühl, n.
**Reserve**, v. a. vorbehalten, zurückhalten.
**Reside**, v. n. sich aufhalten, wohnen.
**Residence**, s. Aufenthalt, Wohnsitz, m., Wohnung, f.
**Resign**, v. a. überlassen.
**Resignation**, s. Ergebung, f.
**Resist**, v. a. widerstehen.
**Resolute**, a. entschlossen.
**Resolution**, s. Entschluß, m.
**Resolve**, v. n. beschließen, sich entschließen.
**Resound**, v. n. wiederhallen.
**Resource**, s. Hülfsmittel, n., Geldmittel, n., Auskunft, f.
**Respect**, v. a. hochachten. s. Rücksicht, Hinsicht, Beziehung, Ehrerbietung, Achtung (vor), f. with respect to, in Beziehung auf.
**Respectable**, a. ansehnlich.
**Respectful**, a. ehrerbietig, höflich.
**Respecting**, pr. betreffend.
**Respective**, a. besonder.
**Rest**, s. Rest, m. the rest (pl.), die übrigen; der, die, das übrige. as for the rest, übrigens. v. n. ruhen.
**Restoration**, s. Restauration, f., Wiederherstellung, f.
**Restore**, v. a. zurückgeben, wiederherstellen.
**Restrain**, v. a. zurückhalten.
**Result**, v. n. entstehen. s. Ausgang, m.
**Resume**, v. a. zurücknehmen.
**Retain**, v. a. zurückhalten, halten.
**Retake**, v. a. wieder nehmen.
**Retaking**, s. Wieder-Einnahme, f.
**Retinue**, s. Gefolge, n.
**Retire**, v. n. sich zurückziehen, weggehen.
**Retired**, a. eingezogen.
**Retirement**, s. Zurückgezogenheit, f.
**Retreat**, s. Rückzug, Zufluchtsort, m.
**Return**, v. n. zurückkehren, wiederkommen, erwiedern, zurückkommen. v. a. zurückschicken. (thanks), sagen, bringen. return thanks, danken. s. Rückgabe, f.; Rückkehr, f. in return for, als Vergeltung für.
**Revelling**, s. Schmausen, n.
**Revenge**, s. Rache, f. v. a. rächen. have revenge, Rache nehmen.
**Reverence**, v. a. verehren.
**Review**, s. Heerschau, f.
**Revile**, v. a. schmähen.
**Revise**, v. a. durchsehen.
**Revive**, v. n. wieder aufleben; v. a. wiederbeleben.
**Revolution**, s. Revolution, f.
**Revolve**, v. n. sich drehen.
**Reward**, v. a. belohnen. s. Belohnung, f.
**Ribbon**, s. Band, n.
**Rich**, a. reich.
**Riches**, s. Reichthum, m.
**Rid, get rid of**, v. a. loswerden, ablegen.
**Ride**, v. n. reiten, fahren. riding in

"traineaux," *s.* Schlitten fahren. ride off, fortreiten.
Ridicule, *s.* Spott, *m.*
Ridiculous, *a.* lächerlich.
Rigging, *s.* Takelwerk, *n.*
Right, *a.* recht. *s.* Recht, *n.*
Riot, *s.* Aufruhr, *m.*
Rise, *v. n.* aufstehen, gelangen, kommen, sich emporschwingen, steigen.
Rising, *a.* steigend.
Risk, *s.* Gefahr, *f.*, Wagniß, *n.*
River, *s.* Fluß, *m.*
Rivulet, *s.* Bach, *m.*
Road, *s.* Weg, *m.*, Straße, Landstraße, *f.*
Roastbeef, *s.* geröstetes Rindfleisch, *n.*
Rob, *v. a.* berauben.
Robber, *s.* Räuber, *m.*
Robust, *a.* stark.
Rock, *s.* Felsen, *m.*
Rocky, *a.* felsig.
Rogue, *s.* Schelm, *m.*
Roll, *v. n.* sich bewegen.
Roman, *s.* Römer, *m.* *a.* römisch.
Rome, *s.* Rom, *n.*
Roof, *s.* Dach, *n.*
Room, *s.* Zimmer, *n.*
Rose, *s.* Rose, *f.*
Round, *pr. um. v. a.* rund machen.
Rouse, *v. a.* wecken.
Route, *s.* Marschstrecke, *f.*
Royal, *a. -ly. ad.* königlich.
Rude, *a. -ly. ad.* roh, rauh.
Ruin, *s.* Ruine, *f.*; Verderben, *n. v. a.* zu Grunde richten.
Rule, *s.* Regel, *f.*
Rumbling, *s.* Rumpeln, *n.*
Ruminate, *v. n.* nachsinnen.
Run, *v. n.* laufen; eilen. run up (a wall), aufführen. run about, umlaufen.
Runaway, *s.* Flüchtling, Ausreißer, *m.*
Runic, *a.* runisch.
Rush, *s.* Sturz, *m. v. n.* stürzen.
Russia, *s.* Rußland, *n.*
Russian, *s.* Russe, *m. a.* russisch.

## S.

Sable, *s.* Zobel, *m.*
Sacred, *a.* heilig.
Sacrifice, *v. a.* opfern.
Sad *a. -ly. ad.* traurig.
Safe, *a. -ly. ad.* sicher; wohlbehalten.
Safety, *s.* Sicherheit, *f.*
Sagacity, *s.* Scharfsinn. *m.*
Sail, *s.* Segel, *n.* set sail, *v. n.* absegeln.
Sailor, *s.* Matrose, *m.*
Saint, *a.* Sankt. *s.* Heilige(r), *m.*
Sake, for my sake, um meinetwillen. for the sake of, um — willen, wegen, um — zu, *infn.*
Salary, *s.* Gehalt, *m.*
Sale, *s.* Verkauf, *m.* for sale, zum Verkauf.
Salt, *v. a.* salzen.
Salutation, *s.* Gruß, *m.*

Salute, *v. a.* grüßen.
Same, *pn.* derselbe. at the same time, zugleich.
Sample, *s.* Muster, *n.*
Sand, *s.* Sand, *m.*
Sanguine, *a.* leichtblütig.
Saracen, *s.* Saracene, *m.*
Sarcastic, *a.* beißend, sarkastisch.
Satan, *s.* Satan, *m.*
Satisfaction, *s.* Genugthuung, *f.*
Satisfied, *a.* zufrieden.
Satisfy, *v. a.* genügen, befriedigen, stillen.
Satyr, *s.* Satyr, *m.*; Waldgott, *m.*
Saucepan, *s.* Pfanne, *f.*; Kessel, *m.*
Savage, *a.* wild, grausam.
Save, *v. a.* retten; ersparen.
Saving, *s.* Rettung, *f.*
Savoury, *a.* schmackhaft.
Saw, *s.* Säge, *f.*
Say, *v. a. & n.* sagen. to be said, sollen. say (= add), beizufügen.
Scale, *s.* Wagschale, *f.*
Scanty, *a.* sparsam.
Scarce, *a. -ly. ad.* selten, spärlich.
Scarred, *a.* narbig.
Scene, *s.* Gemälde, *n.*; Scene, *f.* country-scene, Landleben, *n.*
Scenery, *s.* Anblick, *m.*
Scheme, *s.* Entwurf, *m.*
Scholar, *s.* Schüler, Gelehrte(r), *m.*
School, *s.* Schule, *f.* at school, in der Schule.
Schoolmaster, *s.* Schullehrer, *m.*
Science, *s.* Wissenschaft, *f.*
Sclavonian, *a.* slavonisch.
Scope, *s.* Spielraum, *m.*
Scotland, *s.* Schottland, *n.*
Scotsman, Scotchman, *s.* Schotte, *m.*, Schottländer, *m.*
Scottish, *a.* schottisch.
Scoundrel, *s.* Schurke, *m.*
Scratch, *v. a.* scharren. *s.* Schramme, *f.*
Scream, *v. n.* schreien.
Screech-owl, *s.* Nachteule, *f.*
Screen, *s.* Schirm, *m.*
Scruple, *v. n.* Bedenken tragen (über), zaudern.
Scrupulous, *a.* bedenklich.
Sculptor, *s.* Bildhauer, *m.*
Sea, *s.* Meer, *n.* (to bring up) at sea, im Seedienst. at sea, auf der See.
Seefowl, *s.* Seevogel, *m.*
Search, *v. a.* untersuchen. *s.* Untersuchung, *f.*
Sea-shore, *s.* Meeres-Ufer, *n.*
Season, *s.* Jahreszeit, Zeit, *f.*
Seat, *s.* Sitz, *m.*
Second, *a.* der, die, das zweite. *v. a.* beistehen, unterstützen.
Secret, *a. -ly. ad.* geheim, verborgen, heimlich. *s.* Geheimniß, *n.*
Secretary, of State, *s.* Staatssekretär, Minister, *m.* secretary's office, *s.* Ministerium, *m.*
Secure, *v. a.* versichern, sicher stellen.

**Security,** s. Bürgschaft, f.
**Seditious,** a. aufrührerisch.
**See,** v. a. sehen; einsehen. **worth seeing,** sehenswürdig.
**Seek,** v. a. suchen. **seek out,** aussuchen.
**Seem,** v. n. scheinen.
**Seize,** v. a. ergreifen.
**Seldom,** ad. selten.
**Select,** v. a. auswählen. a. auserlesen.
**Selection,** s. Auswahl, f.
**Selector,** s. Auswähler, m.
**Self,** pn. a. selbst.
**Self-condemnation,** s. Selbstverdammung, f.
**Self-love,** s. Selbstliebe, f.
**Sell,** v. a. verkaufen.
**Senate,** s. Senat, m.
**Send,** v. a. senden, schicken. **send out,** ausschicken. **send to walk,** auf den Spaziergang schicken. **send for,** rufen lassen, schicken nach. **send for (a physician),** holen.
**Sensations,** (pl.) s. Genüsse, (pl.) m.
**Sense,** s. Sinn, m. **good-sense,** s. Verstand, m.
**Senseless,** a. sinnlos.
**Sensible,** a. klug; im Gefühl, im Bewußtsein. **to be sensible of,** erkennen.
**Sentiment,** s. Empfindung, f., Gefühl, n. **religious sentiment,** Glauben(n), m.
**Separate,** v. a. zertheilen.
**Separate,** a. getrennt, geschieden.
**Separation,** s. Trennung, f.
**Sepulchre,** s. Grab, n.
**Sequestered,** a. entfernt.
**Serene,** a. heiter.
**Sergeant,** s. Feldwebel, m.
**Series,** s. Reihe, f.
**Serious,** a. ernsthaft.
**Servant,** s. Diener, Bediente(r), m., Magd, f.
**Serve,** v. a. dienen, bedienen, auftragen.
**Service,** s. Dienst, m. **to be of service,** dienen.
**Set,** v. a. setzen, stellen. **set out on (a journey),** antreten. **set up (a business).** treiben. **set down,** niederstellen. **set off (out),** abreisen (nach = for), sich machen auf den Weg, sich machen (auf). **set off,** ausgehen, fortgehen. **set (a trap),** stellen. **set sail,** absegeln. **set foot on,** Fuß setzen.
**Set,** s. Sammlung, f.
**Settle,** v. a. bezahlen, erledigen, sich entschließen (zu). v. n. sich setzen.
**Settlement,** s. Ansiedelung, f.
**Seven,** a. sieben.
**Seventeen,** a. siebzehn.
**Seventy,** a. siebzig..
**Several,** a. einige, mehrere.
**Severe,** a. streng, schwer, hart.
**Severity,** s. Strenge, Härte, f.
**Sew,** v. a. nähen.
**Sex,** s. Geschlecht, n.
**Shade,** s. Schatten, m.
**Shake,** v. a. schütteln, schütten.

**Shallow,** a. seicht.
**Shame,** s. Scham, Schande, f.
**Shape,** s. Form, Gestalt, f.
**Shaped,** a. gestaltet.
**Share,** v. a. theilen. **share in,** Theil nehmen an.
**Shark,** s. Haifisch, m.
**Sharp-set,** a. hungrig, in großer Verlegenheit.
**Sheathing-board,** s. kupferner Beschlag, m.
**Sheep'sdung,** s. Schafmist, m.
**Shift,** v. n. helfen, sorgen (für), **make shift to live,** sich (dat.) helfen durchs Leben, sich durchbringen.
**Shilling,** s. Schilling, m.
**Ship,** s. Schiff, n.
**Shirt,** s. Hemd, n.
**Shock,** v. a. empören, beleidigen. **to be shocked at,** sich entsetzen über.
**Shocking,** a. gräulich.
**Shos,** s. (sledge-runner), Lauf, m.
**Shoot,** v. a. schießen. **go a shooting,** auf die Jagd gehen.
**Shooting-bag,** s. Jagdtasche, f.
**Shooting-excursion,** s. Jagd=Ausflug, m.
**Shop,** s. Laden, m.
**Shopboy,** s. Ladenjunge, Gehilfe, m.
**Shopkeeper,** s. Krämer, m.
**Shopwoman,** s. Krämerin, f.
**Short,** a. kurz. **to be short of,** Mangel haben an. **in short,** kürzlich, kurz. **in a short time,** in kurzem.
**Shot,** s. Schuß, n.
**Shoulder,** s. Schulter, Achsel, f.
**Shout,** v. n. rufen. s. Freudengeschrei, n.
**Show,** v. a. zeigen, beweisen, bekannt machen. **show as if,** Miene machen. s. Anschein, m.
**Shrub,** s. Staude, m.
**Shrug up,** v. a. Zucken mit.
**Shut up,** v. refl. sich verschließen.
**Shy,** a. scheu.
**Sicily,** s. Sicilien, n.
**Sick,** a. krank.
**Sickness,** s. Krankheit, f.
**Side,** s. Seite, Partei, f. **by the side of,** neben.
**Sideboard,** s. Schenktisch, m.
**Siege,** s. Belagerung, f. **lay siege to,** (anfangen zu) belagern.
**Sieve,** s. Sieb, n.
**Sift,** v. a. sieben.
**Sight,** s. Anblick, m. **lose sight of,** aus den Augen verlieren. **in sight,** in Sicht. **get a sight of,** sehen, erblicken. **at first sight,** auf den ersten Anblick.
**Sign,** s. Zeichen, n. v. a. unterzeichnen.
**Signal,** s. Zeichen, n... Signal; n.
**Signature,** s. Unterschrift, f.
**Signify,** v. a. bedeuten.
**Silence,** s. Stillschweigen, n.
**Silent,** a. schweigend.
**Silver,** s. Silber, Silbergeld, n. a. silbern.
**Similar,** a. ähnlich.
**Similitude,** s. Aehnlichkeit, f., Gleichniß, n.

Simple, a. einfach, einfältig, schlicht.
Simplicity, s. Einfachheit, Einfalt, f.
Simulate, a. nachgeahmt, verstellt.
Since, pr. seit, (ago), vor. c. seitdem; da.
Sincere, a. ad. aufrichtig.
Sing, v. n. singen.
Single, a. einzig. [m.
Single-combat, s. Einzelkampf, Zweikampf,
Singular, a. -ly, ad. besonders, besonder, seltsam.
Sink, v. n. versinken.
Sir, s. Herr, Mein Herr.
Sire, s. Majestät, f.
Sister, s. Schwester, f. sister-in-law, Schwägerin, f.
Sit, v. n. sitzen, sich setzen. sit down, sich setzen, sich niedersetzen.
Situation, s. Lage, f., Zustand, m., Stelle, f., Stellung, f.
Sixteen, a. sechszehn.
Sixth, a. sechste.
Sixty, a. sechzig.
Skate, v. n. Schlittschuh laufen.
Sketch, s. Skizze, f.
Skill, s. Geschicklichkeit, Fertigkeit, f.
Skirmish, s. Scharmützel, n.
Sky, s. Luft, f., Himmel, m.
Slave, s. Sklave, m.
Slavemarket, s. Sklavenmarkt, m.
Slay, v. a. erschlagen.
Sledge, s. Schlitten, m.
Sleep, v. n. schlafen. s. Schlaf, m.
Slight, a. leicht.
Sly, ad. schlau.
Slip, v. n. gleiten, schlüpfen, entschlüpfen. slip off (from), herabgleiten (von).
Slow, a. langsam. slow of belief, schwergläubig.
Smacking, s. Knallen, n.
Small, a. klein, gering.
Smart, a. lebhaft.
Smelling-bottle, s. Riechfläschchen, n.
Smile, v. n. lächeln. s. Lächeln, n. smile at, lächeln über.
Smiling, a. lächelnd; -ly, ad. mit Lächeln.
Smite, v. a. schmeißen.
Smith, s. Schmied, m.
Smoke, s. Rauch, m.
Smooth, a. glatt.
Snatch, v. a. wegnehmen, abreißen.
Snore, v. n. schnarchen. snore away, verschnarchen.
Snow, s. Schnee, m.
Snuff, s. Schnupftabak, m.
Snuffbox, s. Schnupftabaksdose, f.
Snug, a. bescheiden.
So, ad. & c. so. — as to, so daß. pr. (the same) das Gleiche.
Soap, s. Seife, f.
Soapboiler, s. Seifensieder, m.
Sob, v. n. seufzen.
Society, s. Gesellschaft, f.
Softly, int. sachte.
Soil, s. Erdreich, n.
Solar system, s. Solarsystem, n.

Soldier, s. Soldat, m.
Solemn, a. -ly. ad. feierlich; ernsthaft.
Solemnize, v. a. feiern.
Solicit, v. a. bitten, suchen.
Solicitation, s. Anliegen, n. — of marriage, Heiraths-Anerbieten, n.
Solicitor, s. Bittsteller, m.
Solicitous, a. besorgt.
Solicitude, s. Besorgniß, f.
Solid, a. fest; gründlich; ernst.
Solitary, a. einsam.
Solitude, s. Einsamkeit, f.
Some, a. einige, welcher, irgend ein; somebody, jemand; einer; something, etwas; sometimes, zuweilen, manchmal. sometimes — sometimes, bald — bald. somewhat, ein wenig, etwas.
Son, s. Sohn, m.
Soon, ad. bald. as soon as, so bald als.
Soothe, v. a. besänftigen.
Sorcerer, s. Zauberer, m.
Sorcery, s. Zauberei, f.
Sorely, ad. tief (betrübt).
Sorrow, s. Kummer, m. [impers.
Sorry, to be, v. n. einem leid thun (sein),
Sort, s. Art, Sorte, f. what — of, was für...
Soul, s. Seele, f., Geist, m.
Sound, a. gesund. s. Klang, m.
Sounding-line, s. Bleischnur, f.
Soup, s. Suppe, f.
Southern, a. südlich.
Southwest, s. Südwest, m.
Sovereign, s. Oberherr, m.; Herrscher, König, Souverain, m.
Space, s. Raum, m. space of time, Zeitraum.
Spade, s. Spaten, m.
Spain, s. Spanien, n.
Spaniard, s. Spanier, m.
Spanish, a. spanisch.
Spare, v. a. ersparen; entbehren.
Sparkle, v. n. funkeln.
Sparrow, s. Sperling, m.
Speak, v. n. sprechen, sagen.
Spear, v. Lanze, f.
Special, a. besonder.
Spectacle, s. Anblick, m.; -s, pl. Brille, f.
Spectator, s. Zuschauer, m.
Speculation, s. Gewinnspähen, n.
Speech, s. Sprechen, n. [topp.
Speed, s. Eile, f. at full speed, im Galopp.
Speedy, a. eilig.
Spend, v. a. (of time), zubringen.
Spendthrift, s. Verschwender, m.
Spin, v. a. spinnen.
Spirit, s. Geist, m. -s, pl. Feuer, n., Stimmung, f.
Spite, s. Ärger, m. in spite of, trotz.
Splendid, a. prachtvoll, prächtig.
Spoil, s. Beute, f.
Sport, s. Spiel, n.; Spaß, m.; Unterhaltung, f.; Jagd, f. v. n. scherzen.
Spot, s. Platz, m., Stelle, f. on the spot, auf der Stelle.

**Spread**, v. a. bretten, ausbreiten; beschmieren. v. n. sich ausdehnen.
**Spring**, v. n. springen. s. Frühling, m.
**Spy**, s. Spion, m.
**Squeeze**, v. a. pressen.
**Squib**, s. Spöttelei, f.
**Stab**, v. a. erstechen.
**Stable**, s. Stall, m.
**Staff**, s. Stab, m., Generalstab, m.
**Stag**, s. Hirsch, m.
**Stage**, s. Schaubühne, f.: Schauplatz, m.
**Stage-coach**, s. Landkutsche, f., Postkutsche, f.
**Stagger**, v. n. wanken.
**Stand**, v. n. stehen, Stand halten. make —, stellen; —at the top, oben sitzen.
**Standard**, s. Fahne, f.
**Star**, s. Stern, m.
**State**, s. Zustand; Staat, m.
**Station**, s. Lebensstellung, f.
**Statuary**, s. Bildhauer, m.
**Statue**, s. Bildsäule, f.; Standbild, n.
**Stay**, v. n. bleiben; warten. s. Aufenthalt, m.
**Steadfast**, a. -ly. ad. fest.
**Steal**, v. a. stehlen. v. n. steal away, entwischen; schleichen.
**Steam-packet**, s. Dampfpaddelboot, n.
**Steed**, s. Hengst, m.
**Steer**, v. a. steuern.
**Step**, v. n. treten. step in, einschreiten; s. Stufe, f.; Schritt, m.
**Sterling**, s. Sterling, (20 Schilling), m. a pound sterling. ein Pfund Sterling.
**Stern**, a. -ly. ad. finster, strenge.
**Stick**, s. Reisig, n. v. n. stocken. v. a. — full of. beschlagen mit. — up, ankleben.
**Still**, ad. noch, noch einmal.
**Stillness**, s. Stille, f.
**Sting**, v. a. schmerzen.
**Stitch**, v. a. nähen.
**Stork**, s. Stamm, m.; Vorrath, Waaren-Vorrath, m. — of cash, Kassen-Vorrath, m.
**Stocking**, s. Strumpf, m.
**Stone**, s. Stein, m.
**Stoop**, v. n. sich bücken.
**Stop**, v. a. anhalten, aufhalten; zum Schweigen bringen; verstopfen. put a — to, ein Ende machen, Einhalt thun, verhindern. v. n. anhalten; (at an inn), einkehren.
**Store**, s. Vorrath, Buchladen, m. v. a. aufhäufen.
**Stork**, s. Storch, m.
**Story**, s. Geschichte, f.; Mährchen, n.
**Stout**, a. derb; heftig.
**Strait**, s. Enge, f.
**Strange**, a. fremd; seltsam.
**Stranger**, s. Fremdling, m.
**Stratagem**, s. Kriegslist, f.
**Straw**, s. Stroh, m.
**Stray**, v. n. sich verirren.
**Stream**, s. Strom, m. up the stream, stromaufwärts.

**Street**, s. Straße, f.
**Strength**, s. Stärke, Kraft, f.
**Stretch**, v. a. strecken, übertreiben. —forth, ausstrecken.
**Strict**, a. genau, scharf, streng, pünktlich.
**Strike**, v. a. schlagen, stoßen; treffen. strike with terror, Schrecken einflößen. (a blow). geben. strike off, absägen. to be struck with, betroffen werden von.
**Striking**, a. treffend.
**Strong**, a. stark, kräftig.
**Struggle**, v. n. ringen. s. Kampf, m.
**Student**, s. Student, m.
**Studied**, a. ausgesucht.
**Study**, s. Nachdenken, n.; Studirzimmer, n.; Studium, n.; Studirstube, f. v. a. aussinnen, studiren.
**Stupidity**, s. Dummheit, f.
**Style**, s. Schreibart, f.
**Subaltern**, officer, s. Unteroffizier, m.
**Subject**, s. Unterthan, m.; Gegenstand, m.
**Submission**, s. Unterwerfung, f.
**Submit**, v. n. sich unterwerfen.
**Subordinate**, a. untergeordnet.
**Subordination**, s. Unterordnung, f.
**Subscription**, s. Unterschrift, f.
**Subside**, v. n. sinken, schwinden.
**Subsist**, v. n. bestehen.
**Subsistence**, s. Unterhalt, m., Lebensunterhalt, m.
**Substitute**, v. a. aufstellen. s. Stellvertreter, m.
**Succeed**, v. n. gelingen, Glück haben.
**Success**, s. Erfolg, m.
**Successful**, a. glücklich.
**Succession**, s. Aufeinanderfolge, f.
**Sudden**, a. -ly. ad. plötzlich. of a sudden, plötzlich.
**Suffer**, v. a. & n. leiden, ertragen.
**Sufferance**, s. Ertragen, n.
**Suffering**, s. Leiden, n.
**Suffice**, v. n. genügen.
**Sufficient**, a. genügend, genug, hinlänglich.
**Suffocate**, v. a. ersticken.
**Suggest**, v. a. rathen.
**Suit**, v. a. & n. passen (für), gefallen. at the —, auf die Klage.
**Sultry**, a. schwül.
**Sum**, s. Summe, f.
**Summer**, s. Sommer, m.
**Summon**, v. a. herbeirufen, vorladen.
**Sun**, s. Sonne, f. Sun's disk, s. Sonnenscheibe, f.
**Sunday**, s. Sonntag, m.
**Sunday-scholar**, s. Sonntagsschüler, m.
**Sunrise**, s. Sonnenaufgang, m.
**Sunshine**, s. Sonnenschein, m.
**Superb**, a. prächtig, herrlich.
**Supereminent**, a. übertreffend, ausgezeichnet.
**Superficial**, a. seicht.
**Superintend**, v. a. die Oberaufsicht führen, vorstehen.
**Superintendent**, s. Oberaufseher, m.
**Superior**, a. höher; vorzüglicher.

Superiority, *s.* Ueberlegenheit, *f.*; Vorrang, *m.*
Superstition, *s.* Aberglaube, *m.*
Superstitious, *a.* abergläubig.
Supper, *s.* Abendessen, *n.* the Lord's supper, das heilige Abendmahl, *n.*
Supplant, *v. a.* hinunter bringen.
Supplicating, *a.* bittend.
Supplication, *s.* demüthige Bitte, *f.*, Anflehen, *n.*
Support, *v. a.* unterstützen; ernähren; ertragen.
Suppose, *v. a.* glauben, vermuthen. suppose to be, halten für.
Supposed, *a.* vermeintlich.
Supposition, *s.* Theorie, *f.*
Suppress, *v. a.* unterdrücken.
Sure, *a.* sicherlich. to be sure, allerdings. surely, doch.
Surgeon, *s.* Wundarzt, *m.*
Surname, *s.* Beinamen, *m.*
Surpass, *v. a.* übertreffen.
Surprise, *s.* Ueberraschung, *f.*; Erstaunen, *n.*, Erstaunung, *f.* *v. a.* bestürzen, erstaunen.
Surprising, *a.* erstaunlich.
Surround, *v. a.* einschließen.
Survey, *v. a.* überblicken.
Surveyor, *s.* Feldmesser, *m.*
Survive, *v. a.* überleben.
Survivor, *s.* Ueberlebende(r), *m.*
Suspect, *v. a.* in Verdacht nehmen, bezweifeln.
Suspense, *s.* Aufschub, *m.*; Ungewißheit, *f.*
Suspicious, *s. pl.* Verdacht, *m.*
Suspicious, *a.* argwöhnisch.
Sustain, *v. a.* ertragen, erleiden.
Swallow, *v. a.* verschlingen.
Swan, *s.* Schwan, *m.*
Swear, *v. n.* schwören.
Swede, *s.* Schwede, *m.*
Sweden, *s.* Schweden, *n.*
Sweep, *s.* Schornsteinfeger, *m.*
Sweeper, *s.* Schornsteinfeger, *m.*
Sweetheart, *s.* Liebchen, *n.*
Sweet-tempered, *a.* freundlich.
Swiftness, *s.* Schnelligkeit, *f.*
Swim, *v. n.* schwimmen.
Sword, *s.* Schwert, *n.*
Sympathy, *s.* Mitgefühl, *n.*
Symptom, *s.* Anzeichen, *n.*
System, *s.* System, *n.*; Zusammenhang, *m.*

## T.

Table, *s.* Tafel *f.*; Tisch, *m.*
Tack, *v. n.* — about, umlegen.
Tailor, *s.* Schneider, *m.*
Take, *v. a.* nehmen; bringen; (= conduct), führen; (= carry,) tragen. (advice), annehmen. (fire), fangen. (opportunity), ergreifen. (precautions), treffen. (one's place), einnehmen. (from water), auffischen. — across, over, übersetzen. — advantage, Nutzen ziehen. — away, wegnehmen. — a degree, Examen machen. — down, hinunterbringen, herabnehmen. — (one) for, halten für, glauben. — from, abnehmen. — into one's head, sich in den Kopf setzen. — place, Statt finden, geschehen. — prisoner, zum Gefangenen machen. — the trouble, sich die Mühe geben, sich bemühen. — up, nehmen, aufschlagen; (= occupy), in Anspruch nehmen; (lodging), aufschlagen. — up arms, die Waffen ergreifen. — up lodging, sich einmiethen.
Talent, *s.* Begabung, *f.*, Talent, *n.*
Talisman, *s.* Zaubermittel, *n.*
Tall, *a.* groß.
Tallow-chandler, *s.* Lichtgießer, *m.*
Tame, *a.* zahm.
Tap, *v. a.* einen leichten Schlag geben.
Tarnish, *v. a.* beflecken.
Tartary, *s.* Tartarei, *f.*
Task, *s.* Tagewerk, *n.*
Taste, *v. a. & n.* kosten, schmecken, versuchen.
Tax, *v. a.* beschuldigen, besteuern.
Tea-table, *s.* Theetisch, *m.*
Teach, *v. a.* lehren, unterrichten.
Teacher, *s.* Lehrer, *m.*
Tear, *s.* Thräne, *f.*
Tear, *v. a.* reißen. tear to pieces, tear up, *v. a.* zerreißen.
Telescope, *s.* Fernrohr, *n.*
Tell, *v. a. & n.* sagen, erzählen.
Temper, *s.* Sinn, *m.*, Gemüthsart, *f.*
Temple, *s.* Schlaf, *m.*
Temporary, *a.* zeitlich, vorübergehend.
Tempt, *v. a.* versuchen.
Ten, *a.* zehn.
Tender, *a.* zärtlich.
Term, *s.* Wort, *n.* —s, *pl.* Bedingungen, *f. pl.*
Terminate, *v. a.* beendigen. *v. n.* sich endigen.
Terrible, *a.* fürchterlich, schrecklich, entsetzlich.
Terrify, *v. a.* erschrecken.
Terror, *s.* Schrecken, *m.* strike with terror, Schrecken einflößen.
Test, *s.* Probe, *f.* put to the test, auf die Probe stellen.
Testify, *v. a.* bezeugen.
Than, *c.* als.
Thank, *v. a.* danken, dankbar sein. —s, *s. pl.* Dank, *m.* return thanks, danken, Dank sagen (abstatten).
Thankfulness, *s.* Dankbarkeit, *f.*
Thanksgiving, hymn of, *s.* Loblied, *n.*
That, *c.* daß, damit. *pn.* dieser, jener, der, derjenige. for all that, dessen ungeachtet.
Theatre, *s.* Schauplatz, *m.*, Schaubühne, *f.*, Theater, *n.*
Theft, *s.* Diebstahl, *m.*
Then, *ad.* dann, damals, da. *c.* denn, also.
There, *ad.* da, dort. there is, there are, es gibt, es sind. therefore, daher, also. therein, darin.

Thickness, s. Dicke, f.
Thief, s. Dieb, m.
Thievish, a. diebisch.
Think, v. a. denken, glauben, halten, wofür halten. think proper, für angemessen halten.
Third, a. dritte.
Thirst, s. Durst, m.
Thirsty, a. -ily, ad. durstig.
Thither, ad. bis dahin, dahin.
Thorn, s. Dorn, m.
Thorough, -ly, ad. gänzlich, durchaus.
Though, c. obschon, obgleich. even though, wenn gleich.
Thought, s. Gedanke, m. turn of thought, Gedankengang, m.
Thousand, a. tausend. s. Tausend, n.
Threat, s. Drohung, f.
Threaten, v. a. drohen.
Three, a. drei.
Threefold, a. dreifach.
Thrive, v. n. gedeihen.
Throne, s. Thron, m.
Through, pr. durch.
Throughout, pr. ganz durch.
Throw, v. a. werfen; (lead), führen. throw off, abwerfen.
Thunder, s. Donner, m.
Thus, ad. so, auf diese Weise.
Tide, s. Fluth, f.
Tie, v. a. binden, knüpfen. s. Band, n.
Till, ad. bis. not till, erst.
Timber, s. Bauholz, n.
Time, s. Zeit, f., Mal, n. for the time, zeitweilig. at that time, damalig. space of time, Zeitraum. economizer of time, Zeitsparer, m.. in a short time, in kurzem. beat time, den Takt schlagen. all the time, die ganze Zeit. by this time, um diese Zeit. at times, zeitweise. at the same time, zugleich.
Timid, a. furchtsam.
Tiresome, a. langweilig.
Title, s. Titel, Name, m.
To, pr. an. in order to, um — zu. to and fro, hin und her.
Together, ad. zusammen. get together, sammeln. together with, sammt, mit, nebst.
Tomb, s. Grabstein, m., Gruft, f.
Tone, s. Ton, m.
Tongs, s. pl. Zange, f.
Too, ad. allzu, zu sehr; auch.
Tool, s. Werkzeug, n.
Tooth, s. Zahn, m. front tooth, Vorderzahn, m.
Torment, v. a. quälen.
Torment, s. Qual, f.
Torrent, s. reißender Strom, m., Gießbach, m.
Torture, s. Marter, f. v. a. martern.
Toss, v. a. werfen.
Total, -ly, ad. gänzlich.
Touch, v. a. berühren, rühren. touch at, landen.

Touching, a. rührend. pr. betreffend.
Tour, s. Rundreise, f.
Toward, Towards, pr. gegen.
Towering, a. hoch.
Town, s. Stadt, f.
Town-residence, s. Wohnhaus in der Stadt.
Toy, s. Spielzeug, n., Spielsache, f.
Trace, v. a. folgen; (steps) lenken.
Track, s. Spur, f.
Trade, s. Handel, m., Geschäft, n. by trade, von Profession.
Tradesman, s. Handelsmann, m.
Traineau, s. Schlitten, m.
Traitor, s. Verräther, m.
Tranquillity, s. Ruhe, f.
Transaction, s. Geschäft, n.
Transfer, v. a. übertragen.
Transit, s. Durchgang, m.
Transmit, v. a. überschicken.
Transport, v. a. transportiren; entzücken (über).
Transport, s. Entzückung, f.
Travel, v. n. reisen. s. Reise, f. passion for travel, Reiselust, f.
Traveller, s. Reisende(r), m.
Traverse, v. a. durchwandern.
Treasure, s. Schatz, m.
Treasure-digger, s. Schatzgräber, m.
Treat, v. a. behandeln, bewirthen. treat with ill language, verleumden, schelten (über).
Treatment, s. Behandlung, f.
Treaty, s. Vertrag, m.
Tree, s. Baum, m.
Tremble, v. n. zittern.
Trembling, a. zitternd.
Tremor, s. Zittern, n.
Tress, s. Haarlocke, f.
Trial, s. Versuch, m., Probe, Prüfung, f. day of trial, s. Gerichtstag, m. stand (take trial, gerichtet werden.
Tribunal, s. Gericht, n.
Trick, s. Streich, m.
Trifle, s. Kleinigkeit, f.
Trifling, a. klein, unbedeutend, gering.
Triumphant, a. siegreich.
Trivial, a. gemein, trivial.
Troops, s. pl. Truppen, f. pl.
Trot, v. n. traben. trot off, forttraben.
Trouble, v. a. trüben. s. Mühe, f.
Trowsers, s. pl. Hosen, f. pl.
Troy, s. Troja, n.
True, a. wahr, ächt. that's true, recht.
Truly, ad. treulich, wahrlich, wirklich. most truly, ergebenst.
Trumpet, s. Trompete, f.
Trunk, s. Stamm, Koffer, m.
Truss, s. Bündel, Bund, n.
Trust, v. a. anvertrauen, vertrauen, sich verlassen.
Truth, s. Wahrheit, f.
Try, v. a. probiren, prüfen, versuchen, aburtheilen.
Tuft, s. Büschel, m.
Tug, s. Zupfen, n.

VOCABULARY. 165

Tumultuous, a. aufrührerisch.
Tune, s. Tonstück, n.
Turbot, s. Steinbutte, f.
Turkey, s. Türkei, f.
Turkey, s. Truthahn, m.
Turn, v. n. sich wenden, sich neigen. turn pale, erbleichen. turn out, ausfallen. turn upon, sich wenden gegen. to be turned to good account, gut ausfallen. turn up, umwenden.
Turn, s. Reihe, f. turn of thought, Gedankengang, m. in her turn, ihrerseits.
Tutor, s. Vormund, m.
Twelve, a. zwölf.
Twelvemonth, s. Jahr, n.
Twenty, a. zwanzig.
Twice, ad. zweimal.
Two, a. zwei.
Twofold, a. zweifach.
Tyranny, s. Tyrannei, f.
Tyrant, s. Tyrann, m.

## U.

Unable, a. unfähig.
Unaccounted for, a. unerklärt.
Unacquainted, a. unbekannt.
Unbounded, a. unbegränzt.
Uncertainty, s. Ungewißheit, f.
Uncle, s. Oheim, m.
Uncleaned, a. unreinigt, unpolirt.
Uncommon, a. ungewöhnlich.
Unconscious, a. nichts denkend, (ahnend); to be —, nicht denken an..
Uncorrupted, a. unverdorben.
Uncurled, a. ungelockt.
Under, ad. nieder. pr. unter.
Understand, v. a. verstehen, erfahren; make one understand, einem begreiflich machen.
Understanding, s. Verstand, m.
Undertake, v. a. unternehmen, besorgen.
Undertaking, s. Unternehmen, n.
Undiscerning, a. nicht unterscheidend.
Undisturbed, a. ungestört.
Undone, a. ungeschehen.
Uneasiness, s. Unruhe, f.
Uneasy, a. unruhig, beunruhigt.
Unequal, a. ungleich, uneben; parteiisch.
Unerring, a. untrüglich.
Unexpected, a. -ly. ad. unerwartet.
Unfailing, a. unfehlbar.
Unfit, a. unschicklich.
Unfortunate, a. -ly. ad. unglücklich; unglücklicherweise.
Unfriendly, a. unfreundlich.
Ungrateful, a. undankbar.
Unguarded, a. unvorsichtig.
Unhappy, a. unglücklich.
Uninjured, a. unverletzt.
Union, s. Vereinigung, f.
Unite, v. a vereinigen. [ten, m.
United States, s. die Vereinigten Staa-

Universal, a. allgemein.
Universe, s. Universum, n.; Weltall, n.
University, s. Universität, f.
Unknown, a. unbekannt.
Unless, c. wenn nicht, außer, außer etwa.
Unlike, a. ungleich.
Unloud, v. a. abladen.
Unnecessary, a. unnöthig.
Unpleasant, a. unangenehm, mißfällig.
Unreasonable, a. unvernünftig.
Unresisting, a. ohne Widerstand.
Unsuccessful, a. unglücklich.
Until, ad. bis.
Unworthy, a. -ly. ad. unwürdig.
Up, pr. auf. ad. herauf, hinauf.
Upbraiding, s. Vorrückung, f.
Upon, pr. auf.
Upper, a. ober, höher.
Urge, v. a. treiben, darauf bestehen.
Use, s. Gebrauch, Zweck, Nutzen, m.
Use, v. a. verbrauchen. v. n. pflegen; gewohnt sein.
Useful, a. nützlich.
Useless, a. nutzlos, vergeblich.
Usual, a. -ly. ad. gebräuchlich, gewöhnlich.
Utmost, a. äußerst, höchst.
Utter, v. a. hervorbringen, ausstoßen.

## V.

Vacuity, s. leerer Raum, m.
Vain, a. vergeblich; in vain, vergebens.
Valiant, a. tapfer.
Valor, s. Tapferkeit, f.
Valuable, a. schätzbar, werthvoll, kostbar.
Value, s. Werth, m.
Vanity, s. Eitelkeit, f.
Vanquish, v. a. besiegen.
Variable, a. unbeständig.
Various, a. verschieden, wechselnd.
Vary, v. a. verändern.
Vast, a. groß.
Vegetable, s. Gemüse, n.
Vehement, -ly. ad. heftig.
Veil, s. Schleier, m.
Vein, s. Ader, f.
Velvet, s. Sammet, m.
Vengeance, s. Rache, f.
Vent, give, v. n. freien Lauf lassen.
Ventriloquist, s. Bauchredner, m.
Ventriloquy, s. Bauchrednerkunst, f.
Venture, s. Wagniß, n. at a venture, auf's Gerathewohl. v. n. wagen, sich wagen.
Verdant, a. grünend.
Verily, ad. schon.
Verse, s. Vers, m.
Very, ad. sehr.
Vessel, s. Fahrzeug, n.
Vest, s. Gewand, n.
Vexation, s. Aerger, m.; Verdruß, m.
Viand, s. Speise, f.
Vicar, s. Stellvertreter, m.
Vicissitude, s. Abwechselung, f.; Wechselfall, m.

Victim, s. Opfer, n.
Victorious, a. siegreich.
Victory, s. Sieg, m.
View, s. Aussicht, Gegenwart, f.; Ansicht, f.; Absicht, f.; to have in view, vorhaben, in Aussicht haben. v. n. besehen, betrachten.
Village, s. Dorf, n.
Village-school, s. Dorfschule, f.
Villager, s. Dorfbewohner, m.
Vindictive, a. rachsüchtig.
Vine, s. Weinstock, m.
Vine-culture, s. Weinbau, m.
Vinegar, s. Essig, m.
Vineyard, s. Weinberg, m.
Violate, v. a. verletzen, brechen.
Violence, s. Gewaltthätigkeit, f.; Gewalt, f.
Violent, a. heftig, gewaltthätig.
Virgin, s. Jungfrau, f.
Virtue, s. Tugend, f.
Visit, s. Besuch, m.; to be on a visit (to) zum Besuch sein (bei). v. a. besuchen.
Vivacity, s. Lebhaftigkeit, f.
Vociferate, v. n. brüllen.
Voice, s. Stimme, f.
Volley, s. Flug, m.
Volume, s. Band, m.
Voluntary, -lly. ad. freiwillig.
Vow, s. feierliches Versprechen, n.
Voyage, s. Seereise, f.
Vulgarity, s. Gemeinheit, f.

## W.

Waistcoat, s. Weste, f.
Wait, v. n. warten; aufwarten. wait on, bedienen, aufwarten.
Walk, v. n. gehen. s. Spaziergang, m.; send to walk, auf den Spaziergang schicken.
Wall, s. Mauer, f.
Wallet, s. Reisesack, m.
Wander, v. n. wandern; herumschweifen.
Wanderer, s. Wanderer, m.
Want, v. a. bedürfen, nöthig haben, brauchen; wünschen. to be much in want of, sehr nothwendig brauchen. v. n. fehlen. s. Mangel, m.
War, s. Krieg, m.
Wardrobe, s. Kleidervorrath, m.
Warlike, a. kriegerisch.
Warm, a. warm. v. n. durchglühen (von).
Warmth, s. Wärme, f.
Warn, v. a. warnen; warn of, erinnern an.
War-office, s. Kriegsministerium, n.
Wash, v. a. waschen.
Waste, v. a. verwüsten; verschwenden.
Watch, s. Taschenuhr, f.; keep watch, Acht geben. v. a. wachen.
Watchman, s. Nachtwächter, m.
Water, s. Wasser, n. v. a. wässern.
Water-spout, s. Wasserhose, f.
Wave, s. Woge, f. v. n. winken.
Waving, s. Winken, n.

Wax, s. Wachs, n.; cake of wax, s. Wachsboden, m.
Way, s. Weg, m.; Richtung, f. every way, adv. in jeder Beziehung. no way, adv. keineswegs. make one's way, seinen Weg nehmen; give way to, freien Lauf lassen, (dat.); by the wayside, am Wege; in a way, auf eine Weise.
Weak, a. schwach.
Weakness, s. Schwäche, Schwachheit, f.
Wealth, s. Reichthum, m.
Weapon, s. Waffe, f.
Wear, v. a. tragen.
Weary, Wearied, a. müde; überdrüssig.
Weather, s. Wetter, n.
Wedding-day, s. Hochzeittag, m.
Wedge, v. a. durchzwängen. — together, zusammenzwängen.
Week, s. Woche, f.
Weep, v. n. weinen.
Weigh, v. a. wägen. v. n. wiegen.
Weight, s. Gewicht, n.
Weighty, a. wichtig.
Welcome, a. willkommen.
Welfare, s. Wohlfahrt, f.; Wohlergehen, n.
Well, ad. wohl, leicht. do —, wohl daran thun. as — se, so gut als, so wohl als auch. int. Ei gut.
Well-earned, a. wohlverdient.
Well-known, a. wohlbekannt.
West, s. West, m.; to the west, westwärts.
Western, a. westlich.
West-Indian, a. westindisch.
West Indies, s. Westindien, n.
Westphalia, s. Westphalen, n.
What, pn. was. a. welcher. int. was! what sort of, was für ein.
Whatever, ad. was nur, was auch immer. nor any.... whatever, durchaus kein....
Wheat, s. Weizen, m.
Wheel, s. Rad, n.
When, ad. & c. als; da, ba doch.
When(so)ever, ad. wenn auch immer.
Where, ad. wo. (whither), wohin.
Whereas, c. da, indem; weil. [wohin.
Wherever, ad. (whithersoever) überall
Wherein, ad. worin.
Whereupon, ad. worauf, worüber.
Whether, c. ob.
Whichsoever, pn. wer auch.
While, Whilst, c. indem, während.
Whimsical, a. launisch.
Whip, s. Peitsche, f.
Whisper, s. Geflüster, n.
Whisperingly, ad. leise.
Whistle, v. n. pfeifen. s. Pfeife, f.
Whiteness, s. Weiße, f.
Who, pn. welcher, der.
Whoever, pn. wer auch immer, jeder, der.
Whole, a. ganz. s. Ganze, n.
Why, ad. warum, et, nun, aber.
Wide, a. -ly. ad. weit; breit.
Wife, s. Frau, f., Gemahlin, f.
Will, s. Wille(n), m.; Testament, n. v. a. wollen, wünschen.

**William,** s. Wilhelm, m.
**Willing,** a. willig, gern.
**Wind,** s. Wind, m.
**Window,** s. Fenster, n.
**Wine,** s. Wein, m.
**Wing,** s. Flügel, m.
**Winter,** s. Winter, m.
**Wisdom,** s. Klugheit, f. learn wisdom, klug werden.
**Wise,** a. weise.
**Wish,** v. a. & n. wünschen. s. Wunsch, m.
**Wit,** s. Witz; Verstand; Schöngeist, m.; Wizling, m.; frightened out of one's wits, außer Fassung gebracht.
**With,** pr. mit.
**Withdraw,** v. a. zurückziehen.
**Withdrawal,** s. Abzug, Rückzug, m.
**Without,** pr. ohne. ad. draußen.
**Withstand,** v. a. widerstehen.
**Witness,** s. Zeuge, m. v. a. bezeugen.
**Wolf,** s. Wolf, m.
**Woman,** s. Frau, f.; Frauenzimmer, Weib, n.
**Wonder,** s. Verwunderung, f. v. n. sich (ver)wundern (über).
**Wood,** s. Wald, m.; Holz, n. bundle of wood, Holzbündel, n.
**Wooden,** a. hölzern.
**Woodman,** s. Holzhauer, m.
**Wool,** s. Wolle, f.
**Word,** s. Wort, n.; by word of mouth, mündlich.
**Work,** s. Werk, n. v. n. wirken (upon), (auf).
**Workman,** s. Arbeiter, m.
**World,** s. Welt; Erde, f.; on the world at large, in der weiten Welt; world of letters, literarische Welt, f.
**Worldly,** a. weltlich; irdisch.

**Worse,** a. schlimmer; grow worse, sich verschlimmern.
**Worshipful,** a. verehrungswürdig.
**Worst,** a. schlechtest.
**Worth,** a. würdig; worth mentioning, erwähnenswerth. worth seeing, sehenswürdig. to be worth, verdienen.
**Worthy,** a. würdig; worthy of notice, sehenswürdig.
**Would,** (= used to), imperf. pflegen.
**Wound,** s. Wunde, f. v. a. verwunden.
**Wrap,** v. a. wickeln, einwickeln; wrap up, einwickeln, einhüllen.
**Wretchedness,** s. Elend; Unglück, n.
**Write,** v. a. schreiben.
**Writing** s. Schrift, f.
**Written,** a. schriftlich.
**Wrong,** a. unrecht, verkehrt. s. Unrecht, n. to be wrong, Unrecht haben.

## Y.

**Yarn,** s. Garn, n.; cottonyarn, Baumwollengarn.
**Year,** s. Jahr, n.
**Yes,** adv. ja. yes indeed, ja wohl.
**Yesterday,** ad. gestern.
**Yet,** ad. & c. noch; sogar. yet but, erst.
**Yoke,** s. Joch, n.
**Young,** a. jung.
**Your,** a. euer.
**Youth,** s. Jugend, f.; Jüngling, m.
**Youthful,** a. jugendlich.

## Z.

**Zeal,** s. Eifer, m.

# HENRY HOLT & CO'S
# EDUCATIONAL WORKS.

### ENGLISH.

☞ *The prices are for cloth lettered, unless otherwise expressed.*

American Science Series, for High Schools and Colleges. In large 12mo volumes..................................................................
Bain. Brief English Grammar. 18mo. Boards, 45c.; Key............. $0 45
—— Higher English Grammar..................................... 80
—— Composition Grammar......................................... 1 40
Corson. Handbook of Anglo-Saxon and Early English. 12mo........... 2 50
Cox. Mythology. 16mo. Cloth...................................... 90
Freeman. Historical Course for Schools. 16mo.
    I. General Sketch of History, $1.40. II. History of England, $1.00. III. History of Scotland, $1.00. IV. History of Italy, $1.00. V. History of Germany, $1.00. VI. History of the United States, $1.25. VII. History of France........................... 1 00
Gostwick and Harrison. Outlines of German Literature. 12mo........ 2 50
Handbooks for Students and General Readers:—Astronomy, 60c.; Practical Physics, 60c.; The Studio Arts, 60c.; Zoölogy of the Invertebrates, 60c.; Zoölogy of the Vertebrates, 60c.; Zoölogy, $1.00; Handbook of American Politics, 75c.; History of the English Language, $1.00; Mechanics', 60c. *Other volumes in preparation.*
Koehler. Practical Botany. 12mo.................................. 2 50
Sewell and Urbino. Dictation Exercises. 16mo. Boards.............. 55
Shute. Anglo-Saxon Manual. 12mo................................. 1 50
Skinner. Approximate Computations. 16mo......................... 1 20
Siglar. English Grammar. 12mo. Boards........................... 70
Taine. English Literature. Condensed for Schools. 12mo............ 2 00
White. Classic Literature. 12mo.................................. 2 25
Yonge (Miss). Landmarks of History. I. Ancient, 12mo, 95c.; II. Mediæval, 12mo, $1.10; III. Modern, 12mo............................... 1 40

### FRENCH.

Æsop. Fables in French. With a Dictionary. 18mo................... $0 65
Bibliotheque d'Instruction et de Récréation.
    *Achard.* Clos-Pommier, et les Prisonniers, par Xavier de Maistre.... 85
    *Bédoliere.* Mère Michel. New Vocabulary, by Pylodet.............. 75
    *Biographies* des Musiciens Célèbres............................. 1 25
    *Erckman-Chatrian* Conscrit de 1813. With Notes.................. 1 10
    *Fallet.* Princes de l'Art....................................... 1 50
    *Feuillet.* Roman d'un Jeune Homme Pauvre....................... 1 10
    *Foa.* Contes Biographiques. With Vocabulary.................... 1 00
    —— Petit Robinson de Paris. With Vocabulary.................... 85
    *Macé.* Bouchée de Pain. With Vocabulary....................... 1 25
    *Porchat.* Trois Mois sous la Neige.............................. 85
    *Pressensé.* Rosa. With Vocabulary. By L. Pylodet.............. 1 25
    *Saint Germain.* Pour une Epigle. With Vocabulary............... 1 00
    *Sand.* Petite Fadette.......................................... 1 25
    *Segur.* Contes (Petites Filles Modèles; Les Gouters de la Grand'-Mère) 1 00
    *Souvestre.* Philosophe sous les Toits........................... 75

# STANDARD EDUCATIONAL WORKS.

| | |
|---|---|
| Borel. Cours de Thèmes. 12mo | $0 75 |
| Borel. Grammaire Française. 12mo | 1 60 |
| Delille. Condensed French Instruction. 18mo | 50 |
| Fisher. Easy French Reading. With Vocabulary. 16mo | 95 |
| Fleury. Histoire de France. 12mo | 1 40 |
| Fleury. Ancient History. Translated, with Notes. 12mo | 85 |
| Gasc. French-English Dictionary. 8vo. | 3 75 |
| —— Do do 18mo. Pocket edition, $1.40; 2 vols. | 1 60 |
| —— Translator. (English into French) | 1 25 |
| Gibert. Introductory French Manual. 12mo | 85 |
| Janes'. French Grammar. 12mo | 1 25 |
| Lacombe. Histoire du Peuple Française | 75 |
| Le Jeu des Auteurs. (Game of Authors) in a box | 1 00 |
| Maistre (X. de). Œuvres Complètes | 1 40 |
| Maistre (X. de.) Voyage autour de ma Chambre. 12mo. Paper | 40 |
| Musset. Un Caprice Comédie. 12mo. Paper | 30 |
| Otto. French Conversation Grammar. 12mo. Roan, $1.60; Key | 75 |
| —— Bôcher's French Reader. 12mo. Roan | 1 40 |
| —— First Book in French. 16mo. Boards | 40 |
| —— Introductory French Lessons | 1 25 |
| —— Introductory French Reader. 12mo. Boards | 1 00 |
| Parlez-vous Français? or, Do You Speak French? 18mo. Boards | 50 |
| Plays. *College Series of Modern French Plays.* With English Notes by Prof. Bôcher. 12mo. Paper La Joie Fait Peur, 30 cents; La Bataille des Dames, 35 cents; La Maison de Penarvan, 35 cents; La Poudre aux Yeux, 35 cents; Les Petis Oiseaux, 35 cents; Mademoiselle de la Seiglière, 35 cents; Le Roman d'un Jeune Homme Pauvre, 35 cents; Les Doigts de Fée, 35 cents; Jean Baudry, 35 cents. The foregoing in two volumes. 12mo. Cloth. Each vol | 1 60 |
| *Modern French Comedies.* Le Village, 25 cents; La Cagnotte, 35 cents; Les Femmes qui pleurent, 25 cents; Les Petites Misères de la Vie Humaine, 25 cents; La Niaise de St. Flour, 25 cents; Trois Proverbes, 30 cents; Valerie, 30 cents; Le Collier de Perles, 30 cents. The three last named have vocabularies. | |
| *French Plays for Children.* With Vocabularies. 12mo. Paper. La Vieille Cousine; Les Ricochets, 25 cents; Le Testament de Madame Patural; La Mademoiselle de St. Cyr, 25 cents; La Petite Maman; Le Bracelet, 25 cents; La Loterie de Francfort; Jeune Savante, 25 cents. | |
| *Students' Collection of Classic French Plays.* 12mo. Paper. With full Notes, by Prof. E. S. Joyne. Corneille. Le Cid, 50 cents. Racine. Athalie, 50 cents. Molière. Le Misanthrope, 50 cents. The foregoing in one vol. 12mo. Cloth | 1 50 |
| Pylodet's Beginning French. 16mo. Boards | 55 |
| —— Beginner's French Reader. With illustrations. 16mo. Boards | 55 |
| —— Second French Reader. With illustrations | 1 10 |
| —— La Literature Française Classique. 12mo | 1 60 |
| —— La Literature Française Contemporaine, 12mo | 1 40 |
| —— Gouttes de Rosée. French Lyric Poetry. 18mo | 65 |
| —— Mere L'Oie. Illustrated. 8vo. Boards | 50 |
| Riodu. Lucie. French and English Conversations. 12mo | 75 |
| Sadler. Translating English into French. 12mo | 1 25 |
| Sauveur. Introduction to Teaching. 12mo. Paper | 25 |
| —— Entretiens sur la Grammaire. 12mo | 1 75 |
| —— Causeries avec mes Élèves. 12mo. Illustrated | 1 50 |

# STANDARD EDUCATIONAL WORKS.

| | |
|---|---|
| Sauveur. Petites Causeries. 12mo | $1 25 |
| —— Causeries avec les Enfants. 12mo | 1 25 |
| —— Fables de la Fontaine. 12mo | 1 50 |
| Witcomb and Bellenger. French Conversation. 18mo | 65 |
| Zender. Abécédaire. French and English Primer. 12mo. Boards | 50 |

## GERMAN.

☞ *The prices are for paper covers, unless otherwise expressed.*

| | |
|---|---|
| Andersen. Bilderbuch ohne Bilder. With Notes. 12mo | $0 30 |
| —— Die Eisjungfrau, etc. With Notes. 12mo | 50 |
| Carove. Das Maerchen ohne Ende | 25 |
| Evans. Otto's German Reader. Half roan | 1 35 |
| —— Deutsche Literaturgeschichte. 12mo. Cloth | 1 40 |
| Eichendorff. Aus dem Leben eines Taugenichts. 12mo | 50 |
| Elz. Three German Comedies. 12mo | 35 |
| Fouque. Undine. With Vocabulary. 12mo | 40 |
| Goethe. Egmont. With Notes | 50 |
| —— Herrman und Dorothea. With Notes. 12mo | 35 |
| Grimm. Venus von Milo; Raphael und Michael Angelo. 12mo | 50 |
| Heness. Der Leitfaden. 12mo. Cloth | 1 50 |
| —— Der Sprechlehrer unter seinen Schülern | 1 35 |
| Heyse. Anfang und Ende. 12mo | 30 |
| —— Die Einsamen. 12mo | 25 |
| Keetels. Oral Method with German. 12mo. Half roan | 1 60 |
| Koerner. Zriny. With Notes | 60 |
| Klemm. Lese und Sprachbuecher. In 8 concentrischen Kreisen. 12mo | |
| —— Geschichte der Deutschen Literatur | 1 50 |
| Krauss. Introductory German Grammar. 12mo. Cloth | 95 |
| Lessing. Minna von Barnhelm. In English, with German Notes. 12mo | 50 |
| —— Emilia Galotti. 12mo | 40 |
| Lodeman. German Conversation Tables. 12mo. Boards | 35 |
| Mügge. Riukan Voss. 12mo | 30 |
| —— Signa die Seterin. 12mo | 30 |
| Nathusius. Tagebuch eines Armen Fraeuleins. 12mo | 60 |
| Otto. German Grammar. 12mo. Roan, $1.60; Key | 75 |
| —— Evans' German Reader. With Notes and Vocab. 12mo. Roan | 1 35 |
| —— First Book in German. 12mo. Boards | 35 |
| —— Introductory Lessons; or, Beginning German. 12mo. Cloth | 95 |
| —— Introductory Reader. With Notes and Vocabulary. 12mo. Cloth | 1 20 |
| —— Translating English into German | 1 00 |
| Prinzessin Ilse. With Notes. 12mo | 25 |
| Putlitz. Was sich der Wald Erzaehlt. 12mo | 30 |
| —— Badekuren. With Notes. 12mo | 30 |
| —— Das Herz Vergessen. With Notes. 12mo | 30 |
| —— Vergissmeinnicht. With Notes. 12mo | 25 |
| Schiller. Jungfrau von Orleans. With Notes. 12mo | 50 |
| —— Wallenstein's Lager. With Notes. 12mo | 40 |
| —— Die Piccolomini. With Notes. 12mo | 50 |
| —— Wallenstein's Tod. With Notes. 12mo | 50 |
| —— Wallenstein. Complete. 12mo. Cloth | 1 50 |
| —— Der Neffe als Onkel. With Notes and Vocabulary | 50 |
| Simonson. German Ballad Book. With Notes. 12mo. Cloth | 1 40 |

## STANDARD EDUCATIONAL WORKS.

Sprechen Sie Deutsch? or, Do You Speak German? 18mo. Boards..... $0 50
Stern. Studien und Plaudereien.......................................... 1 35
Storme. Easy German Reading. 16mo. Cloth......................... 95
——— Immensee. With Notes. 12mo.................................. 25
Tieck. Die Elfen. Das Rothkaeppchen. With Notes. 12mo......... 35
Whitney. Prof. W. D. German Grammar. 12mo. Roan............. 1 50
——— German Reader. 12mo. Roan ................................. 1 80
——— German-English and English-German Dictionary. 12mo. Cloth... 3 50
——— The same in 2 vols. Fine edition.................................. 5 50
——— German Texts:—Annotated by leading instructors and edited by Prof. W. D. Whitney. 12mo. Cloth. I. Lessing's Minna von Barnhelm, 95 cts.—II. Schiller's Wilhelm Tell, $1.15—III. Goethe's Faust, $1.20 —IV. Goethe's Iphigenie auf Tauris, 95 cts.—V. Schiller's Maria Stuart.
Wilhelmi. Einer muss heirathen, and Benedix, Eigensinn. 12mo........ 30
Witcomb and Otto's German Conversations. By L. Pylodet. 18mo. Cloth 65

### LATIN.

Ammen. Beginner's Latin Grammar. 12mo. Cloth................... $ 75
Sauveur. Introduction to the Teaching of Ancient Languages, 25 cts.; The Vade Mecum of the Latinist, 25 cts.; Talks with Cæsar de Bello Gallico ........................................................... 1 50
Wiley. The Ordo Series of Classics. 12mo: Cæsar's Gallic War, $1.20; Cicero's Select Orations, $1.40; Virgil's Æneid..................... 1 60

### ITALIAN.

Cuore. Italian Grammar. 12mo. Roan $1.50; Key................ $ 75
Ongaro. La Rosa Dell' Alpi. With Notes. 12mo. Paper............. 75
James and Grassi. Italian-English Dictionary. 8vo. Half roan....... 2 00
Montague. Italian Grammar. 12mo.................................. 1 25
Nota (Alberto). La Fiera With Notes. 12mo. Paper................ 75
Parlate Italiano? or, Do You Speak Italian? 16mo. Boards........... 50
Pellico. Francesca da Rimini. 12mo. Paper........................ 75

### SPANISH AND PORTUGUESE.

Caballero. La Familia de Alvareda. 12mo. Paper.................. $ 95
Habla Vd. Español? or, Do You Speak Spanish? 16mo. Boards....... 50
Habla Vd. Ingles? or, Do You Speak English? 18mo. Boards........ 50
Lope de Vega y Calderon. Obras Maestras. 12mo. Cloth........... 1 90
Montague. Spanish Grammar. 12mo................................ 1 25
Spanish Hive; or, Select Pieces from Spanish Authors. 16mo. Cloth.... 1 25
Fallais Portuguez? or, Do You Speak Portuguese? 16mo. Boards...... 50
Fallais Ingles? or, Do You Speak English? 12mo. Boards............ 50

### HEBREW.

Deutsch. Hebrew Grammar. 8vo. Cloth........................... $2 50
——— Key to the Pentateuch. 3 parts (1 now published). Per part...... 1 50
Fuerst. Hebrew and Chaldee Lexicon. 8vo. Half morocco ........... 9 00

☞ *Send for a Descriptive Catalogue.*

## HENRY HOLT & CO., PUBLISHERS, NEW YORK.

www.ingramcontent.com/pod-product-compliance
Lightning Source LLC
Chambersburg PA
CBHW031445160426
43195CB00010BB/856